Regional Economic Change in Russia

ECONOMIES AND SOCIETIES IN TRANSITION

General Editor: **Ronald J. Hill**
*Professor of Comparative Government
and Fellow of Trinity College
Dublin, Ireland*

Economies and Societies in Transition is an important series which applies academic analysis and clarity of thought to the recent traumatic events in Eastern and Central Europe. As many of the preconceptions of the past half century are cast aside, newly independent and autonomous sovereign states are being forced to address long-term organic problems which had been suppressed by, or appeased within, the Communist system of rule.

The series is edited under the sponsorship of Lorton House, an independent charitable association which exists to promote the academic study of communism and related concepts.

Regional Economic Change in Russia

Edited by

Philip Hanson

Professor of the Political Economy of Russia and Eastern Europe, University of Birmingham, UK

and

Michael Bradshaw

Reader in Regional Geography, University of Birmingham, UK

ECONOMIES AND SOCIETIES IN TRANSITION

Edward Elgar
Cheltenham, UK • Northampton, MA, USA

Published by
Edward Elgar Publishing Limited
Glensanda House
Montpellier Parade
Cheltenham
Glos GL50 1UA
UK

Edward Elgar Publishing, Inc.
136 West Street
Suite 202
Northampton
Massachusetts 01060
USA

A catalogue record for this book
is available from the British Library

Library of Congress Cataloguing in Publication Data

Regional economic change in Russia / edited by Philip Hanson and Michael
    Bradshaw. (Economies and societies in transition)
  Includes bibliographical references.
    1. Russia (Federation)—Economic conditions—1991—Regional
disparities. 2. Regionalism—Russia (Federation) I. Hanson, Philip. II.
Bradshaw, Michael, 1959– III. Series.

  HC340.12.R444 2000
  330.947'086—dc21

                                           99–087190

ISBN 1 84064 107 X

Electronic typesetting by Lorton Hall
Printed and bound in Great Britain by MPG Books Ltd, Bodmin, Cornwall

Contents

Figures

Maps

Tables

Editors and Contributors

ABOUT THE EDITORS

Philip Hanson is currently Professor of the Political Economy of Russia and Eastern Europe at the University of Birmingham's Centre for Russian and East European Studies. He has been a visiting professor at the Universities of Michigan and Harvard, and has served as a Senior Research Officer at the Foreign and Commonwealth Office, a Senior Economic Affairs Officer at the UN Economic Commission for Europe and a visiting scholar at the Radio Free Europe/Radio Liberty Research Institute. His work has been mostly on the economies of the Soviet Union and Russia. His books include *Western Economic Statecraft in East–West Relations* (RIIA, 1988), *From Stagnation to Catastroika* (CSIS, 1992), and *Transformation from Below* (co-edited with John Gibson; Edward Elgar, 1996). He has published papers in, amongst other journals, *Soviet Studies/ Europe–Asia Studies*, *Journal of Comparative Economics*, *European Economic Review* and *Communist Economies and Economic Transformation*. He has served as a Senior Expert on EU Tacis projects and as coordinator of a UK Know How Fund project.

Michael Bradshaw is currently Reader in Regional Geography at the University of Birmingham's School of Geography and Environmental Sciences and an Associate Member of the Centre for Russian and East European Studies. Most of his work has been on the relationship between geography and economic transition in the former Soviet Union, with a particular focus on Russia. His books include *The Soviet Union: A New Regional Geography* (Belhaven, 1991) and *Geography and Transition in the Former Soviet Union* (John Wiley, 1997). He has published papers in, amongst other journals, *Post-Soviet Geography and Economics*, *Europe–Asia Studies* and *Geoforum*. He is currently the Editor of the geography journal *Area*.

THE OTHER CONTRIBUTORS

Sergei Artobolevskiy, Institute of Geography, Russian Academy of Sciences, Moscow.

Alexandr Chernikov, Institute of Economics of the Russian Academy of Sciences, Siberian Division, Irkutsk, Russia.

Vladimir Gel'man, European University, St Petersburg, Russia.

Peter Kirkow, ICE Securities, London.

Olga Kouznetsova, Working Centre of Economic Reform, Russian Government, Moscow.

Arbakhan Magomedov, Department of History and Cultural Studies, Technical University of Ul'yanovsk/Slavic Research Centre, University of Hokkaido.

Pavel Romanov, Institute for Comparative Labour Studies, Samara, Russia.

Douglas Sutherland, OECD, Paris.

Irina Tartakovskaya, Institute for Comparative Labour Studies, Samara, Russia.

Andrei Tatarinov, Department of International Economics, Sochi State University, Russia.

Andrey Treyvish, Institute of Geography, Russian Academy of Sciences, Moscow.

Tamara Troyakova, Institute of History, Far Eastern Division, Russian Academy of Sciences, Vladivostok, Russia.

Dmitri Zimine, School of Geography and Environmental Sciences, University of Birmingham.

Preface and Acknowledgements

This book is primarily about the Russian economy. It is, however, the product of cooperation among economists, political scientists, sociologists and geographers. We believe the nature of change in ex-communist countries is especially hard to understand from the perspective of one social science alone. In countries where the general framework of social existence is comparatively well established, separate economic or political analysis can achieve a good deal; when most of the rules of most of the games are being altered, however, economists quickly find themselves appealing to notions such as 'the rule of law' and 'informal networks', in order to make sense of what they observe. And in Russia, especially, once resource allocation ceases to be dictated in Moscow, new spatial issues arise, of a kind that geographers are accustomed to thinking about. Cooperation among specialists makes sense.

The research presented here was mostly funded by the UK Economic and Social Research Council, for a project entitled 'Understanding Regional Patterns of Economic Change in Russia' (grant R000 236 398). On that project we worked with Peter Kirkow, Douglas Sutherland and Jonathan Oldfield, who were part of the home team in Birmingham; their contributions were very substantial indeed. Thanks also to Dmitri Zimine for his assistance in compiling the bibliography. Our (formal as well as informal) network of Russian colleagues and co-authors from seven regions provided not only their own expertise but access and guidance that were vital for the project. The Sakhalin component of the case studies was funded by a second ESRC project entitled 'The Russian Far East: Resource Frontier for the Pacific Century?' (grant L324253005). Some of our other field work was supported by other sources, including the EU Tacis project on the re-structuring of Kaliningrad *oblast'*, led by the Espace Europe team of Grenoble University, and some developed as a spin-off from other activities, including a UK Know How Fund project to provide training

xiii

for junior staff of the Institute of the Economy in Transition (the 'Gaidar' Institute). In this connection, we are indebted to several people who provided insights as well as access, including Vladimir Mau of the Gaidar Institute and Ivan Samson of Grenoble.

For administrative help with the project – characteristically, beyond the call of duty – we are particularly indebted to three Birmingham colleagues: Marea Arries, Tricia Carr and David Robertson.

Birmingham, January 2000   MICHAEL BRADSHAW
                                              PHILIP HANSON

1. Introduction

Philip Hanson and Michael Bradshaw

Our aim in this book is to summarize the findings of a three-year project entitled 'Understanding Regional Patterns of Economic Change in Russia'.* With the words 'post-Soviet' inserted before 'Russia', that title conveys pretty well what this book is about. Sadly, we cannot after three years cross our hearts and say that we now understand everything about what drives economic change in every Russian region. That would be a tall order in any country, large or small. But we do believe we have learnt something useful.

Before embarking on a description of our findings, we owe the reader answers to four preliminary questions. Why study this subject? What are the issues we have addressed? What methods have we used? What is the shape of the book to come?

The subject matters because post-communist economic change plays out differently in different regions of a country; and regional differences in adaptation both shed light on the micro-economics of post-communist change and feed back to macro-economic adjustment in the country as a whole. And these considerations loom particularly large in Russia.

It is not merely that differences in average real incomes across Russia's 78 provinces (oblasts, krays and republics) increased in 1992–8 – though they did. There were large regional differences in real income under communism.[1] It is above all that central planning has gone, and much economic decision-making is now territorially

---

* Funded by the British Economic and Social Research Council, grant R 000 236389.

1. This was partly because of great differences in the availability of goods in the shops. A Muscovite could buy a great many things that a resident of Kuybyshev (now Samara) with the same income could not. In general, the change from shortage to rationing by price makes the comparison of real incomes between communist times and the present impossible.

devolved. Economic activities in Sakhalin, Kemerovo or Tyumen' are still affected by macro-economic policies made in Moscow and, in some cases, by decisions made in company head offices in the capital. But they are also now driven by the decisions of local households, firms and politicians, in ways that were largely absent in the communist era. They are also directly influenced by foreign firms and movements in foreign markets. Under communism such influences were either modified or completely blocked out by the central planners.

This change began before communism collapsed. In the summer of 1990 there was a trade war going on between the city of Moscow and the surrounding regions (a similar conflict was occurring in St Petersburg). A system of so-called *vizitki* (literally 'visiting cards') had been introduced in the capital: Muscovites had to show a Moscow residence permit to buy a wide range of rationed goods in the stores. Many people from central European Russian regions outside Moscow, accustomed in the past to shopping in the metropolis for basic items that were not available in their home towns, were angered. Following the first competitive local elections, in March 1990, every region had local officials who for once had a reason to pay attention to what local residents said. The result was a number of 'export' embargoes on deliveries of food to the capital.[2]

So long as top-down Communist Party rule and central planning prevailed, such developments would have been unthinkable. Both these institutions, however, were crumbling. Some territorial devolution of decision-making was already under way. The initial results, in what was still a shortage economy, were messy.

With the price liberalization of 2 January 1992, a more systematic process of devolution began. This attempt at transforming Russia into a functioning market economy also included the removal of most administrative controls on foreign trade, the privatization of housing, small business, large enterprises and (with massive failures in implementation) land and agriculture. The liberalization extended to rouble exchange rates, and an attempt was made to stabilize both the internal and the external value of the currency.

By mid-1999 the results of this whole transformation attempt could best be described as messy. The scale and character of the mess had not been anticipated by orthodox economic theory. Efforts to repair the damage, both to Russia and to mainstream economics, are now

2. Ryazan', Tula, Kaluga and Oryol all took such action: *Izvestiya*, 1 June 1993: 3.

under way. Part of that necessary repair work is a closer examination of what has been going on within the regions.

To say that the transformation attempt in Russia has been a failure would be to over-dramatize events. The transformation attempts of 1992–8 were incomplete and fitful. The fall of the 'last government of reformers', that of Sergey Kirienko, in August 1998 demonstrated that there was in fact a consensus on economic policy within the Russian political elite. This consensus held across the supposed divide between 'reformers' and 'traditionalists', even though the inclinations and perceptions of these two groups really were different. The post-reform governments of Yevgeniy Primakov and Sergei Stepashin continued to restrict money-supply growth and thereby inflation, and sought to restore Western financial assistance by trying, like their predecessors, to meet International Monetary Fund (IMF) loan conditions. To that extent, they did not depart from reformist policies. If they have been soft on bank and enterprise bankruptcies, that, too, was no departure from past practice. The so-called reformers also flinched from imposing hard budget constraints on large enterprises or large banks. They thus allowed the restructuring of privatized enterprises and the banking system to be postponed. Because of the flaky nature of this policy consensus – and not because reformers were outgunned by traditionalists – the economic changes in Russia after 1991 have had strikingly poor outcomes by comparison with similar transformation attempts in Poland, Estonia, Hungary and the Czech Republic. The fact that the economies of Ukraine, Belarus and Uzbekistan, for instance, are in yet worse shape is not particularly encouraging. In Russia in 1998, officially measured total output was about 44 per cent down from the peak level of 1989. With an occasional, brief respite, recorded GDP has been falling for nine years. Poland, in contrast, is on track to enter the next millennium with its GDP 25 per cent up on 1989.[3]

This comparative failure of transformation in Russia, and indeed in the whole of the former USSR except the Baltic States, presents a challenge to orthodox economics. Simplifying, but not distorting, one could say that received economic doctrine predicts that liberalization and privatization in a former communist, centrally administered economy, supported by macro-economic stabilization, would reduce information and incentive problems associated with central administration, enabling the existing capital and labour inputs, with the existing

3. See the data and forecasts in EBRD (1998).

technology, to produce more. This would not happen overnight, and the changes in resource allocation would be so extensive that the period of adjustment would be more than trivial. But only people who had escaped a good training in economics talked, around 1990, of a decade or more. And the mainstream view has not been undermined by the outcomes in every ex-communist country. In the more successful transforming economies, output fell more moderately, and for 'only' two to three years, before recovery began – far less than in Russia.

Even when they made some allowance for disruption arising from the break-up of the Council of Mutual Economic Assistance trading bloc and the rouble area of the former USSR, for time needed for market-economy legislation and institutions to be in place, and for an element of statistical illusion in the reported decline, few economists anticipated such a deep and prolonged output fall. As the Commonwealth of Independent States' crisis continued, two approaches have been developed to account for it. What has been happening in the regions is relevant to both of them.

The first approach is to look more carefully at the economics of structural adjustment in ex-communist countries and to reconsider some of the standard assumptions that are made about it. Peter Murrell (1991) and others have stressed the difficulties of radical institutional change. Standard neo-classical writings had tended to assume that liberalization, stabilization and privatization policies, changing the incentives of economic actors, would elicit rapid institutional change: that, for example, these policies would quickly impose hard budget constraints on producers, and these in turn would rather swiftly elicit radical changes in the product profiles, internal organization, workforces and array of customers and suppliers of enterprises; also, that enterprises that did not change appropriately would close. Those who stress the difficulty of institutional change have pointed to evidence of the impediments to making radical alterations in roles, rules and procedures within any social organization. This is all the more problematic when the environment in which producers operate is itself being reconstructed, with new property rights, new legislation and new institutions (commercial banks, securities markets, private contracts and so on).

One exercise in modelling the prolonged ex-Soviet output decline, which is compatible with this approach, stresses the role of Soviet industrial structure, chains of suppliers, incomplete information and incomplete contracts. A large final-assembly enterprise has numerous suppliers, perhaps forming a vertical chain, each of which is specialized and not easily replaced (in part perhaps because of the weak state of market information services). Some of those suppliers have alternative demands for their output, perhaps from the new private sector. A scenario in which they switch their output to alternative customers even though the net effect is a drop in total production is possible if the information available to all parties is incomplete and it is not possible to draw up complete contracts, between customers and suppliers, that would handle the problem (Blanchard and Kremer 1997; this paragraph is a very rough and partial summary of two variants of the model they put forward).

In other words, the first approach to accounting for the long fall in Russian output involves repairs and extensions to economic theory, to allow more fully for institution-building problems and for the bad equilibria that can exist while market institutions are weak.

The other way of accounting for the depth and duration of Russia's transformation crisis is to put the blame on politics: in other words, to argue that the standard policies were appropriate, but they have not been implemented. Liberalization in 1992 was incomplete because regional authorities were allowed, at their own financial risk, to keep a range of price controls; and at federal level one key price, that of oil, also remained under control. The privatization of farming and farm land was blocked by parliamentary opposition. Mass, voucher privatization of large and medium state enterprises was done in ways that favoured control by insiders. Those insiders managed to resist the development of a contestable market for corporate control. Therefore industrial assets did not pass into the hands of those who would use them most efficiently – or rather, they did not do so swiftly and systematically. The manager-insiders who gained uncontested control of privatized assets, usually with less than 20 per cent of equity ownership, understood that their hold on this wealth was not widely held to be legitimate. They also knew that much depended on the support of political cronies. In general, they had little reason to believe that the control they exercised was secure, and little incentive to restructure 'their' enterprises and make the value of these businesses grow. On the contrary, they had every incentive to funnel funds out of the business and into their own privately held wealth in Cyprus or London. (For an account that stresses this role of a flawed mass privatization, see Stiglitz 1999.)

At the same time, macro-economic stabilization was an affair of smoke and mirrors: some of the more salient IMF conditions were met – inflation was reduced, monetary growth was reduced, the government deficit ceased in 1995 to be money-financed. But these targets were met by skipping others and by sleight of hand: keeping the cash-flow deficit down by simply not paying state employees and suppliers; ceasing to monetize the deficit, without sufficiently reducing it, and therefore allowing a rapid build-up of short-term government debt and a rising debt-service problem; capping the federal budget deficit while sub-national budget balances went into deficit. Above all, the Russian political and business elites, which overlapped substantially, took care not to translate financial discipline in a macro-economic sense into financial discipline in a micro-economic sense: the growth of the rouble money supply was restricted, while large enterprises continued to operate under soft budget constraints.

In August 1998, the Asian financial crisis and the rickety state of Russian public finances produced a forced devaluation of the rouble and a partial default on domestic debt. At this point, the peculiar, smoke-and-mirrors stabilization was identified by some economists as the critical policy failure. Inflation had been reduced without a serious restructuring of production. Loss-making enterprises had been allowed to stagger on by building up arrears of payment amongst themselves, plus tax and wage arrears. Some payables due had been cancelled with barter deals and the use of money surrogates. At the centre of the payment arrears were manufacturing enterprises not paying electricity suppliers, who in turn did not pay the monopoly natural gas supplier, Gazprom. Gazprom and the electricity industry therefore underpaid their taxes, and regional budgets consequently lacked the 'live money' (*zhivyye den'gi*) to pay teachers, doctors and so on. Explicit budget subsidies had been cut, but a large part of the economy was kept going with implicit subsidies – unpaid tax bills and unpaid bills to energy suppliers – those energy suppliers being partly state-owned (see Bradshaw and Kirkow 1998 for the case of the Russian Far East). By these means, the state surreptitiously made a net injection of credit into the manufacturing sector in 1995–8, while giving the appearance of exercising financial restraint (see Smith 1998; Gaddy and Ickes 1998; Commander and Mummsen 1999).

As ways of making sense of the prolonged Russian transformation crisis, both approaches are quite persuasive. And they are not

necessarily incompatible. Market institutions have been taking shape in
Russia, but property rights, capital markets, bankruptcy procedures and
the enforcement of contracts through the courts all remain problematic.
The problems associated with long supply chains, highly specific inter-
enterprise connexions and poor market information may well loom
larger in the CIS countries than in the Baltic States and Central and
Eastern Europe, perhaps because the industrial structure in the CIS
region is to a greater extent a product of central planning. At the same
time, the failures in policy implementation are real enough; indeed,
they are glaring.

Critics of IMF–World Bank recipes have pointed out that the social
cost of implementing them may indeed be enormous. It should not be
assumed that proper application of orthodox policies must have a
happy ending (Clarke 1997). Others have taken a rather different tack:
the shifts and evasions (as they seem) in Russian economic policy have
a certain social logic. Soviet-era interest coalitions were not broken up
by the collapse of communism, but in many cases survived in rather
different forms. This continuity has left policy at the mercy of elites for
whom insider control of assets and a lack of transparency in property
rights, financial reporting and capital markets were desirable. As
a result, recovery and development are restricted (Olson 1995;
Colombatto and Macey 1995; Hanson 1997c).

A less bleak view would be that, despite the disarray and economic
depression, market institutions and rules of the game are developing.
Local price controls have been eroded. More companies are controlled
by outside investors than superficial indicators show (Earle and Estrin
1997). Pressures on large companies to be more open about their
finances are strong and are having some effect. The regulation of banks
and securities markets has been improving. There is a large and rapidly
growing new middle class (Balzer 1998). Official statistics overstate the
fall in output. Not only Moscow city, but a number of other regions as
well, began to show signs of strong economic recovery in 1997
(Romanov and Tartakovskaya 1998).

A close look at what is happening in the regions can help us make a
better assessment of these processes of change in Russia. The issues to
be addressed in this book all have a bearing on the character of
economic change in post-communist Russia.

First of all, they shed light on the micro-economic processes that
underlie the macro problems. Is there a single Russian economic

space, without administrative barriers to the movement of goods and resources? Is resource reallocation occurring amongst regions in ways that resemble those to be found in established market economies? In so far as inter-regional resource reallocation of a productive kind is occurring, what part is played in this by market adjustment by firms and households, and what part by policy intervention? The gaps between (relatively) rich and poor regions have been increasing (Hanson 1999); but are they increasing in ways that could produce a patchwork of successful and languishing slices of territory that might threaten Russia's integrity? Why have some regions adapted more successfully than others? Is it all to do with what each inherited (location, resources, population size, human capital, conurbation size, initial economic structure)? Or, given those differences, is there evidence that local reformers can affect local outcomes? Can we observe, close up, interest coalitions of local political and business elites that misappropriate public funds, prop up loss-making enterprises and impede the restructuring of production? Or do we see business and political elites disengaging from one another and forced to respond to market pressures by abandoning local cronyism and reliance on federal hand-outs? (Or do we see both these tendencies, but in different places?)

Second, an examination of regional change sheds light on the feed-backs from local problems to the development of macro-economic policies. By what channels and to what effect, if any, do local business and political elites influence federal policies? Can the centre effectively control overall levels of public spending (including federal budgets, regional and local budgets, federal off-budget funds and regional and local off-budget funds)? Is an 'internal IMF' strategy feasible? In other words, can the federal government use conditionality to monitor and restrict sub-national spending, as an analysis by Freinkman and Haney (1997) suggests? Or is the reality closer to that depicted by several political scientists, of a weak centre desperate to strengthen support in the provinces by providing hand-outs to whichever regional leaders seem to threaten the most political damage (Slider 1997a; Treisman 1998)?

It will be obvious from this summary of the issues that the methods used in this study are not solely those of economics. The University of Birmingham team included two economists (Hanson and Sutherland), one economic geographer (Bradshaw) and one political scientist (Kirkow). The Russian colleagues with whom we have been working include economists (Chernikov, Kouznetsova, Tatarinov), geographers (Artobolevsky, Bylov, Treyvish, Zimine), political scientists (Gel'man, Magomedov, Troyakova) and sociologists (Romanov, Tartakovskaya).

The approach we have adopted is as follows. First, we have focused on the regional level, and on regional–national links. We have not, with one exception, explored the local level, of municipalities and rural districts. This does not mean that we consider processes of change at the local level to be unimportant; merely that we consider that such processes at the regional level are important in themselves, and not everything can be tackled at once.

What that has meant in practice is that we have been looking at Russia's 77 oblasts, krays and republics (Chechnya being the seventy-eighth). We have not tried to deal separately with the ten autonomous okrugs and one autonomous oblast that make up the 88 (or more frequently quoted 89) 'federal subjects'. This is because, in many of the statistical series available, separate data for the 'AOs' are not published; they are included in the data for the oblasts and krays where they are located.[4]

These regions, and the differences between them, provide a rich field of study. Their average population size is 1.9 million. That is bigger than one transition economy (Estonia), and by coincidence the same as the average of the European Union's 'second-tier' regions. The variation around that average size is huge. Moscow city has over 8 million inhabitants, Altai Republic little more than 200,000. The variance in real per capita personal income levels is also enormous: a coefficient of variation of 49.8 per cent in the third quarter of 1997, with a ratio of almost 1:8 between Dagestan and Moscow city (Hanson 1998) – well above the 1993 range of per capita GDP between the richest and the poorest second-tier region of the twelve-nation European Union, which was 1:5.5 (European Commission 1994).

Second, in trying to understand the processes of change at regional level, we have drawn on theory and evidence from a number of fields: theories of location in both economic geography and economics; the literature on migration, small firm development and other components of structural change in the economy; literature on the (sub-national)

---

4. The odd one out is the autonomous oblast of Chukotka, which is not simultaneously a federal subject and a component part of a kray or oblast. Where separate data were available for Chukotka, we have added them into those for Magadan.

regional consequences of increases in international economic inter-dependence; literature on economic networks; the political sociology of elite formation.

Third, to get a handle on the processes of adaptation that are at work, we have used a combination of case-studies of a few regions and statistical analysis (mostly cross-section, since few useable time-series are yet available) of them all.[5] The idea was to conduct a pincer movement on – for want of a better word – reality. Theory plus statistical analysis might have taken us quite a long way, as Douglas Sutherland (1997) has shown. But we hoped that case-studies would provide insights that could direct the statistical analysis and make it more productive.

This could come about in a number of ways.[6] To begin with, the data on Russian regions are abundant but problematic. An acquaintance with day-to-day life in a few provinces can help to decide whether this or that series is useable, and how best to make some sort of rough and ready adjustment in some other series for particular types of region. So far as Russian regions in the 1990s are concerned, a spatial equivalent of Alec Nove's law of equal cheating is, unfortunately, not very persuasive. Nove famously suggested, about Soviet economic statistics, that rates of change over time in many series (steel production, say, or money wages, not the intentionally misleading aggregates like national income or industrial production) might be reasonably reliable even if the level in any one year was likely to be inflated. All that one needed to believe was that the proportionate amount of report-padding did not change significantly over time. Nove acknowledged that the law of equal cheating might not always hold, but perhaps, with a bit of *ad hoc* tweaking of the numbers, it might serve. It would be nice to be able to make the same conjecture about cross-section differences in Russian regional data. Unfortunately, for at least some series, there are some obvious catches. Real household incomes by region, which can be derived from official series of money incomes and regional costs of living (the subsistence minimum or baskets of 19 or 25 food items) are likely to understate real incomes in more rural regions relatively to more urbanized regions, because of the greater importance in the

5. For most purposes, 76 regions, since data for both Ingushetia and Chechnya were often lacking. Sometimes data for one or two other regions were also lacking. But *n* was always more than 70.
6. This subject is discussed in more detail in Hanson (1998).

former of subsistence food production. The same applies to the weight of the black and grey economies in different regions. Any adjustment made for the unofficial economy by the Russian State Statistics Committee (Goskomstat Rossii) seems not to be reliably done region by region – whatever view one takes of the plausibility of the aggregate adjustment.

Then there are data for a region that may be hard to obtain except by going there. Such data, admittedly, do not help the cross-region statistical analysis directly, unless one has the resources to go to all regions. But they can help interpret the other numbers.

More fundamentally, the evidence of one's own eyes and ears can and should help to make sense of the number-crunching. *A priori* reasoning might suggest a number of hypotheses, and simply running regressions on lots of alternative specifications until nice-looking adjusted R^2s and significance measures pop up is a questionable tactic: it increases the likelihood that a good-looking result can arise by chance. Even if such analysis identifies significant relationships, it often conveys no understanding of the processes generating them. Selecting amongst hypotheses on the basis of insights gained on the ground is preferable.

How to gain those insights? In our case-studies we did the usual things: went there, looked around us, talked to people, read the local press, watched local TV, tried to visit the local Goskomstat office.[7] Talking to people meant talking, for the most part, to well-placed sources of information in local business and the regional administration. We conducted only one survey, and we cannot claim that it is based on a sample representative of the population or of some clearly defined elite group. That survey, and other interviews, was designed to elicit from expert informants what they considered to be important in the economic changes in their particular region. The survey produced a picture of networking patterns in the business and political elites of seven regions in 1996 and 1997 (Kirkow *et al.* 1998). ('We' in this case means the Birmingham team and our Russian colleagues.)

We also cannot claim that the regions we have studied closely are in some sense representative of all Russian regions. They were Kaliningrad, St Petersburg, Kostroma, Samara, Krasnodar, Novosibirsk,

---

7. Local Goskomstat offices are not welcoming to outsiders. Typically, even their routine publications are marked 'For official use [only]' (*Dlya sluzhebnogo pol'zovaniya*), and are not easily obtained.

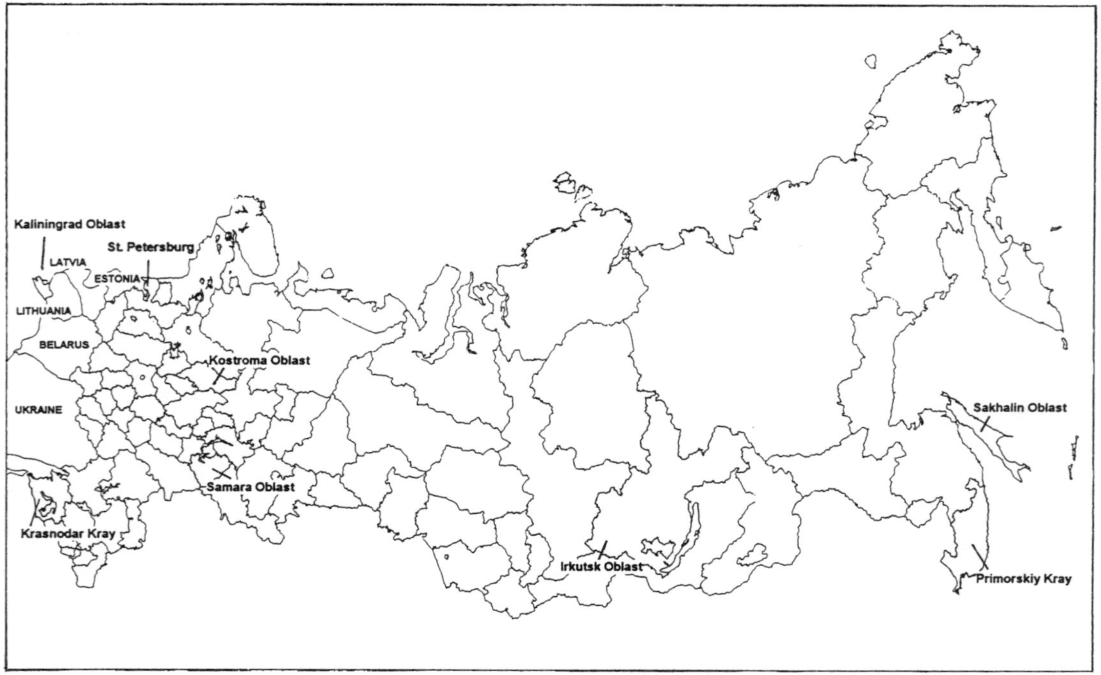

Map 1.1 Case-study regions

Irkutsk, Sakhalin and Primorskiy kray (see Map 1.1). Our initial choice of seven regions (the above less Kaliningrad and Sakhalin) was guided by a conjecture that there could be an important cleavage in economic adjustment between gateway and hinterland regions. We aimed to take a close look at some of both. We did not make a special effort to include leading natural-resource regions (Tyumen' and Sakha, for instance). Fortunately, however, Irkutsk comes into that category, though it is a less prominent example. We reckoned that Moscow city was too well known and too special. We included no republics because ethnic issues were not on our agenda. Kaliningrad and Sakhalin were added to the portfolio when members of the Birmingham team were invited to contribute to other projects.[8]

What might constitute a representative selection of Russian regions? We doubt if there is any satisfactory answer to that question. Various classification schemes have been tried (for example, DeBardeleben and Galkin 1997). Our own early thought of gateways versus hinterland, conceived as border regions with major ports versus the rest, did not serve well. Moscow is a vastly more important commercial gateway than Murmansk or Krasnodar. One tentative classification that we have tried is a four-way division between major natural-resource regions, emerging commercial-hub regions, mainly rural regions and the rest (for details, see Hanson 1997a). This is fairly close to the categories used by DeBardeleben and Galkin, though the two classification schemes were thought up independently. But often the differences within a category seem at least as interesting as the differences between categories. And, on some non-exclusive criteria, a few regions would fall into more than one category: for instance, Krasnodar can be treated both as mainly rural (the Kuban') and as containing a major commercial hub (Novorosiisk with its port and oil terminals); and Primorskiy kray can be classed as both a natural-resource region and a commercial hub. Map 1.2, showing major transport links, gives some guidance about hubs.

The eight regions that are considered closely in this book do include at least one representative of each of those four categories; provided, that is, that Krasnodar is allowed to serve in two of them. But as the economic changes proceeded, it became clear that our bunch of case-studies was tilted towards regions that were less depressed than the Russian average. This was not our intention, but there it is. In the

8. Hanson and Kirkow (1998) also did a study of Tomsk for the OECD.

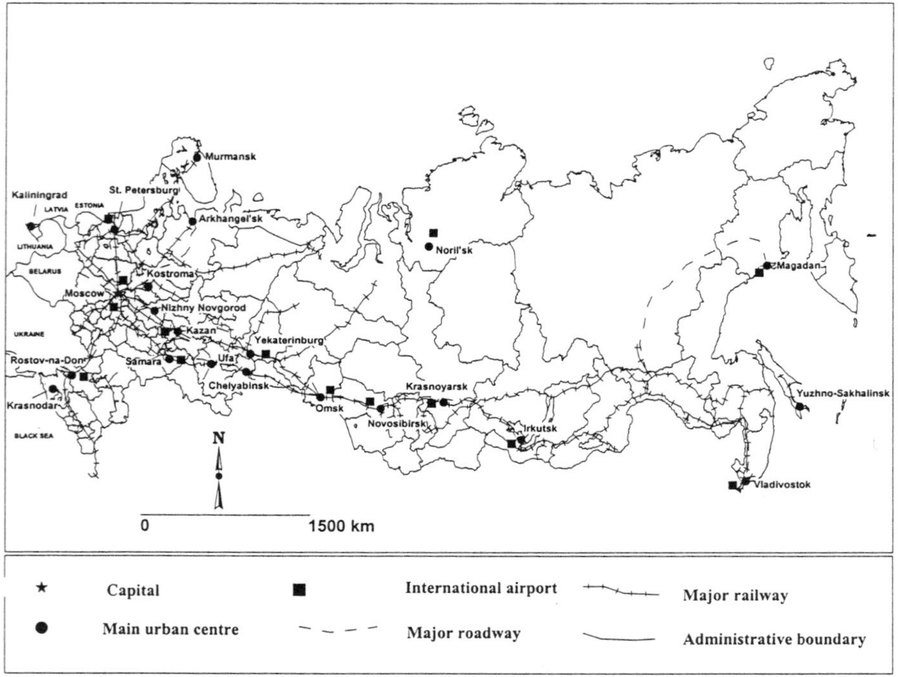

Map 1.2 The Russian Federation

Capital — ★

Main urban centre — ●

Major urban centre — ■

International airport

Major roadway

Major railway

Administrative boundary

0 ———— 1500 km

Labels on map: Murmansk, Kaliningrad, ESTONIA, LATVIA, LITHUANIA, BELARUS, UKRAINE, St. Petersburg, Arkhangel'sk, Kostroma, Nizhny Novgorod, Kazan, Moscow, Rostov-na-Donu, Krasnodar, BLACK SEA, Samara, Ufa, Yekaterinburg, Chelyabinsk, Noril'sk, Omsk, Novosibirsk, Krasnoyarsk, Irkutsk, Magadan, Yuzhno-Sakhalinsk, Vladivostok

N

14

various investment ratings and rankings of Russian regions (the rating of regions having become a new Russian industry), only Kostroma, from our case-study portfolio, regularly ranks in the bottom third (see, for example, 'Reyting ...' 1997). It is also fair to say that our case-studies covered rather little on the problems of rural areas and the farm sector.

With those caveats, we consider that the case-studies have provided ideas and conjectures that have helped in the quantitative analysis. At the same time, the case-studies are of interest in their own right. They provide concrete illustrations of general problems and processes. And they can also be useful for anyone who, for research or commercial or any other reasons, has a particular interest in a particular region. They therefore form a substantial part of this book.

The shape of the book is as follows. We begin with a review of the Western literature on the Russian regions in the post-Soviet era. Then there are three thematic chapters. First, there is a review of our findings on the regional dynamics of economic restructuring in Russia: how differences in the rate of industrial decline, in small-firm development, in agricultural adjustment, in changes in employment and unemployment, and in regional real income levels might be accounted for. Then there is an assessment of one form of adjustment by households: inter-regional migration. The last thematic chapter reviews the economic games played between the centre and the regions: what are federal-government policies on the regions, and especially the patterns of budgetary transfers? Are these tending to reduce inequalities in public provision? How substantial are they, and what do regional policy-makers do to influence them? Conversely, how might an 'internal IMF' strategy of top-down conditionality work out?

The second main part of the book is a set of four case-study chapters, each one dealing with a pair of regions: St Petersburg and Kostroma; Samara and Krasnodar; Sakhalin and Irkutsk; Primorskiy kray and Kaliningrad. The first pair are a relatively rich and a relatively poor region in the more northerly part of European Russia. The second are an emerging commercial hub region and one that is fairly poor and problem-ridden but strategically important, both south of Moscow in European Russia. The next pair, Sakhalin and Irkutsk, are resource-rich regions east of the Urals and far from Moscow. The last pair, Primorskiy and Kaliningrad, are maritime gateways with major fishing fleets, at opposite ends of the country, both under pressure to re-orient their economies to foreign transactions – Primorskiy because of its sheer distance from the centre of gravity of the Russian economy and its proximity to the Asian–Pacific countries, whose gravitational pull[9] exceeds that of European Russia; Kaliningrad because, exceptionally, it is a Russian exclave, physically separated from the rest of Russia and on track to be surrounded by an enlarged European Union.

In each case, we aim in these paired case-studies to describe their initial economic structures around 1990, the main changes in structure and levels of activity that have occurred since then, the nature of the main issues that have arisen, and the roles of major players in their evolution, including local political and economic elites, Moscow policy-makers, Moscow banks, foreign trade and foreign investment. The book ends, predictably, with a summary of the main conclusions.

9.   As it would be represented in a gravity model of trade that treated the Russian Far East and European Russia as though they were separate countries, and used just population size, GDP and distance as explanatory variables.

2. Russia's Regions in the 'Triple Transition'

Michael Bradshaw and Andrey Treyvish

INTRODUCTION

The aim of this review chapter is two-fold: first, to place our research project within the broader context of research on the regional dimensions of systemic transformation in Russia; and second, to use that review to identify the key questions being addressed by current research on Russia's regions. The following review makes no claim to be comprehensive. The focus is upon published material, principally in English and Russian. The review seeks to identify the key questions being addressed by the growing literature on Russia's regions. It should hardly be surprising that this body of research defies simple classification.

The review is divided into two sections. The first section examines the English-language literature on regional issues in Russia.[1] The notion of the triple transition is employed to organize the review, but it is recognized that much of this research, explicitly or implicitly, crosses the boundaries between the economic, the political and the socio-cultural. There are, of course, certain areas and approaches that remain

---

1. The section is a revised and updated version of a review that was published as part of M. J. Bradshaw and P. Hanson, 'Understanding Regional Patterns of Economic Change in Russia: An Introduction', *Communist Economies and Economic Transformation*, 10 (3) (1998), 285–304. For an extended bibliography, see Löwenhardt and White (1999). Neil Melvin of Leeds University's Department of Politics also maintains a web-based bibliography on research on Russia's regions, and this can be found at http//:www.leeds.ac.uk/polis/index3.htm. The same site also contains a bibliography on Russian research on politics and regionalism compiled by Vladimir Gel'man of the European University in St Petersburg and Sergey Ryzhenkov of the Institute of Humanitarian and Political Studies in Moscow.

the sole purview of specific disciplines, for example, an econometric analysis of regional prices or social-anthropological research on ethnic identity in Sakha. But even here one could argue that the findings of such research could only be understood in the broader contexts of regional change in Russia. Thus, the use of the triple transition represents a framework around which we organize our review of the Western literature; it does not imply a compartmentalized discipline-based approach to understanding patterns of regional change in Russia.

The first part of the review is organized around three sub-headings: political, economic and social transition. In each instance the review identifies the key issues relating to that aspect of transition and identifies the relevant literature. The second section of the review examines Russian research on regional economic change in Russia. This part of the review begins by presenting the results of a content analysis of the leading Russian geography and economics journals. This is then followed by a discussion of the theoretical challenges posed by systemic transformation. The final two sections consider the findings of recent empirical research on regional patterns of economic change. The conclusion identifies the key issues that are the focus of contemporary research on Russia's region. It also considers the methodological issues raised by what is a very wide range of research activity.

2.1 RUSSIAN REGIONS IN THE TRIPLE TRANSITION: THE VIEW FROM THE WEST

2.1.1 Political Transition: Building a Federation

Research on the regional dimensions of transition in Russia has focused upon two broad issues: the construction of a working federal system and the process of democratization. The literature on federalism in Russia seems to be addressing two broad issues: the building of a federal system in Russia and the specifics of centre–periphery or centre–region relations (see Slider 1994a; Solnick 1996). Discussion at the Russia-wide scale has examined the asymmetrical nature of Russian federalism (see Debardeleben 1997; Lynn and Novikov 1997; Lapidus and Walker 1995; Lapidus 1999; and Smith 1995a, 1995b, 1999). All regions are created equal by the constitution, but the reality is rather different. Case-study research examines how individual regions have managed their relations with the federal authorities in Moscow (Teague 1996; Tolz 1993a). Particular attention has been paid to the role of the ethnic republics, such as Tatarstan and Sakha (Yakutiya), which have been granted special privileges (see Balzer 1995; Balzer and Vinokurova 1996; Broxup 1996; Frank and Wixman 1997; Khakimov 1996; McAuley, M. 1997; Moukhariamov 1997; Ormond 1997; and Tolz 1993b). Thus, a region's relative position and strength in Russia's federal structure appears to be an important factor affecting its ability to attract federal support and retain income generated on its territory. Here the political issues merge into the economic and the issue of fiscal federalism is a good example of the interrelationship between politics and economics (see Kirkow 1996a; Le Houerou and Rutkowski 1996; McAuley, A. 1997; and Chapter 5 of this study). Furthermore, efforts by the federal authorities to promote local self-government at the municipal and district level further complicate the situation (see Campbell, 1995, 1994; Kirkow 1996b; Mitchneck 1997a, 1995, 1994; Solnick 1996, 1995; Stewart 1997; Treisman 1998, 1996a, 1996b, 1995; Young 1997, 1994; and Wallich 1995, 1992). Now centre–region conflict is played out within each oblast-level unit as well as between the oblast and the centre. Consequently, the internal political configuration of each region is becoming an increasingly important factor shaping the behaviour of the governor, the administration and the oblast duma (this issue is addressed in some of the case-studies that follow).

The second major dimension of regional work on political transition in Russia relates to the process of democratization (Andrews and Stoner-Weiss 1995). This encapsulates work on the elections, both at the federal and regional scale, work on the development of regional and local political regimes, which pays particular attention to the role of elites, and work on the emergence of regional associations. If the number of elections held measured the state of democracy, then since 1991 Russia has made great progress on the road to democracy (Hahn 1997a). There have been nation-wide polls to elect the president and the federal duma, nation-wide referendums on the progress of reform and polls to elect regional dumas and governors (Hahn 1997b). All of these events have generated a wealth of information on the voting habits of the Russian electorate. Political geographers and political scientists have produce a substantial literature analysing those patterns

(Clem and Craumer 1996, 1995; Debardeleben and Galkin 1997; Gimpelson *et al.* 1994; Helf 1994; O'Loughlin *et al.* 1996; and White *et al.* 1997). The electoral geography of national voting seems to have become relatively stable and the literature talks of a 'red belt'. However, it is also clear that voting behaviour in national polls does not explain regional or local political behaviour. Evidence from the last round of gubernatorial elections suggests that local issues, rather than national politics, are foremost in voters' minds (see Slider 1996; Solnick 1998; and Zlotnik 1996). Thus, governors are very conscious of the need to deliver the goods to the local electorate. National party affiliations are far less significant than a demonstrated ability to bring material improvements, either through lobbying the central government, providing local subsidies or introducing reforms that work (Berkowitz 1996, 1994a; Freinkman and Haney 1997; Freinkman and Yossifov 1999). Consequently, regions labelled as 'conservative' on the basis of national electoral behaviour may now have governors and administration that are introducing more 'radical' market-oriented reforms. The fact that local leaders are now accountable to their electorate raises the question of their loyalty to the central government and introduces a new dimension to the centre–region struggle in Russia (Stoner-Weiss 1999).

The issues raised above come together in regional case-studies of political behaviour in Russia. This literature contains research into electoral behaviour at the regional and rayon scale and on the formation and behaviour of local political elites (Cline 1994; Moses 1994; and Young 1994). It is the latter which has been the subject of greatest study. The literature suggests that there is as much continuity as change in the membership of the political elite at the regional level (Hahn 1994a, 1994b, 1993, 1991; Helf and Hahn 1992; and Melvin 1998). Many of the individuals who did well in the Soviet system have survived to form the new governments in Russia's regions. However, research also suggests that new coalitions are being forged between the political and economic elites in the regions (Mitchneck 1997a, 1997b). The strength and intent of these linkages also seem to vary from region to region. Rather than a single model of regional governance in Russia, it is apparent that there are a number of models (Gel'man and Senatova 1995; McAuley, M. 1997; and Stoner-Weiss 1997).

Finally, there has been some research at the inter-regional level that has examined attempts to create associations between regions. Most of this work has focused upon the 'Siberian Association' (Bradshaw 1992; Hughes 1994; Tolz 1993b; Radvanyi 1992; and Zhdanov 1995). It is fair to say that interest in such associations has declined as the constituent regions have refused to cooperate for fear that they might lose out in their individual efforts to lobby for support from the centre. However, renewed interest in the territorial-administrative structure of the federation and the possible introduction of a meso-level between the centre and the 89 subjects might revive the role of these associations. Equally, economic recovery may lead regions to see benefit in such coalitions.

In sum, research on the political dimensions of transition in Russia serves to highlight the complexity of the current situation. It suggests that it is difficult, and often dangerous, to generalize. For example, voting behaviour at the national level tells one very little of attitudes at the regional level. The situation in one region cannot be used to generalize about others. Equally, the political landscape is changing so quickly that past behaviour is no measure of a region's likely position in the future. Furthermore, case-study analysis reveals as much complexity and variation within regions as between them. However, the current complexity does not mean that one cannot identify key issues that are common to all regions. This has been one of the aims of our case-study research, to identify key questions that can be applied to analyses at the national scale.

2.1.2 Economic Transition: Regional Differentiation

It is fair to say that to date far less work has been done on the regional economic aspects of transition than the political aspects. It is this research gap that the current project seeks to address.[2] The reason for this relative neglect is in part due to the nature of economics as a discipline, traditionally macro-economic analysis has tended to dominate research on the Soviet Union and now on post-Soviet Russia. During the Soviet period regional studies were more concerned with the development of the Union Republics rather than the internal structure of the Russian Federation. However, there is a related literature in economic geography, which has always been concerned with the

---

2. See also the special edition of the *Communist Economies and Economic Transformation*, 10 (3) (1998), which contains a number of papers that are also based on this project.

process of regional development. In the Soviet era this literature focused upon the development of Siberia and the Far East. In the current context of economic transition, the fact that regions and regional administrations are so involved in the local economy is seen as a negative distortion. In a market economy it is firms and enterprises that are the key actors, not local politicians and bureaucrats. The literature that exists on what one might call regional aspects of economic transition can be organized around a number of issues: fiscal federalism, market fragmentation and regional economic performance (Mau and Stupin 1997).

The literature on fiscal federalism brings together analysis of the workings of the federal system in Russia with an assessment of the logic underlying the redistribution of federal tax revenues between regions. Initially the flow of tax revenues between donor and deficit regions was explained on the basis of political patronage (Kirkow 1996a; Solnick 1995; Treisman 1998, 1996a, 1996b). More recent analysis suggests that such flows do have an equalizing effect, funds from the richer regions are being transferred to the poorer regions (Stewart 1997; McAuley, A. 1997; and Kouznetsova *et al.* 1999). However, it is also recognized that such federal transfers account for only a minority of federal expenditures in any one region and only around 1 per cent of Russian GDP (see Chapter 5). Other forms of federal expenditure, such as special development programmes and the support of the military, also have a distinct geography. Data on these other expenditures cannot be obtained and therefore the analysis of explicit transfers is, at best, only a partial indicator of the level of federal support for individual regions. Such transfers are, however, worthy of study because they are the main instrument of federal policy designed specifically to alter regional outcomes. At the same time, a high level of federal government activity in a region is as much a hindrance as a help if the government cannot pay its bills. This has been the case in the Russian Far East (see Chapter 8 on Sakhalin) and in Krasnodar (see Chapter 7).

During the initial period of economic transition, the activities of regional administrations coupled with rapid increases in transportation costs served to break up the national market into a series of regional or fragmented markets. Local price subsidies and rationing were used to retain scarce goods within the local market. At the same time regional politicians used subsidies to cushion the voters against increasing living costs. Clearly, within the context of transition economics, such behaviour is seen as deviant and irrational and efforts are now being made to remove such subsidies (Freinkman and Haney 1997). An analysis of prices and capital markets suggests that a national market is now re-emerging as market mechanisms are replacing local control (Slider 1997b; and Pyle 1997). Quite simply, regional actors can no longer afford to subsidize, as the federal government is no longer providing them with funds. However, the gradual emergence of a single market economy across Russia does not mean that all regions will perform well. In fact, economic geography tells us that we can expect even greater variations in regional economic performance than during the Soviet period.

Analysis of patterns of regional economic performance has tended to be conducted at either the Russia-wide scale or on the basis of case-study research (Hanson 1997a; Kirkow 1998, 1997a, 1996b, 1996c, 1994, 1995; Kirkow and Hanson 1994; and Stoner-Weiss 1997). Russia-wide analysis has been based on the collection and analysis of various economic indicators, which are then subjected to statistical analysis (Bradshaw and Hanson 1994; and Bradshaw and Palacin 1996). Such analysis seldom produced rigorous results; however, there does seem to be a relationship between initial economic structure and regional economic performance in the 1990s (Sutherland and Hanson 1996; Bradshaw *et al.* 1998; Van Selm 1998; and Chapter 3 of this study). In the initial transition period regions dominated by heavy industry performed worst, while resource regions seemed to perform best (Hanson 1997b).

Much of this research sought to explain the geography of the transitional recession. See, for example, Gaddy's (1996) study of the regional dimensions of the military-industrial complex. The process of privatization did attract some attention (Filatochev and Bradshaw 1995; and Slider 1994b). Now attention is being focused upon aspects of economic recovery, such as the emergence of the service sector and patterns of foreign investment activity (Bradshaw *et al.* 1998; Bradshaw 1997a, 1995; and Sutherland 1996). A combination of such research provides a picture of relative winners and losers. Analyses rating and ranking regions on the basis of a variety of criteria now throw up the usual suspects as a relatively small number of regions are seen to be emerging as relative winners (for an early attempt, see Nagaev and Woergoetter 1995). Some regions, such as Primorskiy kray, are seen to be underperforming as they have certain natural advantages which are not being exploited to full advantage (Moltz 1996; Rozman 1997; and Troyakova 1995). In other regions the abilities of the local leadership are seen as a key factor in promoting economic recovery; Nizhnii Novgorod is the most often quoted example (Brown 1993). Analysis of regional economic performance reveals a complex interplay of inherited advantages and constraints, which combine with the ability of the regional elite to orchestrate economic recovery (see also Zimine 1998; and Zimine and Bradshaw 1999, on the case of Novgorod oblast). The relative failure of the statistical analysis of indicators at the Russia-wide scale reveals that there is no simple reason why some regions are winners and other are losers. Case-studies offer some explanations, but it is difficult to test these at the national scale, though we have in this volume been able to test some insights from case-studies on cross-regional data (see Chapter 3). Furthermore, the transition is far from over and some of the current front-runners may yet fall from favour while new winners may emerge. There is already evidence to suggest that the August 1998 economic crisis had a more significant impact upon the 'reforming regions' which were most involved in Russia's fledgling financial system. The more peripheral regions were essentially isolated from financial shocks because they were not involved in monetary exchange or had been ignored by the Moscow-based financial groups.

2.1.3   Social Transition: Identity and Inequality

The political and economic processes discussed above are having a major impact on the living standards and life chances of the Russian population. Yet those studying Russia's regions have tended to neglect the cultural and social consequences of transition. Of course, research on the ethnic republics and autonomous regions has focused on issues of language and identity and the resurgence of local identities (Balzer 1995; Balzer and Vinokurova 1996; Fondahl 1997, 1996; and Vitebskiy 1996). In the ethnic homeland ethnicity and regionalism go hand-in-hand, but Russia as a whole seems to lack a strong sense of regional identities. The failure of the regional economic associations suggests the lack of wider regional affiliations (Novikov 1997).

It is generally accepted that economic transition has widened the gap between the rich and the poor, both in terms of individuals in society and of regions in the federation (the increase in income differential is analysed in Chapter 3). Yet there is a relative lack of academic research examining the relationship between transition and regional inequality. Rather, research has focused on the symptoms of poverty and inequality by examining the changing demographics of Russia's regions. Decline in living standards, environmental problems and decline in welfare provision are all implicated in the geography of population change in Russia (Field 1997; Pryde 1995; and Chapter 4 of this study). Despite the limited nature of the housing market and the high cost of transportation, people are voting with their feet and migration flows are seen as a key indicator of the health of regional economies (Heleniak 1997). The Russian north is emptying and people are moving from the east to the west. It seems that southern Russia, with the exception of the North Caucasus, is the favoured destination. Thus, Russia may be experiencing a 'permafrost-sunbelt' shift as the economy of the hyper-industrialized north declines and a more manufacturing and service-based south starts to emerge. This suggests that the relative position of Russia's regions, in terms of economic success and living standards, is undergoing radical change. Those left behind in the loser regions present a major social problem for the federal government. However, case-study analysis reveals that there is often substantial variation in living standards within individual regions, often along the urban–rural divide (Bradshaw and Shaw 1996). Therefore, social inequality is also an issue for individual oblast administrations.

2.2   RUSSIAN RESEARCH ON REGIONAL ASPECTS OF ECONOMIC CHANGE

This section of our review considers the Russian literature published in the 1990s on regional aspects of economic transformation. By Russian we mean the domestic view presented by Russian researchers and not just Russian-language publications. While the focus is upon economic aspects of regional change, as the previous section revealed, the multi-faceted nature of regional economic change in Russia also requires consideration of political and social issues. For a comprehensive review of indigenous research into the politics of Russian regions see Gel'man and Ryzhenkov (1998). The following review addresses four issues: publication trends in the major journals; the changing conceptual basis of research; explanations of the spatial dimensions of economic restructuring; and models of regional development. The review includes materials from the regions; many of these are not available in Moscow, let alone in the West. They attest to the fact that there is now a good deal of worthwhile research being conducted in the regions by local specialists. It is certainly the case that this project has benefited from the contributions made by our colleagues in our case-study regions: further evidence, if it were needed, of the advantages of cooperative field-based research.

2.2.1   Editorial, Disciplinary and Topical Restructuring

It is fair to say that during the 1990s both decay and renewal have affected Russian academic publishing. Many long-running publications have seen their circulation decline; others have experienced a change in content; and numerous new publications have emerged. The growing interest in regional problems spawned many new periodicals; some soon disappeared, often due to financial problems, and some still remain. Below is a far from comprehensive list of new 'regional-oriented' journals published in Moscow and beyond with, when available, information on their founders, sponsors and years of publication.

Moscow-based journals

- *Rossiya-2010: zhurnal mezhregional'noy gosudarstvennosti* (Komitet Gosdumy RF po ekonomicheskoy politike i dr. Yu. Krupov, 1993–5).
- *Vash Vybor: nauchno-politicheskiy zhurnal regionov* (TOO 'Vash Vybor', A. Mineev, 1993–6).
- *Rossiyskaya provintsiya* (Gorbachev-Fond, V. Kubaldin, 1994–6)
- *Federalizm: teoriya, praktika, istoriya* (Institut Ekonomiki RAN, Finansovo-investitsionnaya korporatsiya 'Yugra', S. Valenteye, since 1995).
- *Regional'noye razvitiye i sotrudnichestvo* (Mezhdunarodnaya Akademiya Regional'nogo Razvitiya i Sotrudnichestva, A. Granberg, since 1997).

Examples of non-Moscow journals (with editors' names)

- *Regional'naya ekologiya* (St Petersburg, Institut Sotsial'no-ekonomicheskikh Problem RAN, O. Litovka, since 1994. Before that *Regional'naya politika* 1991–4).

- *Ekonomika i upravlenie: Vserossiyskiy Nauchno-Informatsionnyy zhurnal* (St Petersburg, Publishing House 'Biznes-Tsentr', Institut Upravleniya i Ekonomiki, V. Gnevko, since 1995).

- *Region: Delovoy zhurnal pravitel'stva respubliki Komi* (Syktyvkar, since 1998).

- *Problemy regional'noy ekonomiki* (Izhevsk, since 1998).

- *Regionologiya: Nauchno-publitsisticheskiy zhurnal* (Saransk, Minobrazovaniya RF, Minnauki RF, NII Regionologii pri Mordovskom Universitete, A. Sukharev, since 1992).

- *Guberniya: Zhurnal informatsii, analiza, ekspertizy* (Penza, Publishers of the journal 'Zemstvo', V. Manuylov, since 1995).

- *Regional'nye agrosistemy: ekonomika i sotsiologiya* (Saratov, 1994–5).

- *Panorama-Forum* (Kazan', Tsentr Gumanitarnykh proyektov i issledovaniy, Moskovskiy Tsentr po issledovaniyu mezhnatsional'nykh i mezhregional'nykh ekonomicheskikh problem, R. Khakimov, since 1997).

- *Ekonomika i reformy Tartarstana* (Kazan', Investitsionno-finansovaya korporatsiya Respubliki Tatarstan, A. Zhigalova, since 1997).

- *Region: ekonomika i sotsiologiya* (Novosibirsk, Institut ekonomiki i organizatsii promyshlennogo proizvodstva SO RAN, Mezhregional'naya assotsiatsiya 'Sibirskoye soglashenie', V. Seliverstov, since 1994).

- *Etika uspekha* (Tyumen', Tsentr prikladnoi etiki SO RAN and Finansovo-investitsionnaya korporatsiya 'Yugra', V. Bakshtanovskiy and V. Chrilov, since 1997).

- *Dal'niy Vostok Rossii: ekonomika, investitsii, kon'yunktura* (Vladivostok, since 1997).

In addition to these journals, a number of useful proceedings and reports have been published. For example, since 1990 the Russian Academy of Sciences and International Academy of Regional Development and Cooperation (Economic Geography Section) have published the proceedings of their annual meetings. The Moscow-based Expert Institute has published a number of reports on regional issues (for example, *Analiz tendentsii...* 1996). Other institutions publishing regionally oriented serials include: the Moscow Scientific Fund (*Nauchnye doklady*, since 1993); the Academic Institute of Geography and Stavropol University *(Rossiya 90-e gody: problemy regional'nogo razvitiya*, since 1994); the Interdisciplinary Centre of Social Science produces an annual report *Kuda idyot Rossiya*; and since 1994 the Moscow Carnegie Centre has produced a series of research reports. Regional issues are also addressed in new periodicals such as: *Ekspert, Kommersant'* and its affiliated publications *Den'gi* and *Vlast', Delovyye Lyudi, Kapital, Polis, Mir Rossii, Migratsiya, Pro et kontra*, as well as in numerous encyclopaedias, data- and textbooks. Daily newspapers often have special regional supplements. Finally, there are numerous business publications, such as the *Biznes-karta* series, providing information and key contacts in the regions. The list is endless and it should already be clear that the 1990s have seen a virtual explosion of publications dealing with regional issues in Russia. Due to their small print runs and often-obscure publishing houses, many of these publications remain beyond the grasp of Western researchers.

The abundance and variety of publications gives the impression of a real innovative boom. At the same time, the relative instability of academic and specialist publishing in Russia results in a lack of continuity. As a consequence, there is no single authoritative source that one can consult to discern trends in regional research. That said, it is possible to chart recent changes within two sub-disciplines: human geography and economics. Petrov (1998) made the first attempt to monitor annual topical change in human geography in the period 1984–96. His analysis had to conform to the rather eclectic sub-headings of the *Referativnyy zhurnal: Geografiya (RZh)*. His analysis was based in two sections in *RZh*: 'economic and social geography' and 'geography of the states upon the territory of the former USSR'. Not surprisingly, he found the topic that had experienced the greatest decline in interest was 'geography of economy and cooperation of socialist states'. This theme accounted for 30 per cent of abstracts in 1984 and zero in 1991! The nature of the *RZh* does not make it possible to identify studies on regions within Russia, but it does show a growth in abstracts on topics related to Russia as a whole. An alternative method has been employed here that involves the analysis of the contents of four leading professional geography journals (see Kolosov *et al.* 1996; Eckert and Treyvish 1995; and Kotlyakov and Preobrazhenskiy 1996, p. 48):

- *Izvestiya Akademii Nauk: seriya geografiya* (RAN, AN SSSR, Moscow);
- *Vestnik Moskovskogo Universiteta: seriya geografiya* (MGU, Moscow);
- *Izvestiya Russkogo/Vsesoyuznogo geograficheskogo obshchestva* (RGO/VGO, St Petersburg); and
- *Geografiya i prirodnye resursy* (Irkutsk).

For the purposes of the present review, an updated content analysis of these four leading journals is now presented. To assist presentation, three-year periods have been used. About 20 per cent of the articles published during each period are identified as *human geography*. This group is then further subdivided on the basis of key words in each article's title, such as economic, population, social, cultural, political and resource-environmental geography. The results of the analysis are shown in Table 2.1. Social, population and cultural geography are slowly replacing economic geography; these are now much more popular topics of enquiry among younger scholars. Within the sub-category of economic geography, it is industrial that has experienced the greatest decline. The other area to suffer substantial decline is

Table 2.1   Topical restructuring of human geography by current publications in four journals (%)

Major topical groups	1980–82	1990–92	1993–95	1996–98
Total number of articles (= 100%)	**417**	**387**	**372**	**354**
General human geography (theory etc.)	22.0	25.9	25.7	24.7
Economic geography:	25.7	20.0	18.1	16.2
Industrial geography	14.4	9.1	7.0	5.8
Geography of tertiary sectors	4.8	4.4	6.0	6.1
Population, social and cultural–political geography:	24.0	25.9	26.2	31.7
Population (settlement)	16.0	10.9	7.7	10.4
Social, cultural and political geography	8.0	15.0	18.5	21.3
Resource–environmental geography	28.3	28.2	30.0	27.4

population geography. The clear winners are social and political geography: together they have experienced a rise from 8 per cent to 21 per cent of articles. The declining 'traditional' areas of industrial and population geography comprised 74 per cent of the content of socio-economic geography in the 1980s, but their share had fallen to 33 per cent by the late 1990s. Thus, human geography, broadly defined, has experienced a significant shift in focus as a consequence of the collapse of the Soviet Union. The decline in interest in industrial geography is understandable, given that it was the mainstay of a highly descriptive 'Soviet geography'; however, demographic issues are a critical element of Russia's post-Soviet geography. What is more likely is that demographic research has developed elsewhere in more specialist research institutes.

A second component of our analysis examines the geographical objects of inquiry, in other words which countries and regions have been studied in the human geography literature. Table 2.2 presents the results of this analysis. The results show a switch in interest away from

Table 2.2   Spatial structure of human geography (4 journals), 1980–82 and 1996–8 (%)

Country, Area	1980–82	1996–8
Total number of articles (= 100%)	**348**	**269**
Globe and foreign countries		
(the '90s 'Far Abroad')	29.3	26.4
USSR/CIS (single republics included)	33.6	10.0
Russia: whole regional spectrum	0.9	24.9
European Russia: regions and localities	13.5	19.7
Asiatic Russia: regions and localities	22.7	19.0

USSR/CIS (the 'Near Abroad') towards Russia. However, the internal distribution of studies on Russia is now more balanced with more studies on European Russia. The decline in studies of the 'Far Abroad' is explained by the collapse of CMEA and a declining interest in developing countries; but there is still a significant interest in the countries of the 'Far Abroad' beyond Central Europe.

A similar analysis was conducted on the contents of four leading economics journals: *Voprosy ekonomiki, Ekonomist* (*Planovoye khoz-zyaystvo* before 1991), *Rossiyskiy ekonomicheskiy zhurnal* (*Ekono-micheskie nauki* before 1992), all published in Moscow, and *EKO* (*Ekonomika i organizatsiya promyshlennogo proizvodstva*), published in Novosibirsk. The results of our analysis show that the share of 'regional economic' topics has more than doubled and that this has been at the expense of sectoral topics (Table 2.3). This trend is observable across all four journals. In *Rossiyskiy ekonomicheskiy zhurnal* regional topics now form 12 per cent of content, four times as much as in the 1980s. A second and totally expected trend is the decline in theoretical Marxist macro-economic studies. Formerly abundant in *Voprosy ekonomiki* and *Ekonomicheskiye nauki* (47 to 59 per cent in 1980–82), they were partly balanced by 'meso-economic', mainly sectoral studies (33 per cent of *Planovoye khozyaystvo* articles examined specific sectors or branches). Now macro-economic studies of a different orthodoxy are balanced by regional studies. Strangely, the micro-level of enterprises and entrepreneurs has experienced an absolute decline and a modest growth in percentage, although many related subjects such as privatization, small business and household economy are well represented (for example, Kleyner 1996; Oleynik 1998). The abundance of business-oriented magazines may also help to explain the relative absence of business topics in the more formal journals.

Table 2.3   Topical/level structure of publications in four economics journals, 1980–82 and 1996–8

Major topics by level and type of analysis	1980–82		1996–8	
	No. of articles	%	No. of articles	%
Totals	**3309**	**100.0**	**1889**	**100.0**
Nation-wide and international	570	17.2	567	30.0
Regional and local	210	6.3	248	13.1
Sectors and branches	677	20.5	233	12.3
Enterprises, households, individuals	328	9.9	228	12.1
Theory, method, education	1131	34.2	423	22.4
Undistributed	393	11.9	190	10.1

Some Russian liberal economists would disagree with the statement that macro-economic analysis has dominated research in both the USSR and Russia today. This depends upon how the term macro-economic is understood: if it is a level or scale of analysis (rather than a doctrine), the statement seems correct. In the journals analysed, the share of macro-level analysis is 37.5 per cent, slightly above the share during the Soviet period. However, interest in relations between the various scales of analysis may increase as many liberal economists are now linking the failures of Russia's reforms to its meso- and micro-economic weaknesses (Popov 1998). The results presented in Table 2.4 show an even stronger 'domestication' of economic than geographical research. In other words, Russian geographers remain more interested

Table 2.4　Spatial structure of nation- and world-wide economy (four journals) (%)

Countries	1980–82	1996–8
Russian Federation	2.3	61.7
USSR/CIS (whole and by republic)	53.2	9.2
World-wide and by foreign country (the '90s 'far abroad')	44.6	29.1
Total number of articles (= 100%)	**570**	**567**

in the outside world than Russian economists are. This could help to explain the tendency of Russian economists to see Russia's problems as different or unique, while geographers seem more interested in the application of general processes such as spatial restructuring. The regional orientation of articles published in the economic journals is seldom apparent from their title and in one-third of cases the title defies topical classification (Table 2.5). As for the rest, the four-fold increase in the share of monetary-fiscal topics is impressive. The share which deals with institutional issues remains stable but has experienced a shift in emphasis. Formerly devoted to managerial problems, institutional analysis now focuses upon regional-level reform. Given the deepening of social problems, the decline in articles related to these issues (10–11 articles annually) looks strange and is at odds with the growth of interest in these issues within geography.

What general observations can be drawn from this content analysis of the leading Russian geographical and economic academic journals?

Table 2.5   Topical structure of regional/local economy (four journals) (%)

Major Topics	1980–82	1996–8
General: allocation of economy, regional development and policy, etc.	35.7	27.6
Social: labour force, employment and human factors	15.2	11.8
Monetary, budgetary and financial	3.8	15.4
Institutional and managerial	10.5	13.8
Regional-sectoral, individual regional and undistributed	34.8	31.3
Total number of articles (= 100%)	**210**	**246**

First, there has been a trend towards more regionally oriented analysis and a reduction in sectoral studies. Second, there has been a shift in the kind of topic addressed by academic research to reflect the new socio-economic situation in the country; never before have so many new topics been introduced simultaneously (in the case of geography, see Baburin and Shuvalov 1996; and Gladkiy 1992). As elsewhere, change has tended to take place within disciplinary and institutional boundaries. It is also interesting to note that so-called 'regional economics', proclaimed since 1970 as an academic and applied discipline (supported by Gosplan), has so far failed to bridge the gap between economics and geography. This failure is despite many attempts to rejuvenate the discipline (see *Regional'nye...* 1991; Granberg 1994; and Bil'chak and Zakharov 1998). The result is that there are groups of geographers, economists and regional economists all studying the same issues, but from different perspectives. These same groups are also tied into collaborative projects with foreign scholars in kindred disciplines. To this can be added the new groups of political scientists and sociologists now involved in similar research projects. Little attention is paid either to problems of duplication of effort or to the constraints of international copyright. Here competition for funding becomes paramount and individuals and institutions, understandably, guard their contacts. The net result is that there is a large, and continually growing, body of research and literature that is by its very nature partial and fragmented and lacks a common theoretical or methodological approach (but the same is also true of Western research).

2.2.2   Conceptual Change or Continuity?

With the benefit of hindsight, we can say that 1992 marked a turning-point from perestroika and 'what to do' disputes (Men'shikov 1990; *Perekhod...* 1990) to real reforms which attracted new criticism and alarm. Some analysts (Petrov *et al.* 1992; Animitsa 1993) argued that the Russian way to democracy and the market economy would inevitably lead to sharp regional problems. The term '*regionalizatsiya*', embracing and elevating regionalism and regional restructuring, was born, together with numerous claims for stronger regional policy in order to soften new inequalities, socio-political pains and risks. Some attempts to initiate an alternative strategy and reintegration from below were also undertaken (*Nizhegorodskiy...* 1992). However, the instigation of a full-scale regional policy under conditions of economic crisis looked unlikely (Ratner *et al.* 1993). The centre–periphery gaps generated by *spatial mobilization* and previous *big jumps* (the spatial consequences of Soviet development strategy) were described and compared with the processes of spatial and economic structuring in Western industrial societies (Gritsay *et al.* 1991; Vishnevskiy 1998, pp. 37–77). Nevertheless, diminishing disparities were not just a slogan for industrial diffusion. The image of Soviet space as a single social-economic-state structure and the region viewed as a section of a single factor, however often criticized (Kaganskiy and Rodoman 1995, pp. 48–9), remains a significant factor in the mass and professional mentality.

The Soviet heritage, especially the concepts of economic region and territorial complex (TPC), became a source of disagreement and a means of identifying particular schools of thought. Attitudes towards the continuing relevance of the TPC concept showed a clear schism within Russian economic geography and regional economics (for criticism, see Petrov *et al.* 1992; Rodoman 1993; Lyubovnyy and Lagutenko 1994). Lyubovnyy and Lagutenko (1994) referred to the TPC as a source of personal well-being for generations of economic geographers and regional economists; and as the source of economic crisis in the TPC regions themselves as they were now over-specialized and lacking high-tech sectors (one of our case-studies, Irkutsk oblast, was the location for one of the first TPCs). At the same time, entire pro-TPC volumes were published (Dmitriyeva 1992; *Problemnoye...* 1993). The TPCs extracting oil, gas and iron ores, and thus supporting

Russia's budget, were given particular attention. The debate over the fate of the TPC was symptomatic of the wider crisis about how to reconcile the intellectual heritage of the Soviet past with a very rapidly changing post-Soviet present. The journals abounded with contradictory messages. For example, one issue of *Mir Rossii* contained an article calling for the revision of post-Soviet boundaries and Russian ethnic-based expansion (Kobuzan 1996), but the same edition also contained an article which suggested a new strategy of Russian domestic development – the compression of intensively used space (Pivovarov 1996). The question of paradigmatic change or continuity remained open, but was supplemented by conciliatory suggestions of a 'healthy balanced approach' (Agafonov and Gladkiy 1994); however, the various sides remained entrenched.

Meanwhile, the attacks of the 'old academicians' and the younger critics (Grigorii Yavlinskiy, Sergei Glazyev and others) on the nature of the reform process became more insistent. Yavlinskiy, in particular, advocates grass-roots institutional reforms as a necessary precondition of successful national-level stabilization. He and his EPItsentr Institute worked closely with Boris Nemtsov in the early 1990s on reforms within Nizhnii Novgorod oblast. The regional dimension may have been missing from much of this debate, but the sectoral concerns had clear regional implications. For example, concern for the plight of Russia's textile industry translated to its impact upon Ivanovo oblast. Russia is neither Kuwait nor Canada: with an economically active population of over 70 million, it cannot survive on its resource industries alone; however, such comparison soon led to the identification of resource-rich and resource-poor regions *Makroekonomicheskiye...* 1996; *Ekonomicheskiye...* 1997).

2.2.3 The Spatial Restructuring of the Russian Economy: Market Adjustment or Degradation?

Dmitriyeva (1992) was the first to use the term *regional diagnostics* in the title of a book. Soon after her initial publication, a whole series of works were dedicated to budgetary relations, transfers and donor-recipient problems (Leksin and Shvetsov 1995; Polishchuk 1996; Lavrov 1997a; *Regiony...* 1997; Pozdnyakov *et al.* 1998; *Ekonomicheskiye...* 1997). Other works have examined the socio-economic infrastructure of regions along west–east, north–south and core–

periphery axes and have concluded that their adaptive potential varies greatly (Tarkhov and Treyvish 1992; Tarkhov 1995; Privalovskaya *et al.* 1995; Analysis... 1996; Levada 1996; Marchenko 1996; Nefyodova 1997; Ioffe and Nefyodova 1997; *Predprinimatel'skiy...* 1997; Rimashevskaya and Yakovleva 1998; Regional... 1999).

It has been observed that the so-called process of industrial *primitivization* (increasing reliance upon the primary sector of industrial activity) has resulted in a renewed eastward shift in the locus of economic activity. The old core region of European Russia has now conceded to a Yamal–Urals–Volga (–Don and Kuban seaports) belt that now provides Russia with half of its outputs and exports (Kazantsev 1996; Treyvish 1998a). Differential adaptation, either creating new markets or adjusting passively (Shtayner 1996; Belyakov 1997), has widened the gap between the centres and and conservative peripheries. Moscow's tertiary sector boom (Gritsay 1996) has supported the Central Region's share of GDP, despite the decline of its manufacturing sectors. Every fifth large Russian enterprise or headquarters and over 40 per cent of their capital are registered in Moscow. Moscow's share of Russian retail trade turnover has increased from 12 per cent in 1990 to 29 per cent in 1998. The city generates high prices and compensates its residents by providing incomes that are substantially higher than the national average. The main losers in this equation are deeply depressed industrial regions such as Ivanovo oblast and backward peripheries such as the North Caucasus. The usage of aggregated resource potential (natural, labour and capital resources expressed in GDP values) calculated by Klotsvog and Kushnikova (1998) was 50 per cent below the national average in the Dagestan and Kalmyk republics, but 100 per cent above the national average in Nizhni Novgorod and Samara oblasts and 187 per cent in Moscow city. The North-west, Centre, South and even Far East economies are better equipped with infrastructure than the Volga–Urals industrial belt (Dronov 1998, p. 182). Transitional recession has not created these problems: their origins lie in the regional consequences of late-Soviet development strategy; rather transition has amplified their effect and deepened the divide between winner and loser regions.

Kaganskiy (1995, 1996, 1997) has used the term *neo-Soviet space* as an extension of the notion of *nomenklatura capitalism* to describe post-Soviet Russia. According to Kaganskiy, money, oil and gas on a Moscow–Tyumen' axis have polarized the country rather than organized it. Vardomskiy (1997) adds that the new openness has divided the Russian economy into two sectors: the larger, failing *introvert* and the smaller, successful *extrovert* represented by 37 regions of central, border, gateway and exporting types. The remaining 52 regions do not constitute a single undifferentiated marginal zone. At the same time, there are also substantial variations within regions. Some calculations show that intra-regional disparities surpass the inter-regional, even if cities alone are compared (not allowing for urban–rural differences) (Nefyodova and Treyvish 1998). According to Rodoman (1998), some 10 million sq km, two-thirds of Russian territory, comprises a 'deep periphery' running wild, cut off from civilization, services and communications. This new, and deepening, inequality is often explained as the inevitable consequence of economic transition and the general crisis within the Russian economy. The ability of the economy to adapt to new conditions has certainly been hindered by the relatively low mobility of the population and labour and the absence of national labour, housing and capital markets (*Makroekonomicheskiye...* 1996; Polishchuk 1998). In other words, the Soviet legacy has hampered and retarded the process of spatial restructuring. The one area where this is not the case is in the largest cities and their suburbs (Nefydova 1998).

Analysis of regional development trends in Russia by Artobolevskiy, Bylov, Lavrovskiy and Treyvish (in *Regional...* 1999, pp. 23–49, 93–118) has identified what they term *regressive divergence* as the dominant but not the only process affecting Russia's regions (see Table 2.6). A process of *progressive convergence* is observable in indicators

Table 2.6   Typology of general and local (regional) development trends

General Trend Dynamic	Progress (Improvement, development, growth, etc.)	Regress (Degradation, decay, decline, etc.)
Convergence (Levelling, equalization, etc.)	Progressive convergence (Levelling up, equalizing growth)	Regressive convergence (Levelling down, equalizing decline)
Divergence (Differentiation, etc.)	Progressive divergence (Unbalanced development, uneven growth)	Regressive divergence (Differentiating, uneven decline)

Source: Artobolevskiy *et al.*, in *Regional...* 1999.

such as housing space per family, phones and car ownership. Downward levelling or *regressive convergence* has accompanied recent consumer and financial crises as they have impacted on previously privileged centres and they have left the already depressed self-supplied periphery relatively untouched. The net result is that those regions that were doing well before the crisis have suffered disproportionately and have moved downward towards the periphery. Measuring the regional impact of industrial decline is complicated by the nature of the pricing system; equally, official statistics cannot account for the contribution of shadow and non-monetary activities. The net result may be to overstate the level of production decline in major industrial centres and to understate the level of economic activity in peripheral rural areas where shadow and non-monetary activities predominate. Therefore, at best, official production statistics provide a partial and biased measure of economic prosperity in a given region and thus fail to capture the real nature of regional development levels in Russia's regions. Many Russian scholars would agree with the Western description of Russia as a 'leopard skin economy' (Sapir 1996) or a 'patchwork quilt of regions too different in their economic and political regimes' (Talbott 1998).

2.2.4   Regional Elites, Interests and Models of Development

A number of Russian studies focus on the delineation of federal and regional powers. Notwithstanding what has been written in the Russian constitution and in various bilateral agreements, the roles are divided in a manner whereby the federal government is responsible for strict financial policy and the provinces (regions) for coping with the effects of those policies and the support of their enterprises and population. In reality, the Kremlin, lacking political resources or the will, had to share its power. Department–sectoral economic control and the spatial rotation of elites (moving them on so they don't turn native) are no longer possible. The result has been the emergence of a form of 'bargaining federalism' and a growth in the power of regional elites (Afanas'yev 1994, 1997, 1998; Duka 1995; Lavrov and Kuznetsova 1996; L. Polishchuk 1996; A. Polishchuk 1998; Pavlenko 1997; *Transformatsiya...* 1999).

It is normally said that civic structures, regional political parties and the mass media are stronger now, but weaker than the former authoritarian and quasi-feudal regimes. Old directors and the new business and political elites are collaborating in search of privilege and enrichment. For some this is creating a second, regional, version of the command economy (Mokhov 1997). Whether it be bureaucrats or business interests in control of the local economy, there is a symbiotic relationship between public politics and private capital. The term lobby does not explain the relationship between business interests and local political processes; there is often no distance between the two (Afanas'yev 1998; Lepekhin in *Transformatsiya...* 1999, p. 57). The nature and extent of interpenetration varies from region to region. Afanas'yev (*Transformatsiya...* 1999, p. 12) suggests that the degree of administrative control is dependent on a region's economic power, with the common rule that weak industry results in a weak business elite and powerful bureaucratic paternalism. Normally stronger regions have more clearly articulated interests, policies and development models. Equally, a special position (Kaliningrad, Sakhalin) or obstinacy (Chechnya) may result in strong local interests.

A number of studies have tried to identify and classify the various regional strategies that have emerged during the 1990s (*Regiony...* 1993; Marchenko 1996; Vardomskiy 1997; *Predpriminatel'skiy...* 1997). Marchenko (1996) proposed the following typology:

1 conservative-communist (basically agrarian);
2 national-liberal (urbanized);
3 international liberal (gateway model);
4 lobbyist (searching for federal support);
5 separatist (strong republics bargaining with Moscow); and
6 paternalist–clientelistic.

Marchenko then compared the regions' industrial rates of change and real incomes and concluded that conservatism and paternalism strategies brought few benefits. The separatist and national-liberal models seemed to be more successful. This could, however, be a suspect conclusion since stronger regions often prefer more open and resolute models. A more recent scheme suggested by Lysenko and Matveev (in *Ekonomicheskiye...* 1997, p. 99) classifies regions on the basis of economic interests and market orientation:

1 mining–exporting regions interested in liberal and open economic policy and relative independence;
2 'manufacturers' interested in a large and unified national market and state protectionism, but protesting against anti-inflation policies;
3 self-sufficient agro-industrial regions interested in internal development and often isolationist;
4 republics whose elites play the ethnic card and enjoy exclusive economic regimes; and
5 border regions in favourable positions interested in most liberal trade policy and an offshore model of development.

The problem with such typologies is that they simplify, and often distort, reality.

If trying to generalize across the 89 federal subjects were not difficult enough, as noted earlier, it is also the case that there is as much variation within each region as amongst the regions. Among the 86 regions with at least two urban settlements, the first in population acts as the regional 'capital' in 80 cases. This status helps it to improve its social infrastructure at the expense of the rest the region. Novikov (1998) has calculated that on average 43 per cent of municipal (district-level) expenditures are accounted for by the regional capital, which in turn, on average, accommodate 31 per cent of the country's population. Within regions, centre–region conflicts are commonplace and a mayor can win a regional election with the help of the capital's 'prosperous image'. The market also elevates the competitiveness of other centres in terms of industrial production and investments. For example, Novgorod is often lauded for its success in attracting foreign investment, but most of that investment is located in the city of Chudovo and not the oblast capital. A study of 950 cities (Brade *et al.* 1999) revealed numerous instances of cities with an economic importance beyond their position in the population hierarchy. For example, there are mining towns in Tyumen and the Kuzbass where the capitals never were the economic leaders; heavy industrial centres (such as Staryy Oskol, Cherepovets, Sayanogorsk, Angarsk and Bratsk) have strengthened their role and control of their region's finances; and there are also new informal centres (such as Monchegorsk in Murmansk oblast, Tol'yatti in Samara oblast and Noril'sk in Krasnoyarsk kray) that have recently eclipsed in some respects their oblast capitals. The existence of such islands of relative prosperity in otherwise depressed regions helps soften the perception of Russia as a country of insuperable centralism. However, Western analysts may find this intra-regional dimension quite difficult to study. In Russia today local self-government and region–local problems are even more haphazardly regulated than federal–regional problems. Hence the shadow rules and bargains which affect the higher level of relations become even more common at the lower level.

2.3 CONCLUSIONS

From this review it is clear that the aggravation of regional problems associated with systemic transformation and growing state, corporate and public interest has challenged the skills of both Western and Russian scholars. In both literatures there is great variety in method and approach and, as yet, no apparent consensus on what should be done and what might happen next. There is a large degree of similarity in terms of the topics being covered: centre–periphery relations; the emergence of regional political elites; spatial restructuring and so on. But it also seems the case there is a greater interest in Russia-wide analysis and generalization in domestic research on regional matters than there is in the Western literature. In fact, it could be concluded that many Russian studies seem too ready to generalize on the basis of large data sets and pay little attention to detailed case-study research, while most Western researchers seem loath to move beyond one or two case-studies. Those who do are often criticized for making generalizations that they cannot substantiate. However, we are aware of a number of survey-based research projects currently under way that involve a large number of case-studies and therefore probably fall somewhere between the two extremes.

Differences in level of analysis are apt to lead to difference in assessments of particular regions. All of us involved in regional case-studies always look to see how the latest typology or ranking has treated 'our' region and then form a judgement on the validity of the exercise on the basis of whether or not they got our region(s) right. As later studies in this volume reveal, a major reason why Russia-wide analyses using Goskomstat Rossii data fail to reflect the story told at the local level is that measures of the same indicator published locally for the same time period are often very different from those published in Moscow. The lesson for those wishing to use such analysis to guide decision-making is that there is no substitute for actually going to the regions themselves. A central aim of this project has been to use regional case-studies to assist us in conducting Russia-wide analysis. Unfortunately, as noted above, the reality on the ground defies simple generalization, but at least we have been able to 'ground' our generalizations and place our case-studies in a broader context.

3. Regional Dynamics of Economic Restructuring Across Russia

Douglas Sutherland, Michael Bradshaw and Philip Hanson

INTRODUCTION

That economic restructuring is taking place in Russia is beyond doubt. What is more open to debate is the actual shape of the economy that will emerge in the medium to long term. Present developments in the Russian regions suggest that the geography of restructuring can be very varied indeed, making it difficult for the observer to construct a coherent picture based on a limited array of information. In this chapter the differing geography of transformation in Russia's regions is addressed, using a wide array of indicators. By examining different indicators of economic decline, the development of new economic activity and measures of the consequences of economic transformation, one can see several, often apparently conflicting, developments occurring simultaneously, even within a single region.

This implies that no holistic measure of economic change is available and that the coexistence of several adaptation strategies within the spatial unit dictates a wider appreciation of these processes and both the mechanisms that drive them and the likely effects of their consequences.

Following Goskomstat reporting we present first the bad news: the scale of aggregate economic decline. We then look at two major established sectors, industry and agriculture, considering the regional implications of their patterns of decline; then at regional patterns of development of new firms; and finally at the bottom line for regions: what has been happening to real personal incomes across Russia.

3.1   ECONOMIC DECLINE

The Russian economy has been in severe and prolonged decline since 1989. Russian GDP as officially measured has fallen over ten years by 47 per cent.[1] There are good reasons to believe that this official picture is somewhat exaggerated: underestimation of the informal sector or black economy by the statistical authorities in more recent years; a decline of Soviet-era output exaggeration in the early years; in welfare terms, the statistical neglect of the benefits of a shift from a shortage economy to rationing by price (decline in queuing); the statistical inclusion of declines in the output of unwanted items. But nobody seriously contends that total Russian output has not fallen substantially.

It has indeed been suggested that since the mid-1990s the reality may have been even worse than the official statistics indicate. This might result from the 'overpricing' of goods delivered in barter settlement and from other non-monetary transactions (tax offsets, bills of exchange); exaggerating reported output, chiefly in industry and construction (Gaddy and Ickes 1998). However, most of these transactions are between firms. If firm A delivers cement or steel to firm B at an accounting price above what the market would bear in a monetary transaction, this will have the (accounting) effect of reducing B's value added, so long as B (or eventually some other firm Z further down the production chain) has to sell final output to Russian consumers or foreign buyers for 'live money' at market prices. It is not clear that the net effect is to exaggerate the sum of every firm's value added, or private-sector GDP measured by output.

The decline, then, is real and substantial, probably somewhat less than the measured decline, but far from a statistical artefact. Meanwhile, at least up until the mid-1990s, this decline was accompanied by a steep increase in inequality amongst personal incomes (on which, more below). It is against this setting that we must review regional patterns of change.

---

1. Derived from EBRD (1998) and *Russian Economic Trends*, monthly update of 10 June 1999.

3.2   THE INDUSTRIAL SECTOR

There is ample evidence to suggest that industrial restructuring was taking place during the 1980s, well before the collapse of the Soviet Union. More advanced manufacturing and light industry were slowly replacing traditional heavy industry and the material intensity of industrial production was declining. The transitional recession that has followed the collapse of the Soviet Union has brought with it an entirely different type of industrial restructuring. Instead of restructuring heralding the advent of a post-industrial, service- and knowledge-based stage of economic development, the Russian economy is now retreating into the resource-production and primary processing sectors. The traditional priority sector of the Soviet economy, machine building and metalworking, has suffered dramatic decline. At the same time, the light industrial and consumer goods sectors have also declined.

The reasons for this are threefold: first, there has been a dramatic decline in domestic demand for all types of industrial goods (both producers' and consumers' goods); second, the liberalization of the economy has allowed some sectors to export production where it was more remunerative to do so; and third, liberalization has introduced import competition into some industrial sectors. The sectoral consequences of these processes are made clear in Table 3.1; it is the resource sectors that have benefited the most from the opportunity to export and the manufacturing sectors that have suffered the most from the collapse in domestic demand and increasing import competition. For many this pattern is no bad thing. Most of that manufacturing activity is written off as inefficient at best and value subtracting at worst (Gaddy and Ickes 1998). Furthermore, the level of industrial collapse would be even greater if enterprises were forced to stop using non-monetary payments and had to face hard budget constraints.

The issue that interests us here is how that sectoral pattern of industrial decline has affected Russia's regional economies. Each oblast-level unit has a particular economic structure and is thus affected differentially by Russia's industrial collapse.

As ever, we are faced with concerns about the data. It is likely that the industrial decline data overstate the problem: for example, they refer to large and medium-sized enterprises only and they are based on

Table 3.1   Sectoral distribution of industrial decline, 1990–97

	Employment ('000 workers)					
	1990	%	1997	%	% change in employment 1990–97	% change in volume of production 1990–97
Total	20,998	100.0	14,009	100.0		
Electricity	545	2.6	810	5.8	3.2	–23
Fuels, energy	801	3.8	821	5.9	2.0	–32
Ferrous metals	785	3.7	683	4.9	1.1	–43
Non-ferrous metals	487	2.3	508	3.6	1.3	–44
Chemicals	1,130	5.4	891	6.4	1.0	–56
Machine-building	9,652	46.0	5,262	37.6	–8.4	–59
Forestry	1,792	8.5	1,138	8.1	–0.4	–64
Construction materials	1,097	5.2	783	5.6	0.4	–65
Light industry	2,288	10.9	1,006	7.2	–3.7	–86
Food industry	1,545	7.4	1,454	10.4	3.0	–50

Sources: Employment data: Goskomstat Rossii (1998b, p. 182); production decline data: Goskomstat Rossii (1998c, p. 162).

rouble values that are subject to distortions in domestic prices. For example, in international terms a Russian tractor may be vastly over-priced, while the domestic price for raw materials may be well below the world price. The data in Table 3.2 present a variety of different ways of looking at aspects of the de-industrialization story. Other variables, such as electricity generation or pollution emissions, could have been used, but the picture would be much the same. The regions that have suffered the lowest industrial decline are resource-based and export-oriented or they are 'hub' and 'gateway regions'. The regions that appear to have suffered the most are the southern periphery of the North Caucasus and the eastern periphery of eastern Siberia and the Russian Far East. However, these are also the least industrialized regions anyway and the impact of de-industrialization is likely to be cushioned by a large informal sector. There are a few regions where industry is very important and where there has been a substantial amount of industrial decline; Ivanovo oblast is the most obvious example.

There is not the space here to conduct a more rigorous analysis of the relationship between industrial restructuring and regional economic performance. Fortunately, such analyses have already been conducted. Sutherland and Hanson (1996) used shift-share analysis to ascertain the extent to which regional economic structure explained the economic performance of particular regions. They concluded that, while economic structure did explain some of the variation in region economic performance, a large amount of the variation was left unexplained. On the basis of further analysis, they concluded that much of the residual variation could be explained by:

> a region's capacity to earn convertible currency (a positive influence), by the degree of its dependence on military production (a negative influence – the larger military industry loomed in a region's employment, other things being equal, the more its total employment fell), and by the average money wage (a negative association, but only partially causal ...). (Sutherland and Hanson 1996, p. 385)

A rather different approach was adopted in Bradshaw *et al.* (1998). Here the emphasis was upon examining the relationship between economic decline (associated with de-industrialization) and economic growth (associated with service development). This analysis concluded that: 'In general, regions with strong raw material bases or an inter-ventionist local administration performed better than the Russian average, while regions more dependent on agriculture and weaker industrial sectors suffered the greatest output declines' (p. 151). On the issue of service sector growth, it was observed that: 'New service growth is strongly associated with total employment growth, suggesting that those regions which show high signs of service sector growth are also showing a growth in the total number employed' (p. 158). Overall, this analysis reached the conclusion that: 'de-industrialization in Russia seems to be spawning both a retreat into the resource economy and the expansion of the service sector, each with a different geography; while the geography of decline seems closely aligned to heavy industry and manufacturing' (p. 161).

The final study of this kind, by Van Selm (1998), also sought to examine the relationship between economic restructuring and regional

Table 3.2 Regional rankings of industrial decline and economic performance, 1990–97

Decline in volume of industrial production, 1990–97 (%)	% employed in industry in 1990	Gross regional product per capita, 1996 ('000 roubles)	Unemployed as % of economically active population	Value of exports to 'Far Abroad', 1997 (US$ million)
Lowest decline	**Highest percentage**	**Highest GRP per capita**	**Lowest unemployment**	**Highest value of exports**
Nenets	Vladimir	Tyumen'	Moscow	Moscow
Yamal-Nenets	Sverdlovsk	Sakha	Kursk	St Petersburg
Sakha	Ivanovo	Chukchi	Voronezh	Komi
Tatarstan	Yaroslavl	Moscow	Tatarstan	Tyumen'
Khakasia	Nizhniy Novgorod	Magadan	Yaroslavl	Arkhangelsk
Volodgda	Chelyabinsk	Komi	Orenburg	Vologda
Ulyanovsk	Udmurt	Kamchatka	St Petersburg	Moscow Oblast
Komi-Permyak	Tula	Krasnoyarsk	Orel	Irkutsk
Belgorod	Kemerovo	Samara	Nizhniy Novgorod	Perm
Tomsk	Moscow oblast	Irkutsk	Kostroma	Tatarstan

Highest decline	Lowest percentage	Lowest GRP per capita	Highest unemployment	Highest value of exports
Jewish	Kalmykia	Ingushetia	Ingushetia	Jewish
Dagestan	Tuva	Dagestan	Jewish	Dagestan
Aginsk-Buryat	Sakha	Kalmykia	North Ossetia	Altay Republic
Karachevo-Cherkess	Tyumen	Tuva	Kalmykia	North Ossetia
Adygeya	Chita	North Ossetia	Dagestan	Chita
Pskov	Amur	Adygeya	Murmansk	Kalmykia
Kabardino-Balkaria	Dagestan	Kabardino-Balkar	Buryatia	Kurgan
Ivanovo	Moscow city	Karachevo-Cherkess	Chita	Mordva
Altay Republic	Stavropol	Marii-El	Tuva	Kabardino-Balkar
Khabarvosk	Krasnodar	Altay Republic	Karachevo-Cherkess	Mary-El

Source: Rankings are based on data obtained from Goskomstat Rossii (1998d).

economic performance. On the issue of de-industrialization, Van Selm (1998, p. 609) notes that: 'The sectors that are doing relatively poorly (foods, textiles) have experienced heavy competition from abroad, whereas the sectors that are doing relatively well (fuels, metals) are the sectors that have found new export markets'. On the basis of his analysis, Van Selm (ibid., p. 610) concludes that '40 per cent of the variation in the regions' rates of industrial decline in the period 1993–1995 can be explained by variation in their industrial sectors'. Like Sutherland and Hanson, he also concludes that a large amount (60 per cent) of variation cannot be explained by industrial structure. Van Selm extends his analysis to consider the impact of economic policy on industrial performance. Here he concludes: 'pro-reform regions perform hardly if at all better than conservative anti-reform regions' (p. 615). Overall, he concludes that 'regions with the right industries did better than regions with the wrong industries, but regions with the right policies did not do better than regions with the wrong policies' (p. 618). Clearly one can debate what constitutes a 'right' and 'wrong' policy', and this is the subject of later discussion; but one could observe that if performing badly is the result of removing subsidies and shutting down inefficient enterprises then there is no contradiction between the 'right policies' and poor performance.

The analysis of the data for the early to mid-1990s suggests that the industrial structure of a region was a significant factor, but far from the only factor, explaining its relative industrial and even economic performance. By the late 1990s things were starting to change: the stabilization of the rouble exchange rate, the lack of new capital investment and rising domestic production costs were all starting to squeeze the profitability of the resource sector. This was most evident in the oil industry where the falling world oil price aggravated the situation. At the same time, there was some evidence that domestic manufacturing and processing sectors were starting to recover, often with foreign assistance. Then came the August 1998 financial crisis. With the benefit of hindsight, we may conclude that this has offered Russia's beleaguered enterprises a last opportunity. By dramatically increasing the domestic cost of imports and reducing production costs in dollar terms, the devaluation of the rouble has once again made the resource sector profitable and offered import-substituting opportunities to domestic manufacturers and food processors. When the dust has settled, the late 1990s will probably be seen as a different phase of restructuring from that experienced in the early 1990s. It remains to be seen whether the new-found profits generated by devaluation will be ploughed back into modernizing the capital stock of a now hopelessly antiquated industrial base or whether they will simply add to the rate of capital flight. If it is the latter, then the patterns of decline apparent in the early 1990s are likely to resurface with additional problems in the resource sector due to a lack of new capital investment. The clear downside of the August 1998 financial crisis is that it seems to have snuffed out the newly emergent service sector and has obviously reduced the confidence of foreign investors.

3.3   AGRICULTURE

The agricultural sector is one that is popularly perceived to be under considerable pressure, if not in outright crisis. Certainly price liberalization, import competition and the effects of macro-economic stabilization efforts have had a detrimental impact on the functioning of this sector, but one should not overlook the considerable adaptation that has occurred. In real terms, farm output has fallen less than industrial output, even as its share of current-price GDP has declined. In other words, part of the sector's difficulties derives from a steep fall in its terms of trade with the rest of the economy. At the same time, the decline in retail-price subsidies from their high Soviet-era levels has particularly affected the livestock sector, where they were concentrated. Thus livestock production has declined relatively to crop production, at least in part as an adjustment to relative price changes that produce a closer approximation to opportunity costs.

In general, the Soviet inheritance has been a great burden on this sector. Farm sizes are very large, but the rationalization of farm size will be hampered by a capital stock more suited to the larger farm.[2] Continual tinkering with the system achieved precious little in terms of substantive gains, though the provision of private plots, and their output, did mean that a private-enterprise agriculture did exist in

---

2. That is of course the capital stock that actually works. Even in 1996 the deputy Prime Minister for Agriculture, Aleksandr Zaveryukha, stated that transfers of new combines from the Don factory to the Siberian fields would be completed, albeit without engines (*Interfax Food and Agriculture Report*, V, issue 35, 23–30 August 1996, pp. 3–4).

embryo – albeit one that is geared mainly to subsistence food production. Even if one argues that the success of the private plots was only achieved through greater labour intensity and the leaching of resources from the larger farm unit to the private plot and that such opportunities will not be available for a greater degree of privatization of agriculture, at the same time it also shows the possibilities for agriculture if these sorts of incentives to the individual are extended further.[3] Some farm reorganization has occurred in addition to the inconsequential renaming of the type of farm organization. Initially the development of small private farms was viewed by local authorities as a neutral development, though subsequently the level of support or degree of obstruction has varied across regions (Alimova *et al.* 1995; Van Atta 1994; and see Chapter 7). In the longer term local authority attitudes to the private sector may become more favourable as the real costs of the controls that are imposed are appreciated, or budgetary pressures force local authorities to consider land taxation as a means to increase local revenue (Shleifer and Boycko 1994, p. 80).

In the realm of agriculture the impact of the local authorities' actions is still generally seen to be very important in helping or hindering the sector's development. Price and extra-regional 'export' controls were all seen as expressions of regional agricultural quasi-autarky. But this impression may be more to do with the intentions of regional administrations than with their effects. A number of studies (Berkowitz and Husted 1995; De Masi and Koen 1996; Loy and Wehrheim 1997) all provide evidence of the presence of food-price convergence across regions, indicating that a single economic space was developing. During 1995, according to one study (Ulanova 1995), the scope of regional price controls fell from covering 37 per cent of goods at the beginning to only 19 per cent at the end.

Although agricultural output has declined, this is not due solely to import penetration or to increasing constraints on the sector. It is also a response to falling herd sizes reducing the needs for feedstuffs and greater efficiency in general (Serova 1999). There is some evidence from the regions that the responses in Russian agriculture to price liberalization, import competition and macro-economic stabilization efforts have been greater than normally attributed to this

3. One should also note that estimations of fuller liberalization do predict substantial gains for the agricultural sector. See, for example, Liefert *et al.* (1993) and Johnson (1993).

sector.[4] Agricultural specialization is beginning to develop, utilizing the advantages of local soil and climatic conditions and running counter to regional governments' notions of autarky. In addition, those regions that have been able to increase labour productivity have also been the regions that were able to increase total output more rapidly. Indirect evidence also suggests that where price controls have been practised most extensively these regions have also recorded lower gains in labour productivity. In this light Russian agriculture has adapted rather well in the face of some serious obstacles.

Agriculture in Russia is a sector that is often considered beyond the reach of reform. The available evidence, however, does suggest that agriculture has adapted quite extensively already. It is true that the state and collective farms have mostly been renamed rather than restructured, becoming joint-stock companies, for example. It is also true that the development of new private farms (*fermy*) has been weak and that the Russian parliament has blocked legislation that would allow a land market to take shape. (Two regions' efforts to get round this impediment are noted in Chapter 7.) But the real organizational change has been the growth of the long-established household 'subsidiary' plots. Heavily restricted in Soviet times, these have been allowed to increase in size and diversify their activity, so that by 1996 they accounted for half of all estimated farm output.

Key problems associated with further liberalization of agriculture, and particularly land privatization, will constrain more positive outcomes in at least the short term, but as and when they do occur it is possible that agriculture will demonstrate more success than some of the moribund privatized industrial enterprises.

The main regional consequence of post-Soviet agricultural change is (unusually for post-Soviet regional developments) a blurring of regional differences. It is true that regional administrations have more independence now from the federal centre, and that many are apt, when the going gets tough, to make declarations about (illegally) restricting the delivery of food outside their regions' borders. But their activities in food procurement have dwindled as private food wholesaling has developed. The traditional Soviet notion of 'food-surplus' and 'food-deficit' regions therefore means less than might, in these days of regional autonomy, be expected.

4. Sutherland (1997) develops some of these ideas further.

On our working definition of 'food-surplus' and 'food-deficit' regions, and using 1997 data, we assess 24 regions as 'food-surplus', 24 as 'food-deficit' and 29 as neither.[5] Amongst the food-deficit regions thus defined are many obvious candidates: Karelia, Komi, Arkhangel'sk and Murmansk in the European North, the cities of Moscow and St Petersburg, and the entire Far East Macro-Region except Amur. Less obvious food-deficit regions were Nizhny Novgorod, Kemerovo, Sverdlovsk and Tyumen' (if its component Khanty-Mansi and Yamal'-Nenets autonomous districts are included), amongst otherwise 'strong' regions, and Dagestan, North Ossetia and Ingushetia amongst economically weak but troublesome regions. Our guess is that the cross-cutting of dependence on food supplies from 'outside' with other factors suggesting a propensity to defy Moscow (relative economic strength, ethnic self-assertion) may help to shore up federal arrangements. Conversely, many 'food-surplus' regions are in other respects economically weak. This pattern, together with the declining ability of regional administrations to control food movements, probably means that the regional politics of food supply matter less than might at first be expected.

At the same time, regional differences in policy certainly show up in agriculture. Apart from the regional initiatives on land markets already mentioned, regional administrations have varied in their readiness to allow private plots, for example, to expand – for example, the traditionalist regime in Krasnodar seems to have been quite restrictive in this respect (see Chapter 7).

3.4   NEW NON-FARM ECONOMIC ACTIVITY

With the growing liberalization of the Russian economy in the early 1990s new incentives for individuals and enterprises were created. In this light we assume that the new economic units and activity seen in

---

5. Data used from *Rossiiskii statisticheskii yezhegodnik*; calculations by Jonathan Oldfield. We classed a region as 'food-surplus' if its output per head of population of at least four out of five product groups (grain, potatoes, green vegetables, meat, dairy products) was equal to or above the all-Russian average. Conversely, we classed a region as 'food-deficit' if in four out of five product groups its per capita output was below the average – in both cases with the condition that grain had to be one of the four, because of the special importance given to grain in Russian politics.

the period of analysis represent adaptations to these opportunities, that the decentralization of economic decision-making resulted in the creation of economic activity that was not formerly included in the planners' scheme of things.[6] Three, overlapping, measures of new employment creation are used here. The criterion for these three categories of new economic activity was that they were either absent or almost completely absent in the centrally administered economy. They are private small enterprises, joint ventures, and the financial and 'commercial' sectors. The importance of each of these varies across regions, and by no means uniformly, despite the links between them.

We concentrate here on the development of new economic activity and neglect the restructuring of existing economic units. Although this is regrettable, it is not serious. Sufficient attention is paid in other places to questions of restructuring for it to be redundant here.[7] Restructuring of the industrial sector is undoubtedly important, but does not deserve the same attention that the planners paid to this sector. The expected composition of the restructured Russian economy would see a marked movement away from one in which industry dominates.[8]

Table 3.3 gives some simple rankings of the top and bottom ten regions for each of these indicators. This gives a hint of the diverse picture that emerges. As one would expect, the city of Moscow is at the top, or near the top, of all these rankings. In terms of employment these new sectors are more important to the Moscow economy than elsewhere in Russia. This is particularly true for the financial and commercial sector, which in 1994 (the last year for which information was available) was significantly larger in terms of employment than for the region with the second largest share, Chukotka. The development of the financial and commercial sector is notable in that the regions with large shares, even though they may in absolute terms be small, are not what are typically considered 'reformist' regions. Partly this may be explained by the fact that the financial sector is subject to increasing returns to scale leading to an agglomeration of such activity in Moscow, while these sectors' employment in regional financial hubs, such as

6. No doubt many economic entities that emerged in the late Gorbachev and early Yel'tsin period may already have existed in the 'coloured markets', and as such do not represent 'new' activities. The opportunity for these actors to be incorporated into the formal economy was, however, new.
7. See, for example, Commander *et al.* (1996)
8. Current proposals for the 'new mobilization economy' will halt this movement in the short to medium term if they are implemented.

Table 3.3 Regional rankings for foreign investment and joint venture activity

Cumulative foreign investment per capita, 1997		Growth of foreign investment per capita, 1993-7		Joint ventures per 1000 population, 1997		Joint ventures as share of labour force, 1995		Joint venture output in gross regional product, 1995		Joint venture labour productivity, 1996	
Moscow	1179.4	Moscow	1093.2	Moscow	0.87	Moscow	2.42	St Petersburg	11.98	Nenetsk	4879
Jewish	836.1	Magadan	568.4	Kaliningrad	0.34	Kaliningrad	2.20	Kaliningrad	9.97	Khanty-Mansi	501
Magadan	726.0	Arkhangel'sk	306.0	St Petersburg	0.31	St Petersburg	2.10	Moscow	8.86	Tyumen'	414
Arkhangel'sk	459.2	Tatarstan	237.7	Karelia	0.16	Karelia	1.48	Moscow oblast*	8.46	Tomsk	380
Tomsk	263.5	Sakhalin	135.5	Primorskii	0.14	Sakhalin	1.38	Primorskii	5.91	Orenburg	351
Krasnoyarsk	254.2	Tomsk	206.2	Sakhalin	0.14	Irkutsk	1.14	Arkhangel'sk	5.38	Arkhangel'sk	350
Sakhalin	253.5	Omsk	168.6	Sverdlovsk	0.13	Murmansk	0.85	Sakhalin	5.00	Smolensk	322
Tatarstan	240.6	Kamchatka	153.6	Astrakhan	0.10	Tyumen'	0.84	Komi	4.97	Komi	270
Kamchatka	197.7	Novgorod	145.9	Kamchatka	0.10	Primorskii	0.81	Tomsk	4.87	Sakha	223
Marii-El	192.1	Krasnoyarsk	120.1	Murmansk	0.10	Komi	0.81	Novgorod	4.82	Novgorod	198
Bryansk	2.4	Chuvash	1.64	Krasnoyarsk	0.01	Ul'yanovsk	0.09	Chita	0.09	Tambov	35
Tuva	2.3	Orenburg	1.35	Aginsk Buryatsk	0.01	Altai Republic	0.08	Kurgan	0.06	Penza	35
Buryatiya	2.2	Kirov	1.18	North Ossetia	0.01	Kurgan	0.06	Penza	0.06	Chita	24
Chuvash	1.8	Penza	0.97	Penza	0.01	Adygei	0.05	Karachaevo-Cherkess	0.05		
Orenburg	1.5	Chita	0.76	Ivanovo	0.01	Dagestan	0.05	Jewish	0.02	Aginsk Buryatsk	24
Kirov	1.2	Astrakhan	0.70	Tambov	0.01	Penza	0.03	Kalmykia	0.00	Vladimir	19
Penza	1.0	Adygei	0.44	Altai Republic	0.01	Karachaevo-Cherkess	0.02			North Ossetia	15
Kurgan	0.7	Kostroma	0.07	Mordova	0.01	Kalmykia	0.01	Dagestan	0.00	Jewish	12
Adygei	0.4	Kurgan	0.04	Kalmykia	0.01	Tula	0.00	Ingush	0.00	Dagestan	5
Kostroma	0.1	Altai Republic	0.02	Dagestan	0.00	Chukotsk	0.00	Tuva	0.00	Koryaksk	0
								Chukotsk	0.00	Altai Republic	0

Sources: Goskomstat Rossii (1997c and 1998b).

Bashkortostan, is much less important. The importance of the banking sector, for later dates, can also be seen in the figures given by the ratio of banks to regional population, and per capita bank lending activity. Again no clear pattern at the extremes emerges. The regions with high ratios of banks to population and relatively high per capita lending are a mixture of some of the richest and poorest regions in Russia.[9] If commercial and financial employment patterns defy simple regional typologies, then the story for joint venture activity shows the attraction of gateways and resource-rich regions.[10] Those regions that attract the fewest joint ventures and least foreign direct investment are typically mainly agricultural regions.

The apparent importance of small private enterprises to local labour markets also shows considerable regional variation and is not apparently linked to any general regional typology. It is possible to examine the factors governing labour demand in small private enterprises to show that much of the growth in employment can be linked to local labour market conditions. Using a somewhat simplified labour demand function it can be seen that real wages, aggregate demand and labour productivity are all influential in expected ways:

$$PSEE = \begin{array}{c} -0.32 - 0.42*M/P - 0.21*U + 0.15*Y/E + 0.02*HK \\ (-0.68)\ (-3.78) \quad\ (-2.09) \quad\ (2.46) \quad\ (3.23) \end{array}$$

$$\begin{array}{c} + 0.30*WSIB - 0.46*NCR \\ (3.65) \qquad\ (-5.90) \end{array}$$

Adj $R^2 = 0.36$, DW $= 2.35$, F-stat $= 7.62$, $n = 72$ (associated *t*-statistic in brackets)

9. This would suggest that the financial sector is relatively integrated and that the number of banks is endogenous to lending behaviour. As such it tends to confirm the findings of Bayoumi and Rose (1993) that at a sub-national level capital is more mobile than Feldstein and Horioka (1980) demonstrated internationally. As a result the complaints that over 80 per cent of banking sector assets are held by Moscow banks are shown to be unsound by the high per capita lending activity in very poor regions.
10. Much as for banking capital, the story for foreign investment often suggests that Moscow is the dominant recipient region. Large discrepancies between officially recorded flows at the regional level and other sources on committed investments suggest that where the flows are registered is not always coterminous with the ultimate recipient region.

where PSEE is growth in employment in private small enterprises, M/P is the regional real wage, U is the unemployment rate, Y/E is regional productivity, HK is the share of the region's population with secondary education, and WSIB and NCR are dummy variables for regions in the West Siberian macro-economic region and the North Caucasian republics, respectively, needed to correct for spatial autocorrelation, and the estimation is for 1994.

The estimated equation for the growth in private small enterprise employment in 1994, the last year when consistent data series could be used for such analysis, is relatively robust and suggests that the growth in private-sector employment was relatively well described by considerations of high real wages and unemployment levels damping down labour demand, while regions with high levels of human capital and productivity were also regions where labour demand from new firms was, *ceteris paribus*, higher.

Although the early growth of the small enterprise sector is relatively well explained by simple neo-classical ideas, what presents a greater difficulty is why the early rapid growth of this sector lasted such a short time, apparently ending in 1994.

It is possible to determine the impact of some of the initial conditions on the growth of small enterprises. New geographical economics stresses the importance of regional size. We specify a functional form that will capture whether increasing returns to scale do play a role in the development of small-enterprise employment. Although regional size may have this role, it is also important to see whether this results from regional size or externalities arising from urban agglomerations. Relative wage costs are fixed by a measure of real monetary income adjusted to give greater weighting for predominantly rural regions. Regional dummy variables are also introduced to correct for spatial autocorrelation. As a dynamic specification cannot be attempted due to the frequent changes in small enterprise reporting definitions, we take the ratio of small-enterprise employment in June 1997 to the labour force size of the region in 1992. This is done to try and minimize the effects of subsequent migration movements. Regions where out-migration has been large have large shares of small-enterprise employment. This, however, merely reflects the fact that what employment is left is in small enterprises. It does not indicate a strong growth of this sector in those regions:

$$\text{Log(PSEE97/LF92)} = -3.76 + 0.0001*\text{POP92} - 0.35*\log(\text{M/P92})$$
$$(-20.87) \quad (4.05) \qquad\qquad (-2.47)$$

$$+ 0.01*\text{URBAN} + 0.38*\text{FEAST} - 0.31*\text{URAL}$$
$$(4.29) \qquad\qquad (3.04) \qquad\qquad (-2.51)$$

Adj $R^2 = 0.43$, DW $= 1.89$, F-stat $= 11.77$, $n = 73$ (associated t-statistic in brackets)

The results from this estimation reveal that as the size of regions increases the share of private small-enterprise employment to total regional population grows more rapidly, indicating that some sort of increasing returns to scale effect is exerting an influence. In addition, the impact of the share of the urban population also has a similar effect. This suggests that it is not only how urban a region is, but also its overall size. Also, as expected, the real wage measure exhibits a negative relationship. Finally, dummy variables for the Far East and the Urals macro-economic regions are required to correct for spatial autocorrelation. The requirement for the inclusion of these dummy variables intuitively makes some sense. In the case of the Far East the rise in transportation costs may have made the importation of some goods prohibitively expensive, allowing the growth of local enterprises filling these needs. In the Urals macro-economic region it is possible that the dominance of heavy industrial sectors has hindered the development of this sector.

Although these results are only suggestive, they do highlight the importance of regional characteristics in the development of small enterprises. We shall see below that the development of small enterprises is important in determining regional real income and, in the following chapter, that real income is an important factor in migration patterns. Such links between all these variables have long been central to the analysis of economic change across space.

3.5 ECONOMIC CONSEQUENCES: REGIONAL EMPLOYMENT AND REAL INCOMES

3.5.1 Unemployment

In any country the success or failure of economic adjustment to new circumstances can only be judged by what happens to the material welfare of the population. In that sense, the overall consequences so far of the collapse of communism are extremely hard to assess because of the shift from a shortage to a market economy – to rationing by price rather than by queue – and because of probable changing biases in the official statistics. Average material welfare probably declined in the early 1990s, and may subsequently have stabilized (see Balzer 1998). But what about regional differences? First, the impact on employment levels is examined, followed by changes in real incomes across the regions.

The spectre of mass unemployment hung over Russia prior to the start of transformation (Nordhaus 1990). Actual developments have shown that the growth of unemployment has been more gradual than anticipated and spatially heterogeneous.[11] The growth of unemployment is related, *inter alia*, to the region's industrial structure. Estimating the relationship between the 1995 unemployment rate and the 1992 share of industrial employment suggests a quadratic relationship. It can be seen that regions with very low and very high shares of industry are those that subsequently experienced larger unemployment rates. This does give an indication of the degree of industrial employment restructuring occurring in Russia's regions, which is distinct from the observation that industrial restructuring is facilitated by the downward flexibility of the real wage. This relationship is, however, weak, suggesting that industrial downsizing in itself is not a major factor in the growth of unemployment.

It can also be seen that certain areas of the country are experiencing far higher degrees of unemployment, particularly in the North Caucasus. Elsewhere there has been considerable fluidity in the growth of unemployment. Partly this is due to 'individual restructuring', as people move from those regions experiencing the greatest downturn in

---

11. Measures to restore financial stabilization in late 1998 may well lead to sharp increases in unemployment rates as the hard choices are finally confronted.

economic fortunes. For example, Chukotka had the highest rate of unemployment in 1992, but by 1995, owing to out-migration, became the region with the second lowest rate. Cross-correlations of unemployment rates given in Table 3.4 show that previous unemployment rates are particularly poor indicators of future rates, arising as a result of the dynamic adjustments taking place simultaneously.

This serves to underline an important point. Even though certain regions can be seen as the areas where unemployment rates are high, there has also been substantial change in the relative impact across Russia. Thus, easy conclusions about unemployment are hard to reach. What one can say is that unemployment rates have increased, while at the same time dispersion in rates also increased. The greater dispersion in regional unemployment rates tends to indicate a greater mismatch between jobs and workers, which is often associated with duration effects, whereby the greater the regional mismatch the greater the probability of long-term unemployment and all the associated problems.

To examine the determinants of the growth of regional unemployment rates a relatively simple set-up is used. The growth of the unemployment rate is a function of the initial unemployment rate, given a particular set of technologies. The set of technologies is proxied by the quadratic of the share of industry in regional employment. However, the dynamic adjustment variables to account for the intuitions of new geographical economics are also included, such as population size, distance, and the likely effects of transportation costs.

$$\text{Unem92-5} = 1.71 - 0.07*\text{Unem92} - 0.03\text{Ind} + 0.001*\text{Ind}^2$$
$$\qquad\quad (6.95)\ (-6.20) \qquad\qquad (-1.92) \qquad (2.03)$$

$$\qquad - 8.05\text{E-5}*\text{Pop92} - 0.0001\text{Migout} + 0.21\text{Distant}$$
$$\qquad\quad (-4.81) \qquad\qquad (-3.72) \qquad\qquad (2.72)$$

Adj R^2 0.71, D-W 1.95, F-stat 31.76, $n = 74$

where Ind is the share of employment in industry, Pop is the regional population size, Migout is the percentage of the population that migrated out of the region in 1993,[12] and Distant is a dummy variable

12. As there has been remarkable consistency in the relative migration rates the choice of year does not affect the overall estimation.

for regions in the North and Far-East macro-economic regions where transportation costs should be of especially great importance.

From this estimation it can be seen that the growth in unemployment can be reasonably explained by the original unemployment rate, even though the cross-correlations were not strong, and the share of industrial employment at the beginning of transformation (Table 3.4). However, this is not the whole story. Population size and migration also seem important in expected ways. Out-migration is associated with lowering the rate of unemployment and larger regions seem more capable of withstanding adverse employment shocks. The impact of distance is also expected in that those regions where inputs are likely to be more expensive are faring worse.

Table 3.4   Cross-correlations of unemployment rates

	1993	1994	1995
1992	0.01	–0.01	0.01
1993		0.55	0.62
1994			0.50

3.5.2   Regional Income Differences[13]

For Russia's regions in the 1990s, we have data from which estimates of real household incomes can be made. The initial conditions in 1991 plus (or, more often, minus) the subsequent changes in each region's economy have generated a shifting pattern of real incomes across the Russian regions during this decade. There are two salient facts about the inter-regional differences in real per capita household incomes in the 1990s: they are large, and they have been increasing. Some observers have speculated that these differences could become a cause of conflict and even territorial fragmentation. Others (notably Jacques Sapir 1996) have raised a rather different question: are we seeing two or more quite different patterns of adjustment in different regions, perhaps entailing a lack of market integration of the Russian economy;

13. This section summarizes Hanson (1999) and adds some additional points. The evidence and arguments are presented more fully in that paper.

might this strongly affect long-term growth prospects, creating a situation rather like that of India, where a number of dynamic regional economies have developed but the weight of a huge, backward hinterland has dragged down the overall growth rate?

To address these questions, we need, first, to see what the evidence of increasing regional inequalities consists of; second, to put it in perspective both in relation to regional inequality elsewhere and in relation to overall (inter-household) inequality in Russia; third, to try to account, if we can, for the differences we observe – what are the factors determining those differences? – and, finally, to see how strong the evidence is of a 'leopard-skin' development in which the spots cannot readily be changed and the economy is not a single economic space.

The information that we have on regional incomes is from Goskomstat. It consists of reported average money incomes in each region. It appears that estimates of income in kind, such as subsistence food production, are not included. In general, the estimation of money income is probably rather weak, since much income is not reported. Goskomstat has also published three series that provide partial measures of the cost of living in each region. Because Russian regional price levels differ greatly, it is important that money income data are adjusted to reflect those differences.

The three series that could be used to assess regional costs of living are: the monthly rouble costs of a so-called subsistence minimum; a 19-item food basket; and (from 1996) a 25-item food basket. The subsistence minimum figure is believed to be a number that has been subject to local manipulation. The food-basket series are in that respect preferable, but they cover only part of the household budget.

Neither the money-income numerator nor the cost-of-living denominator, therefore, is as sound a figure as we would wish. On balance, we have chosen to use money incomes deflated by local food-basket costs wherever possible. In interpreting the picture that emerges, however, we have to take account of other relevant knowledge. In particular, the relative poverty of mainly rural areas is likely to be overstated because of the omission of subsistence food production, which can be assumed to play a larger role in those areas.

At all events, the differences appear to be massive. In November 1997, for example, average money income in Moscow city was 5.8 times the local subsistence minimum, while in the Republic of Tuva it was less than the local subsistence minimum: 0.69.[14] So, on the face of it, the region with the highest average real income had a population 8.4 times better off than the poorest region. Given the likely importance of subsistence food production in Tuva, the real difference will be somewhat less stark. If adding in subsistence food production for Tuva doubled real incomes, and including it for Muscovites added 10 per cent to their real incomes, the ratio would be 4.6:1.[15] The evidence about changes over time in regional inequality is clear: the dispersion has increased sharply during 1992–7. This is shown in Table 3.5.

Table 3.5   Russia: regional variation in real incomes, 1992–7

	1992	1993	1994	1995	1996[a]	1997[a] III
Coefficient of variation (%)	30.6	26.0	32.2	39.5	42.3	49.8
Number of regions	74	74	77	77	76	77
Memorandum RF real *y*	2.54	3.79	2.38	2.3	2.2 (3.24)	

Notes: [a] 1996 and 1997 figures, except the bracketed 1996 figure for Russia as a whole, are for money incomes divided by the subsistence minimum, whereas the figures for 1992–5 are for money incomes divided by the 19-item food basket. Therefore 1992–5 and 1996–7 data are not strictly comparable. However, the bracketed 1996 figure in the bottom row is comparable with earlier years.

Sources: Calculated from Bradshaw and Palacin (1996); Goskomstat (1996a and 1996b); *Izvestiya*, 25 October 1997, p. 5.

The strong and almost continuous increase in the coefficient of variation over six years, albeit across a break in the series, supports the common perception in Russia that the fortunes of different regions have been diverging. Unfortunately, it is impossible to make comparisons

14. Derived from Goskomstat, *Sotsial'no-ekonomicheskoe polozhenie Rossii* (1997), XII, pp. 393–4 and 403–4.
15. A report from the Institute of Living Standards in late 1996 suggested that for rural dwellers subsistence food production added 100 per cent to their incomes, while for the population as a whole it was worth an additional 20 per cent (*Delovoi ekspress*, 21 January 1997, p. 16). That is the basis for the guesstimated adjustments used here.

with regional inequalities in the communist era, when the question of availability of goods would have had greater import. It seems likely that real regional inequalities in the 1970s and 1980s were substantial but less than in the 1990s.

We noted in Chapter 1 that, by happenstance, the average population size of Russian provinces at present is the same as that of the 183 'second-tier' regions of the European Union (EU), as it was before the expansion from 12 to 15 countries. Since data are collected for those regions, a comparison is possible that at any rate juxtaposes regions of similar population size. Unfortunately, the readily available numbers for the EU are for per capita regional GDP, but one would expect per capita real incomes to be fairly well correlated with per capita GDP, as these are regions in different countries and redistribution amongst them by taxes and transfer incomes is limited. In 1993 the range from richest to poorest EU region (Hamburg to Voreio Aigaio in Greece) was 5.5:1 (European Commission 1994). That is less than the officially measured difference given above for Moscow:Tuva, and slightly more than the rather speculatively adjusted alternative figure for that ratio.

It seems fair to say that the range of income levels across Russian regions is of at least a similar order to that amongst similar-sized regions in the whole of the EU as it was in the early 1990s.

Another way of putting current Russian regional inequality into perspective is to ask how significant it is in comparison with inequality *within* regions or, to put it differently, how much regional differences contribute to overall inequality amongst Russian households.

The development during the 1990s of inequality amongst Russian households has apparently followed a different path to inter-regional inequality. The latter appears from the evidence in the last sub-section to have grown continuously through late 1997. The former, according to the official data (which are just for money incomes and ignore cost-of-living differences in different regions), increased sharply in 1992–4, but then levelled off. The ratio of the top 10 per cent of incomes to the bottom 10 per cent (the decile ratio) rose to 14:1 in 1994, declined to 13:1 in 1996 (OMRI *Daily Digest,* 15 January 1997) and to 12.5:1 in February 1998 (*Ekonomika i zhizn'* 1998 (16), p. 19).

Part of the inequality that is now observable in Russian personal incomes generally, and probably part of its likely increase between the Soviet era and the mid-1990s, can be ascribed to the growing regional differentiation shown in Table 3.5. But how much of it?

We approximated an answer to this question by constructing a Russian decile ratio in which it is assumed that there is no inequality within regions: in other words, a reconstruction of the national decile ratio as it would have been if the only differences in incomes had been those between regional averages. This was done by identifying two groups of regions containing, respectively, around the richest tenth and the poorest tenth of the population, as grouped by their regional average incomes.

The following calculation was made for November 1996. A group of richest and a group of poorest regions, on the real-income proxy measure of regional average money income divided by regional subsistence minimum, were found, each of which contained close to 10 per cent of the total Russian population. These were, first, Moscow, Tyumen' and St Petersburg and, second, a much larger number of mainly small regions that contained around the same number of people, about half of them in the North Caucasus.

These groups of regions each contained close to 11 per cent of the population. That was the nearest the regional boundaries permitted to a decile ratio. The population-weighted average measure of real income in the three richest regions was 5.01 (that is, about five times the subsistence minimum locally priced). The average real income of the richest group was 4.4 times that of the poorest group. If incomes within each region were all identical, in other words, the decile ratio for all Russian incomes would be close to 4:1. So inter-regional inequality, thus defined, accounts for something like 33 per cent of overall inter-household inequality.

Thus inter-regional income inequalities are not the dominant source of inequality in Russia. But overall inequality has apparently been falling since 1994–5, while the regional component of it has (apparently) continued to rise. In any established market economy, unless inter-regional transfers were exceptionally large, one would expect regional differences in real income to correspond fairly well with regional per capita GDP. For Russia we have gross regional product (GRP) data only for the years 1994 and 1995. In the latter year, as Figure 3.1 shows, there is indeed a fairly strong, positive relationship between per capita real income (measured here as per capita monthly money income divided by the regional cost of the 19-item food basket) and per capita GRP. For 1994, however, the relationship is far less clear. This is a point to which we shall return shortly.

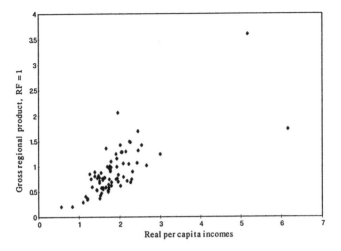

Figure 3.1   Russian regions, 1995: gross product and real personal income levels

In thinking about the sources of regional differentiation in the mid-1990s, we considered a number of possible influences. The most obvious immediate influence should be productivity. GRP per capita represents the overall level of economic activity per head of population. We have reason to suspect, however, that its coverage is biased towards the established, 'old' workplaces, and understates the importance of the new private sector. Also, it excludes by definition not only value added in federal government activities that cannot be redistributed by region but also value added in financial intermediation (information from Andrei Tatarinov). Those two considerations suggest a downward-biased estimation for regions containing the emerging commercial–financial hubs, and especially Moscow city.

Studies of individual regions suggested that two main types of region have adapted best to the new circumstances: major natural resource regions and regions containing the new commercial hubs. What both possess is a capacity for earning revenue from the outside world at a time when domestic demand is depressed. A possible proxy for this can be found in the Goskomstat regional data on inflows of foreign currency (*valyutnye postupleniya*). These numbers are for recorded

inflows to the region, including export revenues that are not left
offshore or in other regions, credits from abroad and foreign investment
in financial form. That there is at least a suggestion of a positive
relationship, across regions, between per capita real income (defined as
before) and per capita foreign exchange inflows (measured here as a
multiple of the average across all regions) is suggested by Figure 3.2.

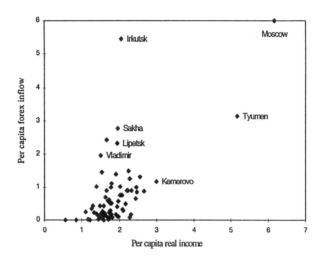

*Figure 3.2   Russian Federation regions: per capita real incomes and
                forex inflows, 1995*

We also considered two other factors. One was agglomeration
effects based on so-called Jacobs externalities (Callejon and Costa
1997). Our case-study observations suggested that the shift of workers
from old to new activities was easier in large cities than in smaller
communities. This could perhaps be attributed to the opportunities for
new firms to grow in an environment where many different skills and
facilities (premises, equipment) were readily to hand, facilitating the
recombining of production inputs in new forms (see the observations on
Samara and Kaliningrad in Chapters 7 and 9, respectively). The core
idea of Jacobs externalities is that the local presence of a wide range of
skills and activities lowers the cost of economic expansion for any one
firm. This seemed to us to be exemplified in the restructuring we

observed in a number of different places. As a proxy measure for such agglomeration effects we used a dummy variable distinguishing regions containing a city of more than 700,000 population from other regions. The other factor was the strength of local demand. As a proxy (and inverse) measure for this we used the regional rate of registered unemployment.

To summarize: we took an index of real per capita personal income (average across all Russian regions = 1) as the dependent variable (REALY). Independent variables were per capita GRP (also as an index, RF = 1), per capita inflows of foreign exchange (also as an index, RF = 1, identified below as HCPC), a dummy variable for the presence/absence of a large city, and the unemployment rate.

All the explanatory variables had the expected signs. In different specifications, however, the unemployment rate was never close to being significant, and the big-city dummy was significant at 10 per cent, but not at the 5 per cent level conventionally required. The interplay of the other two factors, for 1994 and 1995, however, presented an interesting picture:

$$\text{REALY94} = \quad 0.919 + 0.057 \text{HCP94}$$
$$(29.54) \quad (3.19)$$

$$n = 74; \text{adj } R^2 = 0.111; DW = 1.72; F = 10.155$$

where the bracketed figures are t-statistics. Evidently the effect of foreign currency influences is weak, but it is highly significant (at better than 1 per cent).

For the 1995 data, the relative importance of GRP and HCPC is reversed. Here Moscow city was omitted as an outlier, and log form worked better. We get:

$$\ln\text{REALY 95} = \quad 0.003 + 0.519 \ln\text{GRP95}$$
$$(0.13) \quad (11.29)$$

$$n = 75; \text{adj } R^2 = 0.631$$

Here again the bracketed figures are t-statistics, and the coefficient on the explanatory variable is this time both highly significant and strong.[16]

16. If Moscow city is not omitted but instead is assigned its own dummy (Moscow/

The change between the two years is intriguing. A sceptic would say that this is exactly the kind of odd year-to-year change that is to be expected from dodgy data. But a less sceptical interpretation also fits. This is that in 1994–5 the economy was in several important ways adjusting from a period of extreme turbulence. Part of the short-term adjustment to the liberalization of 1992 was a flow of resources into trading in imported consumer goods. This activity was almost certainly under-recorded in GDP and GRP data, relative to the activity of established enterprises. It was also likely to be stronger in regions where there were comparatively large inflows of foreign exchange. It is plausible to suggest that between 1994 and 1995 three things were changing. First, the relative importance of such trading in imports was levelling off or even declining. From separate evidence – see above – we know that the growth of small firms was coming, for the time being, to an end. Second, the established (state and privatized) enterprises were still declining but no longer experiencing a precipitous fall in activity, as they began to cope with the situation – albeit in some very dubious ways (see Chapter 1). Third, the inter-regional market in foreign currency was probably becoming more integrated.

If these conjectures are somewhere near the mark, we have a reason for expecting that the relationship between a region's measured production and its real household incomes was becoming more 'normal'. Conversely, the specific regional incidence of foreign exchange inflows was becoming less critical to regional levels of material welfare.

The fact remains, however, that regional real income levels were continuing to diverge. This phenomenon has led some writers to suggest that rather more than quantitative divergence may be involved: that economic regimes are sharply differentiated across Russian regions, with some more or less adjusting to the market, and others coping in fundamentally different ways.

The (apparent) fact of diverging regional real incomes is important in itself. But if Russia is becoming once again a single economic space, subject to a single economic order, we might expect some countervailing tendencies back towards convergence to become apparent at some

not Moscow), the result is predictable: the Moscow dummy variable has a high coefficient (0.862) and is highly significant. In other words, being Moscow makes a great difference, even allowing for per capita GDP levels. Given our reservations about the Moscow GRP number, this may only reflect the (likely) fact that Moscow's GRP is underestimated relative to all other regions.

point.[17] If it is fragmented into a patchwork of adapting market economies, on the one hand, and Enver Hoxha-style Albanias, on the other, divergence might continue indefinitely. So the evidence about regionally differentiated patterns of economic behaviour needs to be considered.

Jacques Sapir (1996) has suggested that Russian regions may be split into those in which market institutions and more or less conventional patterns of market behaviour have been developing, and those in which adjustment has mostly taken radically different forms – in particular, a strong reliance on barter.

If there are some regions in which barter predominates and other regions in which it does not, one would expect some systematic differences in household behaviour. In barter-dominated regions, recorded personal money incomes would not be the main determinants of consumption. And one indicator of this difference would be that there would be visibly different relationships between recorded saving and recorded money incomes in the two kinds of region.

Sapir showed that, indeed, between early 1993 and early 1996 there were some striking anomalies in recorded regional savings rates (average propensity to save or APS). Other things equal, one would expect high-income regions to show high APSs, and vice versa. The anomalous combinations of a relatively high APS and relatively low per capita incomes tended to become more marked over time. From this evidence he identified two categories of regions.

It is important, however, to adjust the money income data for differences in local prices. The quantitative importance of this is illustrated in Table 3.6. In Figure 3.3 indices of regional APSs for 1995 (unweighted average of Russian regions = 1) are plotted against per capita real incomes (money income as a multiple of the locally priced 19-item food basket).

---

17. Agglomeration effects might by themselves produce diverging regional real incomes. But growing concentration of economic activity produces congestion costs and rising local labour and real-estate prices. These could in time push investment out of the hitherto favoured areas and out to the hinterland. There is some evidence, though it is open to dispute, that the long-term tendency in established market ecoᵤomies is towards convergence of regional income levels (Barro and Sala-I-Martin 1991). Preliminary work on real income determination (Berkowitz and DeJong 1997; Sutherland 1997) does suggest that regional size matters, albeit for very short time spans. In addition, the growth of small enterprises (numbers or employment) also emerges in both studies as an important factor increasing regional real income.

*Table 3.6   Money incomes and cost of living in Ul'yanovsk and
               Magadan, November 1997 ('000 roubles per month)*

	(1) Average money income	(2) Subsistence minimum	(3) Real income (1)/(2)
Ul'yanovsk	654.6	255.2	2.57
Magadan	1735.3	875.8	1.98
RF average	909.8	407.3	2.23

Source: Goskomstat Rossii (1997b), pp. 393–4, 403–4.

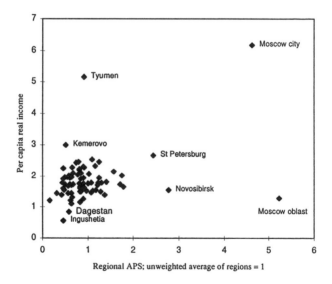

*Figure 3.3   Russian Federation: per capita real incomes and savings
                indexes, 1995*

Evidently, the relationship is not neat and clear, but the scattergram suggests that it may be a rather more orthodox one than would appear if money income data were used. In the regression analysis, Moscow oblast' was excluded as an outlier, and the possibility of a non-linear relationship between APS and real income levels was allowed for. We get:

$$APS95 = 9.408 - 3.53 \, REALY95 + 1.897 \, (REALY95)^2$$
$$(2.66) \quad (-1.20) \qquad\qquad (4.46)$$

$$n = 76; \text{adj } R^2 = 0.47; DW = 1.62; F = 33.77$$

Here the coefficient on the square of real income is highly significant, the equation as a whole works quite well, and almost half of the variance in the dependent variable is accounted for.

This suggests that perhaps, after all, the Russian regions all belong to a population with tolerably homogeneous relationships between savings propensities and average real incomes. It does not follow that market integration is proceeding smoothly in what is or soon will be a single economic space. But it does cast doubt on one piece of evidence to the contrary.

What is clear is that the main uses of barter are in inter-enterprise transactions and in enterprise settlements with regional budgets. It is also clear that the closer an enterprise is to final consumer-goods markets, the less reliant they are on barter (see *The Russian Economic Barometer*, issues during 1997–9 for survey data on barter; also Lavrov 1998b, on barter settlement with the budget). It is not obvious that this particular characteristic of Russian barter transactions from the early 1990s would produce a clear demarcation amongst regions.

In general, the evidence about regional income differences suggests four things. First, there is a growing differentiation across regions. Second, inequality within regions none the less greatly exceeded inequality between regions. Third, initial differences in productivity levels, plus differences in adaptation after 1991, plus (perhaps) reduced inter-regional income redistribution may be the main explanation of the divergence amongst regional income levels observed in the late 1990s. And, finally, there may be hope of subsequent convergence of income levels, because there may be rather more market integration of Russia's regions than is sometimes claimed.

3.7   CONCLUSIONS

Our first conclusion must be that adaptation in Russia is more complex than would be suggested simply by placing different regions in different categories (highly rural, gateway, natural-resource, and so on) and relying on those categories to explain the various observed outcomes.

Second, even in declining sectors such as industry and agriculture there has been considerable structural change that can and does have differential effects across regions.

Third, the growth of new sectors allows for no easy generalizations. New types of employment are concentrated not simply in the 'reformist' regions but in regions whose size, real-wage levels, urbanization and unemployment rates (as proxies for demand) are favourable. For all the disappointment surrounding new business development in Russia, what development there has been looks to be driven by rather standard market-size, labour-market and urban-agglomeration factors, rather than anything specially Russian – or specially policy-determined.

A corollary of this is as follows. Corrupt state regulation and extensive organized crime have severely handicapped the development of new firms in Russia as a whole, in comparison with Central European ex-communist countries; our study suggests that the relative importance of this handicap does not differ greatly across Russian regions. If it did, standard economic explanations of regional variance in new firm development would not work as well as they do.

Similarly, the consequences of all these adjustments for the population seem to be explicable largely by 'market' considerations, with access to hard currency (representing markets in or investment from the outside world) playing a role early on, and becoming less important as currency markets became more integrated, and suggesting a 'normal' relationship by 1995 with regional per capita gross product.

The process of adjustment, with its sharp regional differences, has certainly produced a large and increasing differentiation across regional average real incomes. This, however, remains less important, quantitatively, than inequality within regions. This supports the standard fiscal-federal prescription that 'equalization' should be primarily a federal function (see Chapter 5).

Evidently, a multitude of influences of an impersonal kind are influencing regional outcomes in Russia in the 1990s. It is the comparative normality of our results that is striking, so far as we have accounted for differing patterns of regional adjustment. This is not to say that the situation is not one of disarray and widespread hardship; rather, that, given the initial economic distortions inherited from the Soviet era – of production of unwanted items in daft locations, for a start – the processes by which production and incomes have tended to adjust across Russian regions seem to be processes explicable by standard economic theory.

In this chapter we have looked as far as possible at regional adjustment processes without reference to policies. We have seen that such an approach in fact takes us quite a long way. One autonomous process of adjustment that we have only touched on, however, is migration. That is the subject of the next chapter. In Chapter 5 we go on to look at the federal government's policies intended to affect regional outcomes. The effects of regional governments' policies are judged, in this study, chiefly from the eight case-studies covered in Chapters 6 to 9.

4. Demographic Responses to Regional Economic Change: Inter-Regional Migration

Douglas Sutherland and Philip Hanson

INTRODUCTION

The process of economic transformation has been accompanied by marked demographic changes. For example, life expectancy, particularly for males, plunged after 1992 and is only now beginning to recover somewhat. In this chapter the focus is on patterns of inter-regional migration. This is an important topic. It reveals a 'regional' aspect of the ways in which individuals have responded to economic change as distinct from the responses of firms (Chapter 3) and central government (Chapter 5).

Inter-regional migration shapes, as well as responds to, regional economic change. It is part of the process that determines the location of economic activity and therefore partly shapes the economic potential of the regions. Assuming, reasonably, that the Soviet-era planners placed economic activity, and thereby tried to influence household residence decisions, in sub-optimal locations, this will have resulted in considerable spatial disequilibrium of the workforce and placed question marks over the sustainability of employment in many places. Once firm and individual locational decision-making is decentralized, considerable intra-country migration would be a natural consequence.[1]

---

1. An alternative to migration that may lead to equalization of living standards across the regions is through capital mobility and free trade. *De facto* market segmentation and a less than fully integrated capital market limit the extent that these channels can counteract the pressures to migrate, at least during the period considered here.

What we are concentrating on here are the characteristics of regions that influence individuals' decisions to move within the country to improve their well-being. During a period of profound structural change the location of the labour force would be expected to change as employment possibilities change differentially across the regions. This is driven by changes in the reference markets of economic units as liberalization progresses, making some loci of economic activity unsustainable while favouring others. As a result, one would expect there to be congruent movements of the population and the location of economic activity, although rising unemployment may limit the ability of many to take advantage of the new opportunities that become available.

In describing the migration flows between regions within Russia, use will be made of a distinction between 'push' and 'pull' factors. The 'push' factors governing inter-regional migration are expected to be stronger in those regions with concentrations of types of economic activities that are likely to be uncompetitive as market-type production relations and structures become more firmly embedded in the Russian economy, resulting in higher levels of out-migration. In-migration, reflecting the 'pull' factors, is expected to be related to either the location of inherited economic entities that are proving to be less adversely affected than most by economic transformation or to locations where new economic activity is developing more strongly. In this way more emphasis is given to economic influences on migration decisions, especially the relative importance of local labour and housing markets, which have been shown to be important in studies of migration in other parts of the world.[2]

---

2. International flows of migration, including refugees and forced migrants from former republics of the Soviet Union, are excluded from the analysis. The reason for excluding international migration flows is to attempt to isolate the factors governing the initial decision to migrate and the subsequent choice of destination. Refugees and forced migrants have little choice in their destination, either through considerations of what is the neighbouring region to the country they are leaving or what restrictions are placed on immigration. It is unavoidable that subsequent inter-regional migration by international immigrants will be captured, but it is assumed that the motivation for these migration decisions are on a similar basis to longer-term residents.

4.1   DEMOGRAPHIC CHANGE

Since the mid-1980s the headline demographic indicators in Russia have deteriorated markedly, particularly after 1992 when the natural increase of the population became negative. These indicators worsened until 1994, when Russia had the second largest rate of natural decrease of population in the world. Fertility and mortality rates have been so adversely affected that they have been compared with the effects seen in periods of war (Heleniak 1995, p. 446). As birth rates are declining and death rates increasing, the total population is falling, yet at the same time the dependency ratio, or the ratio of the cohorts younger and older than working age to the cohort of the working age population, is rising.

Such an adverse outcome is also notable in other countries undergoing economic transformation, but not on the scale of Russia (Ellman 1997).[3] Proximate causes of the greater number of deaths are increases in accidents, suicide, cardiovascular disease and alcohol-related deaths. One investigation of the decline in male life expectancy at birth between 1990 and 1994, when it reached its nadir, identified the additional problems of the negative impacts of the lack of social cohesion, the pace of change, and rising inequality. Impoverishment, pollution and changes in health service provision were all found to have little direct influence on the change on life expectancy (Walberg *et al.* 1998). One of the more general findings is that it is mainly middle-aged men who have borne the brunt of the increases in the various measures of the mortality rate.

Fertility has also fallen due to reasons associated with economic transformation.[4] The birth rate between 1989 and 1994 fell by 36 per cent; partly, it is hypothesized, as a result of childbearing being postponed during periods of economic uncertainty. Such motives are compounded by declines in real incomes since late Soviet times and rising costs associated with child rearing. What is more striking is that during this period the falls in the measures of fertility were almost uniform across the Russian regions (Heleniak 1995, p. 450). Thus, the

3. It seems that the marked increase in the crude death rate, rather than changes in fertility rates, is the main factor that distinguisnes Russia from other transformation economies.
4. Ellman (1997) suggests that the decline in fertility throughout transformation economies can also be seen as 'convergence' to fertility rates in Western Europe.

variation in population change across the Russian regions depends on the whole on changes in mortality and the differential impact of migration.

4.2   MIGRATION FLOWS

Even though the natural increase of the population has declined below the levels seen in the late Soviet period the impact on particular regions has been quite different. In regions of the Russian Far East, for example, the population has fallen in the space of half a decade by up to 50 per cent. Partly this is the effect of out-migration but it also reflects the living conditions in some of the more remote areas of Russia where life expectancy is far below the already abysmal Russian average. Immigration, both inter-regional and international, is moderating the population declines in some regions, though a clear pattern is emerging of migration towards the West and South of Russia. In terms of total population change the picture is different, with an absolute growth of regional populations in mainly south Siberia and southern European Russia (compare Map 4.1 with Map 4.2). Thus, in regions of central European Russia the effect of immigration is insufficient to balance the natural declines these regions are experiencing.

The noted southern and westward shift in effect is reversing the push by the Soviet era planners to develop some of the more remote regions of Russia. To some extent the scale of out-migration from these regions reveals just how poor the planners' decision-making was. However, it is not only the planners' preferences for the location of the population and economic activity that has resonance today. Several other legacies from the centrally administered system are also important factors governing migration.

4.2.1   Inter-regional Migration in the Soviet Period

During the period of the centrally administered economy, planning was carried out to match the needs of regional economic activity, meeting with varying degrees of success. The existence of wage coefficients to mobilize the movement of labour to regions with harsher living conditions suggests that market-type incentives were needed in the Soviet

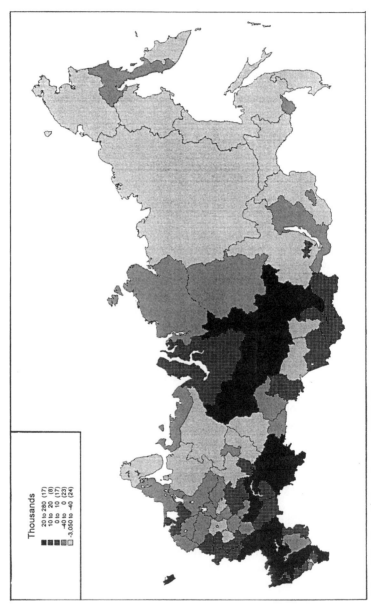

Map 4.1 Population change, 1992–7

Thousands

- 20 to 280 (17)
- 10 to 20 (8)
- 0 to 10 (17)
- -40 to 0 (23)
- -3,050 to -40 (24)

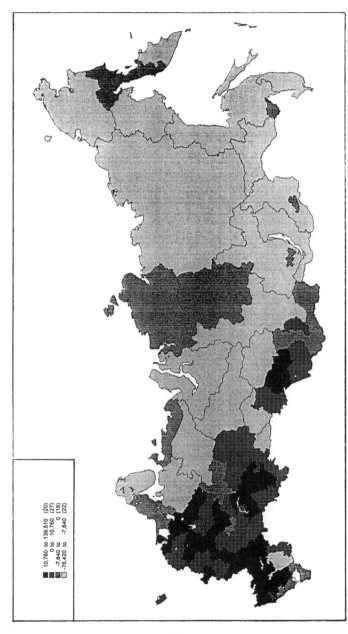

Map 4.2   Net inter-regional migration, 1993–6

10,760 to 139,510   (20)
0 to 10,760   (27)
-7,840 to   0   (18)
-76,420 to -7,840   (22)

labour market. Even when the centrally set differentials in pay were insufficient to attract labour, enterprise directors could adjust the local incentive payments or upgrade the occupational status of the workers: all measures contributing to 'wage drift' in the Soviet economy. This situation was recognized by the planners, exemplified in the *Trudovoe pravo* (labour law): 'The primary influence in determining streams of migration is, not regional requirements for labor, but rather the worker's unrestricted self-interest' (quoted by Grandstaff 1980, p. 20). The importance of stressing this point is that migration during the Soviet period could be understood in market-type terms, implying that we should not expect radically different types of influences on post-liberalization Russian migration.

Even though the planners could not control migration without resorting to market incentives,[5] they left several serious problems in their wake. One aspect of this was extensive, mainly industrial, growth requiring ever more labour. As the opportunities for rural–urban migration declined over time, the regional imbalances on the labour market became apparent. Over-ambitious planning also created workplaces that could not be filled. The attempts to control the migration flows to address these regional imbalances through the use of internal passports is one serious handicap that is a legacy of the Soviet system, mainly through the unconstitutional use of the *propiska* (registration) system.

The second main legacy of the Soviet period is the restrictions on the housing market: at the onset of economic transformation almost 50 per cent of the housing stock was owned by enterprises. (It should be noted, however, that this overestimates the restrictions since many of the apartments were not occupied by the enterprise's workforce.)

4.2.2   Inter-regional Migration During Transformation

The barriers that housing and administrative limitations place on population movement has been raised as an issue inhibiting the development of an effective labour market in Russia (see, for example, Polishchuk 1997, p. 88). In Chapter 3 we saw that the conditions on the Russian labour market may actually be more favourable than in

---

5. Malle (1986, p. 124), indicating how poorly the planners controlled migration, states that the ratio of planned to actual migration was in the range of one to four, and in some cases one to nine.

Western Europe in terms of unemployment duration, even though territorial differentiation in unemployment rates is marked.

To a certain extent, the regional imbalances have been important in determining outcomes for certain regions. Media reports pay attention to the plight of the inhabitants of the Russian far north, but this is not a static problem. Many are indeed locked into eking out a precarious existence in such regions, but many others have left.

The lack of a functioning housing market is a serious problem limiting economic adaptation through inter-regional migration. By the beginning of 1994 46 per cent of the Russian housing stock was said to be privately owned (Kayanova and Mal'gin 1994, p. 20). This figure is likely to be an underestimate when account is taken of the proliferation of private house construction throughout Russia, which is unlikely to be incorporated in official measures of the housing stock. Although house privatization has progressed, Abalkina (1994, p. 113) argues that between 1991 and 1994 the flexibility of the housing market was roughly the same. Such an estimation is probably based on considerations of how flexible the rental market for property is, rather than the proportion of the housing market that has been privatized. If this was the case between these years, then the restrictions on mobility stemming from the lack of available properties for rent remained. In the recent clamp-down on tax evasion one of the groups being targeted are those who rent their apartments in cities while living in their suburban *kottedzhi*, giving indirect evidence that the market for rental has eased somewhat.

Where the situation has eased and inward migration is at least a possibility, the use of the *propiska* system can hamper the movement of the population. Moscow city is notorious for its unconstitutional use of this system to prevent inward migration, as several constitutional courts have ruled. Moscow is not alone in the use of such a system, mainly by charging (illegal) fees which effectively delimit the opportunity to move into the region (the way this system operates is similar to the restrictions on migration to the Channel Islands). The governor of the Komi Republic, Yurii Spiridonov, has also raised this issue with the constitutional court, arguing that the system prevents the return migration of people who have taken short-term jobs in high-wage regions (Katanian 1998). The repeated rulings of the constitutional court have had little impact on actual practice, and the restrictions on mobility will only be reduced once enforcement becomes a reality.

Table 4.1 Russian macro-regions: inter-regional migration flows, 1993–6

| | Total | | | | Percentage of initial population | | | | | | | |
| | Out | In | Out | In | Out | | | | In | | | |
	1993–6	1993–6	1993–6	1993–6	1993	1994	1995	1996	1993	1994	1995	1996
Russia	**5,543,647**	**5,653,175**	**3.73**	**3.80**	**0.96**	**0.96**	**0.98**	**0.83**	**0.94**	**0.99**	**1.00**	**0.89**
North	370,609	234,181	6.09	3.85	1.48	1.69	1.61	1.41	0.97	1.04	1.00	0.90
North-West	330,394	381,660	4.02	4.64	1.05	1.06	1.08	0.87	0.98	1.22	1.30	1.20
Central	843,339	1,057,581	2.79	3.50	0.73	0.71	0.72	0.64	0.77	0.89	0.96	0.90
Volga–Vyatka	212,128	250,766	2.49	2.95	0.65	0.62	0.65	0.58	0.72	0.78	0.77	0.68
Central Chernozem	199,369	285,037	2.55	3.65	0.61	0.64	0.70	0.60	0.90	0.95	0.94	0.84
Volga	519,144	623,422	3.10	3.73	0.77	0.78	0.81	0.73	0.95	0.97	0.95	0.83
North Caucasus	545,536	712,763	3.14	4.10	0.94	0.67	0.86	0.63	1.14	1.10	1.00	0.82
Urals	621,019	656,179	3.03	3.20	0.79	0.76	0.79	0.69	0.80	0.84	0.84	0.73
West Siberia	672,450	651,016	4.45	4.31	1.09	1.15	1.13	1.07	1.06	1.10	1.11	1.04
East Siberia	456,507	379,296	4.94	4.10	1.31	1.30	1.27	1.09	1.05	1.08	1.09	0.90
Far East	737,034	377,129	9.33	4.77	2.23	2.80	2.61	1.91	1.25	1.25	1.27	1.11
Kaliningrad	35,365	44,145	3.90	4.87	1.02	1.00	1.01	0.81	1.13	1.35	1.21	1.11

Source: Goskomstat Rossii (1997a).

During the period from 1993 to the end of 1996, for which data are available, inter-regional immigration and emigration represent about 1 per cent of the region's population. This is almost identical to the out-migration rate from southern Italy during the 1970s and 1980s (Daveri and Faini 1998). In Table 4.1 data are given for the period 1993–6 for the macro-economic regions. This table reveals that the largest flows of migration have been in the Central macro-economic region, followed by the Far East in terms of out-migration and the North Caucasus in terms of in-migration. In the Far East, due to its smaller population, these gross out-migration flows as a percentage of initial population are double the scale of out-migration experienced in southern Italy. Immigration is also high in the Far East in relation to the initial population, resulting from substantial movement away from regions in the north of the Far East.

Table 4.1 also suggests that at the level of the macro-economic region there has been continuity in the pattern of migration. One easy way to examine this at the regional level is to examine the cross-correlations of the various years for which the data are available. These are presented in Table 4.2. As the table reveals, there has been little change in the regions where inter-regional migrants are coming from and going to.

Table 4.2   Russian macro-regions: cross-correlations of inter-regional migration flows

Year	In-migration			Out-migration		
	1994	1995	1996	1994	1995	1996
1993	0.97	0.93	0.87	0.95	0.95	0.91
1994		0.93	0.94		0.97	0.93
1995			0.98			0.93

Source: Derived from Table 4.1.

Map 4.2 reveals visually the overall pattern. From the map the net in-migration into the European part of Russia and to a much lesser extent to the south of the Siberian part of Russia is apparent. The map summarizes the westward and southward shift in the population over the years from the end of 1993 to the end of 1996. Thus, even though gross in-migration as a percentage of the initial population has been relatively high in parts of the North, Siberia and the Far East macro-economic regions, it has not been running at a high enough rate to cover the loss of population through out-migration.

4.3   EXPLAINING MIGRATION FLOWS

The general assumption made about migration is that it results from the desire of migrants to improve their utility, either in the short or long term, by changing their location of residence. This is an implicitly rational decision, although it is unlikely that potential migrants have complete information about relative returns in all regions or that migration is costless and there are no barriers to migration. Thus the simple neo-classical approach to migration is unlikely to hold in its entirety. It does, however, serve as a useful benchmark for examining these flows.

In empirical studies of labour market responses to adverse shocks to regions it has been found that migration is a potent employment response in regions within the United States, whereas in Western Europe regional wage flexibility is the main adjustment mechanism (Abraham 1996, p. 52). The downward flexibility of real wages in Russia has been much noted by analysts, but this may have led to a neglect of the substantial inter-regional migration that has been occurring. It is obvious that Russia does not fit easily with either the paradigmatic North American or Western European labour market adjustment processes.

A standard approach to understand the migration process is the Harris–Todaro (1970) model of inter-regional migration. Even though the positive relationship between real wages and unemployment has been challenged (Blanchflower and Oswald 1994) migration should be considered as a long-term investment and not necessarily as disproving the existence of a wage curve.[6]

6. Blanchflower and Oswald (1994, p. 93) stress that the 'migrant's choices are not likely to respond to transitory movements in economic conditions... it is "permanent" values of pay and joblessness that will be positively related across regions in a long-run equilibrium'. The difficulty is in determining the 'permanent' values. If, however, the transitory movements during economic transformation are

According to the Harris–Todaro approach, migration responds to differences in expected earnings even in the face of considerable unemployment in other regions. What is important with the existence of unemployment is the expected probability of obtaining a job and the associated expected real wage in another region. This is what the criticism of the Harris–Todaro approach is based on: an expected high real wage in a region with high unemployment; whereas the empirical work has tended to show that there is a negative relationship between these variables rather than the positive relationship implied here.

In the case of Russia it may well be the employment differentials rather than the real-wage component that is the more important variable to consider. This would necessitate a relaxation of the assumption made by Harris and Todaro that there is full employment in the marginal migrant's home region, introducing more realism for the present situation in Russia.

Even though the Harris–Todaro approach may suffer from lack of realism in its assumptions, it does usefully highlight the importance of the interdependencies of real wages, or income streams, and unemployment. Extensions of the basic model also allow for the incorporation of important factors such as uncertainty and the informational content of real wages.

The importance of information features in many of the works on migration. The 'migrant stock effect' has the effect of increasing migration into a region as a consequence of information being passed back to other potential migrants about conditions in a destination region. It is also sometimes assumed that the reasons behind the higher propensity for the more educated and skilled to migrate is their greater ability to assimilate and assess information about various regions during the complex migration-related decision-making.[7] Empirical studies reveal that the probability of migration does decrease with distance as a result of, *inter alia*, information problems. The greater the distance, the less likely it is that the potential migrant has full information about conditions in that region. One of the consequences of this is the phenomenon of 'repeat moves', which it is argued stems from the initial imperfect

believed to have long-term impacts by the population then the transitory may be a proxy for the permanent.

7. It is also likely that the employment opportunities for these groups are less constrained at a macro level, as a result of regional mismatch. To balance this, however, is the fact that the more highly skilled are more likely to be able to secure employment in their home region.

information. Short moves, often to neighbouring regions, are therefore the most common; this we saw as a likely explanation for the high levels of both in- and out-migration in the Russian Far East. It should also be noted that migration also incurs non-pecuniary psychic costs, which are incurred when the migrant breaks social links in the home region. When migrants have incurred the initial psychic cost it appears that it is reduced in future moves, as migrants are more likely to remigrate.[8]

A comprehensive estimation of factors influencing migration would require household data to extract the information on how significant the various factors are. Here the approach is to examine the characteristics of regions: why do people leave particular regions and what attracts them to others? In adopting such a procedure some of the informational content that would be available from individuals' decisions is lost. However, the factors that we are trying to identify are important for the region's future. The new geographical economics literature suggests that the impact of migration decisions on a region may have profound results for its development. In the presence of increasing returns to scale, in-migration will benefit the region, attracting more in-migration until congestion costs choke off the incentives to migrate and concurrently base new economic activity in the region. Already in Russia the emergence of regional hubs for sectors of the economy that are likely to be subject to increasing returns, such as financial markets, are documented (see Chapter 3). Therefore, the question of what drives this process is of considerable import for the prospects of particular regions. Regions that are losing population and failing to create new economic activity are likely to be in worse shape as a result of this process. Given that empirical research for other countries tends to reveal that younger and more qualified individuals migrate, this may leave high residual costs for the region in supporting an ageing population that is likely to have poorer economic prospects. With such likely outcomes, the system of fiscal relations in Russia will acquire even greater importance (see Chapter 5).

What influences can be measured? In the following analysis some simple least-squared estimations are used to highlight the influence of various factors on the labour flows. Following the general thrust of the

8. Work on migration in Canada tends to suggest that the first explanation of informational uncertainty is more potent than the imputed psychic costs (Grant and Vanderkamp 1976, pp. 74–7).

Harris–Todaro approach, emphasis is placed on the impact of real income and unemployment on migration flows. Estimates are made for both out- and in- migration, thereby splitting the migration decision into two components: the decision to leave a particular region and the choice of destination region. In this way it is hoped to extract information about what characteristics of regions make them more or less attractive to individuals. This information will be incomplete since the migration decision is an extremely complicated process and by concentrating on economic factors many other important considerations, such as life-cycle effects, are omitted.

We shall first concentrate on influences on out-migration, but limit ourselves to the two main economic influences: real income and employment. The general approach therefore would predict a positive relationship between out-migration from a region and that region's level of unemployment and a negative relationship between a region's real income and inter-regional out-migration from it.

The proportion of the region's population that migrates out of the region is taken as the dependent variable. This is in preference to the total inter-regional out-migration as we are trying to measure the influence of the prevailing conditions in the region on the 'average' resident.

To derive a real income measure several manipulations have been used. First, the measure of monthly monetary income for each region has been deflated by the estimated measure of monetary income necessary to sustain a minimum standard of living. Although there has been some criticism of this measure, in that it may be manipulated by local authorities to increase transfers from the federal authorities, point estimates in the past reveal that using either this data series or the cost of a consumption basket has only marginal impact on the results. The second innovation, which is perhaps more open to criticism, is a modification to take account of the potential impact of subsistence activity in rural areas, which some estimates have indicated may double the average rural household's real income if it were properly taken into consideration. In order to correct for this, a weighting has been used so that the greater the urban population in the total regional population the lower the weighting. Conversely, the larger the share of the rural population in the total the higher the weight.

Another factor that is taken into account is the dependency ratio in the region (the ratio of working-age population to non-working-age population, where the higher the figure the greater the proportion of non-working to working-age population). This factor will implicitly take into consideration family size. For a larger family the costs of migration are higher and this factor may limit the migration possibilities open to those of working age.

A final variable is introduced to take account of distance. In empirical studies of individuals' migration decisions the impact of distance is seen to be important. Given the nature of the data it is impossible to measure where the migrants are going, only that they have left a particular region. However, in larger regions it is likely that a substantial proportion of migration will be intra-regional. To take some account of this, a variable of total population has been used to proxy for regional size. Although this does not explicitly take cognisance of distance, it serves as a proxy for possible alternative locations within a region, and thus meets our purposes of giving some measure of regional 'size' that takes account of more than geographical size.

Table 4.3 gives the results for the years 1993–6 for this estimation. What is apparent is the stability of the influence of several parameters on migration flows. The influence of real income on migration is initially the opposite sign to that expected, though statistically insignificant. In subsequent years the more expected negative relationship is apparent, though again it is statistically insignificant. Measurement error, either at the stage of data collection or in subsequent manipulation, may be responsible for this, although the possibility cannot be ruled out that regional real income plays only a small role in the decision to migrate away from a region. Some indication of this is given by the impact of unemployment on migration. This measure is the residual between the labour force and reported employment. Again this may be a measure that is not the most accurate, but it does have the advantage of being more realistic than the reported levels of unemployment, which for several reasons substantially underestimate the true scale of this problem. In 1993 and 1994 the effect of unemployment on inter-regional out-migration was roughly comparable, and then the coefficient for the rate of unemployment decreased markedly for 1995 and 1996, also losing its statistical significance. One possible reason for the fluctuation may be that large-scale out-migration occurred from regions that initially suffered high levels of unemployment, and once that stock adjustment had taken place it became harder for residents in regions that then experienced growing unemployment to migrate away.

Table 4.3   *Determinants of out-migration by administrative region; dependent variable: annual gross out-migration as a proportion of the population*

Coefficient	1993		1994		1995		1996[a]	
Constant	5.83	(11.75)	6.29	(11.69)	5.62	(11.31)	5.19	(10.03)
Real income	0.18[b]	(1.41)	−0.09	(−0.94)	−0.15	(−1.09)	−0.10	(−0.78)
Unemployment	0.42	(2.23)	0.46	(2.95)	0.13	(0.87)	0.17	(1.26)
Population	−0.20	(−4.00)	−0.24	(−5.03)	−0.27	(−4.71)	−0.25	(−4.86)
Dependency	−2.30	(−5.30)	−2.02	(−5.95)	−1.85	(−2.57)	−1.39	(−9.98)
Far East	0.90	(7.73)	0.93	(6.15)	0.93	(6.09)	0.75	(6.31)
East Siberia	0.51	(6.65)						
Volga–Vyatka			−0.36	(−5.29)	−0.33	(−4.02)	−0.28	(−3.29)
Adjusted R^2	0.72		0.72		0.70		0.63	
Durbin-Watson	1.85		1.82		1.77		2.06	
F-statistic	31.06		33.02		28.70		21.15	
Observations	71		74		73		73	

Notes: [a] Real income, unemployment, and dependency ratio figures are for 1995.
[b] Monthly monetary income deflated by the consumption basket.
Figures in brackets are *t*-statistics.

Residents may have considered that those regions which fared particularly badly during the early 1990s offered few prospects for the future, and so moved away when they could, reducing the rate of unemployment as a result. Residents of other regions which then started to experience more marked economic decline (and the possibility of immigration raising unemployment rates cannot be dismissed) may still have felt that the region continued to offer better possibilities for them than migration would.[9] The high rates of inter-regional migration would tend to lend some support to such a story, that initially there was marked emigration from particularly poorly performing regions, and then more complex decision-making governed the migration process.

9. Investigation of, *inter alia*, real income determinants (see Chapter 3) suggests that a key break occurred in 1995. Thus, a more fundamental change in the operation of the economy, or even perhaps statistical methodologies employed, is the cause of this change.

The size of the region, through the proxy of population, exhibits the expected negative relationship with inter-regional out-migration. This relationship is linear, suggesting that the more populous a region, the more opportunities to move within it. As this suggests that distance is an important consideration for migration, and given the size of Russia and its overpopulation of geographically remote regions, it is likely that repeat migration will be an important feature of the migration process and will considerably lengthen the period of adjustment to regional shocks. For all four years the impact of the dependency ratio was, as expected, a negative constraint on out-migration, though its impact declined over the period.[10]

Finally, three dummy variables were required to address problems of spatial autocorrelation. A dummy for the Far East macro-region was needed for all years, revealing that out-migration was uniformly higher for the federal subjects in the Far East than would have been predicted from the other variables. The same was true for the administrative regions within the East Siberia macro-region in 1993. During 1994–6 the regions in the Volga–Vyatka macro-region showed signs of reduced out-migration even after the other influences had been accounted for.

Investigation of inter-regional in-migration (Table 4.4) requires us to modify some of the variables used in testing the influences. First, the dependent variable is changed to gross in-migration, rather than a proportion of the region's population. This is done as the proposition is that the migration decision is composed of two main decisions: the decision to leave a particular region and the choice of which region to migrate to. In the analysis of the out-migration decision it was assumed that prevailing economic conditions would affect the population of that region in roughly similar ways. The prevailing conditions in the destination region have no such influence on the migrants, who are assumed to view all regions in a roughly similar manner.

The variable for the real income measure is the simple per capita monetary income measure deflated by a measure of the cost of living in the region. Adjustment for subsistence activity is omitted as it is assumed that the migration is in search of paid employment,[11] rather

10. The higher the dependency ratio in a region, other things being equal, the greater the costs for the typical household of moving elsewhere. This influence shows up in analyses of migration in other countries.

11. Although not reported here, real wages have similar estimated coefficients when substituted for the real income measures reported in Tables 4.3 and 4.4.

than subsistence activity. The coefficient of this variable is expected to be positive, with migrants favouring regions with higher real incomes. The converse relationship is expected with respect to unemployment, which is again the wide measure of the residual between reported employment and the labour force. Partly this takes account of the effects of the probability of finding employment in the destination region. In regions with high levels of unemployment it would be expected that the chances of finding employment would be diminished and thus discourage migration to such regions. A variable for the population of the region is again incorporated. This serves two potential purposes, though it is unfortunate that they cannot be identified separately. First, in larger regions the availability of accommodation and employment will be larger and, second, in the presence of increasing returns to scale at the regional level the migrants' decision may be influenced by the potential opportunities offered by a larger agglomeration (see Chapter 3).

A variable to take into account the flexibility of the housing stock has also been included as the number of privatized dwellings in relation to the population of the region. As discussed above, the rigidities of the housing market are seen as a key obstacle to inter-regional migration. Therefore, the degree of liberalization of the housing market should have an impact on migration flows. The degree of privatization of dwellings is a measure that should capture the availability of housing, although a more precise measure of housing available for either rent or perhaps purchase would be a better indicator of the flexibility of the local housing market.

A final variable to examine the impact of the *propiska* system is included by the use of a dummy variable for Moscow. If, as expected, this prevents the free movement of people to the capital, then the coefficient for this variable should be significantly negative. Although other regions do attempt to control the in-migration of people it is only Moscow that has unambiguously clung to the use of such restrictions for the whole period examined in Table 4.4.

Finally, examination of the residuals for the estimated equations revealed problems with spatial auto-correlation that was removed with the inclusion of a dummy for Stavropol', Krasnodar and Rostov, the non-republic federal subjects in the North Caucasus macro-economic region. Given the instability in the region it is perhaps little surprise that these regions show significantly higher levels of inter-regional

Table 4.4   *Determinants of in-migration by region; dependent variable: annual gross in-migration*

Coefficient	1993		1994		1995		1996[a]	
Constant	2.67	(2.42)	6.25	(5.37)	5.16	(7.06)	4.60	(6.37)
Real income	0.26[b]	(1.68)	0.30	(3.24)	0.31	(1.99)	0.49	(2.45)
Unemployment	1.20	(0.91)	-2.92	(-2.01)	-1.09	(-1.22)	-0.84	(-0.91)
Population	0.80	(17.64)	0.88	(21.48)	0.84	(22.01)	0.86	(17.86)
Housing	0.06	(1.45)	0.24	(3.26)	0.33	(3.96)	0.35	(4.05)
Non-republics in Caucasus	0.54	(3.37)	0.43	(2.95)	0.33	(2.26)	0.27	(2.03)
Moscow	-0.41	(-2.46)	-0.69	(-4.34)	-0.38	(-2.17)	-0.41	(-1.78)
Adjusted R^2	0.90		0.91		0.90		0.90	
Durbin–Watson	2.03		2.36		2.32		2.34	
F-Statistic	104		123		113		107	
Observations	70		73		72		73	

Notes: [a] Real income, unemployment and housing figures are for 1995.
[b] monthly monetary income deflated by the consumption basket.
The figure in brackets is the associated *t*-statistic.

in-migration. Partly this may also capture some secondary in-migration of international immigrants from the Caucasus region in general (but see note 2).

In Table 4.4, the results for the years 1993–6 are given. A cursory examination of the table reveals far more instability in the influence of variables governing the choice of destination region. Real income is positively associated with in-migration, with a strengthening of the effect over the period considered. The impact of unemployment is at best weak. Although the coefficient for this variable is negative for three of the four years, it is statistically significant only for 1994. This is perhaps a result of the unemployment rate being an imperfect proxy for the perceived opportunities of obtaining employment in the destination region.

Unsurprisingly, the larger the region the larger the inflow of inter-regional immigrants. The relationship is linear, suggesting that for inter-regional immigration the potential effects of the opportunities associated with increasing returns to scale are not present, or at least not in the time period considered. The effect of barriers to in-migration is shown to be potent over the period considered, as is the inflow of inter-regional migrants to the non-republics of the North Caucasus macro-region.

The results from the estimation of influences on both in- and out-migration come as no real surprise. One can see that there is a tendency to move from low real-income regions towards high real-income regions, and – although this is not quite so clear – away from regions with high unemployment rates. The population of the region is important, partly because in more populous regions more opportunities for intra-regional migration or employment change are available and partly because, for the migrant, larger regions will more easily absorb immigrants. High dependency ratios do inhibit migration in a manner that economic priors suggest, as does the flexibility of the housing market. The strength of the relationship with housing market conditions does suggest that further liberalization will improve the flow of migration within Russia and will help reduce the problems, such as unemployment duration and regional mismatch, associated with barriers to inter-regional migration. Such concerns are also raised by the impact of Moscow's attempt to limit in migration. Finally, the motivation to migrate in the Far East is especially strong, for reasons specific to that macro-region, over and above the influence of other factors.

4.4   CONCLUSIONS

Russia in the 1990s was characterized by extreme turbulence, with worsening demographic indicators and extreme economic dislocation. In this context, inter-regional migration was one response by households to emerging circumstances in the regions. The choices made by individuals and households are important in revealing their assessments about present and expectations of future opportunities in particular regions. It appears that inter-regional migration flows in Russia have been substantial in the 1990s, and that the influences driving both in- and out-migration to or from a Russian region are in the main those that economic theory would predict: away from poorer, smaller regions with relatively high unemployment and towards better-off, larger regions with lower unemployment.

In addition, migration is especially high, other things being equal, from regions especially remote from Moscow and especially affected by the reduction of subsidies to transport, energy and food supplies (in the Russian Far East and East Siberia).

This pattern of inter-regional migration is an important part of Russian economic adjustment in general, and of labour-market adjustment in particular. It helps to keep unemployment levels in check and, probably, to reduce – if only marginally – the problems associated with regional mismatch and long-term unemployment: a decline in individuals' employability and thus their contribution to competition on the supply side of labour markets.

Despite all the impediments to such labour-market adjustment in Russia – the great size of the country and the associated costs of inter-regional migration, the weakness of the housing market and the embryonic state of many labour-market institutions such as private recruitment agencies – the scale of inter-regional migration in 1990s' Russia is quite large by international standards. This probably reflects both the pace of structural change since the fall of communism and the underdeveloped character of social safety nets: in particular, the low level and frequent unavailability of unemployment benefits. At all events, it is at odds with the stereotype of Russians' alleged 'passivity' in the face of sweeping economic change.

The evidence presented in this chapter also suggests that inter-regional migration is tending to correct Soviet-era territorial misallocation of resources. For the positive benefits arising from migration to be realized more fully, however, the constraints need to be addressed. Further liberalization of the housing market and of regional government controls on place of residence (notably, Moscow city's perpetuation of its *propiska* system) would assist this important form of grass-roots adjustment to economic change.

5. Federal Government Responses to Regional Economic Change

Philip Hanson, Sergei Artobolevskiy, Olga Kouznetsova and Douglas Sutherland

INTRODUCTION

The purpose of this chapter is to describe the ways in which the federal government tries to influence regional patterns of economic change in Russia and the effects of these policies. This is just one element in the larger topic of centre–region relations in Russia – a topic that has elicited a massive flow of commentary. The more academic part of that commentary is reviewed in Chapter 2. Here we deal chiefly with the centre's regional policies. We shall touch on the politics of regional lobbying, national cohesion, alliance-building and separatist rhetoric, but they are not our prime concern.

The meaning of 'regional policy' has yet to be settled in Russian practice. It is not surprising, therefore, that there is no established set of institutions for forming and instituting regional policy – let alone a single overlord body such as France's DATAR or the European Union's Directorate-General XVI. We take regional policy to be taxing, spending and legislation by the central authorities, aimed at least in part at achieving economic effects that are differentiated across krays, oblasts and republics.

This does not mean that we are dealing only with so-called 'fiscal-federal' issues of the sharing of budget revenue and the Federal Fund for Support of the Regions (FFPR in its Russian acronym). We have treated these at considerable length elsewhere (Kouznetsova *et al.* 1999), and shall simply summarize and update that review here. Our definition of regional policy does mean, however, that we exclude some federal government actions, despite the fact that they do undoubtedly have regionally differentiated effects. Thus federal purchasing of goods and services and federal maintenance of the regional branches of federal agencies are not treated here as part of regional policy. If we pass lightly around these subjects, it is for two reasons: we assume, perhaps too charitably, that these federal government actions are not directed primarily at benefiting some regions more than others; and systematic information about them is lacking.

The main sections of this chapter deal, in turn, with the location of central government decision-making on regional policies; with the allocation of funds and responsibilities between centre and regions; with the scale of the resource flows involved and their evolution over time in the 1990s; with tax-sharing and FFPR arrangements; and with overall conclusions. Intra-regional issues (cities and rural districts versus regional administrations) are a whole different ball-game, though admittedly one that is closely related; we touch on these only in passing – though a little bit more is included later in the case-study chapters. We take the background of rapidly diverging regional income levels, discussed in Chapter 3, as given. The intricacies of FFPR formulae and their possible revisions are confined to the chapter appendix.

5.1   WHO IS IN CHARGE OF REGIONAL POLICIES?

In Soviet times, the location of economic activity was determined chiefly by the investment and output programmes of branch ministries. There were government agencies that studied the regional allocation of resources. There were at various times specific programmes of development for particular regions. During 1957–64 there was even a territorially- rather than branch-based planning and management system. But for most purposes and for most of the time, outputs and incomes in different parts of the USSR were the outcome of a national planning process in which branch plans played a dominant role. This shaped the development of administrative regions and the State Planning Committee's macro-regions alike (see, for example, Schiffer 1988).

The development and carrying out of regional policies, in our sense, can be initiated and influenced by two executive bodies (the presidential administration and the government), two legislative bodies (the two houses of parliament, with their committees) and a judicial body – the Constitutional Court. Box 5.1 summarizes the main locations of regional policy in the 'centre'. The roles in regional policy of many of these entities are weak. The roles of all of them have fluctuated substantially, because of both a high turnover of leading personnel and a high turnover of these organizations' missions. In late 1998 and early 1999 the following could be said about the various organizations and arrangements indicated in Box 5.1.

Box 5.1   Regional policy in Russia

A.   Presidential Administration
    (a)   Territorial Department
    (b)   Department coordinating presidential envoys
    (c)   Presidential Commission on the preparation of power-sharing agreements

B.   Russian government
    (a)   Branches of federal agencies in regions
    (b)   Department on relations with federal subjects and with the Federation Council
    (c)   Ministry of the Economy, within which:
        (i)   Department of the Economics of Federal Relations
        (ii)   Department of Regional Economic Policy
        (iii) Department of Regional Programmes
    (d)   Ministry of Regional Policy (formed in autumn 1998 from parts of former Ministry of Nationalities and Regional Policy plus former State Committee on the Development of the North)
    (e)   Ministry of Finance
    (f)   Ministry of Taxes
    (g)   Working Centre of Economic Reform
    (h)   Regular consultation by PM/deputy PMs with heads of the eight macro-regional economic associations.

C.   Legislature
    (a)   Federation Council (with Committee on Federation, federal agreements and regional policy
    (b)   Duma (with Committee on Federation and regional policy)

D.   Judiciary
    The Constitutional Court

In the Presidential Administration, the Territorial Department is responsible for information, monitoring and analysis of developments in the regions. It has absorbed some of the work carried out (and in part published) by the now-defunct Presidential Analytical Centre. The coordination of the work of the President's envoys (or representatives) in the regions has been spasmodic, focusing *ad hoc* on particular trouble-spots as events unfold. Presidential representatives in the regions have little influence except when – as happens from time to time – one of them is backed directly and strongly by the President. The work of the Commission has recently been at a low level; many centre–region power-sharing agreements have been signed, but both their desirability in principle and their effectiveness in practice have been questioned. In general, the weakening of the Yeltsin presidency in 1998 has meant that the Presidential Administration ceased for the time being to be a major player in federal policy.

So far as the other part of the federal executive, the Russian government, is concerned, there is a multiplicity of agencies and much overlapping of their roles. The regional presence of federal agencies (including the military) is substantial: not surprisingly, the federal government employs more people outside Moscow than does the sum of regional administrations. It is often suggested, however, that regional political leaders have a strong influence on, and even control of, the local arms of most federal agencies. Poor federal funding is often cited as a reason for taking this view, along with regional administrations' control of buildings and some material supplies. However, in two key areas there is little sign of federal bodies in the provinces defecting to local leaders: military lines of command still function, for all the generally shambolic state of the Russian army; and federal tax collection, using the federal tax service, the federal treasury system and federally authorized banks, still dominates the flows of budget revenues. Attempts by regions to withhold tax revenue due to be transferred to Moscow have been brief and minor (Lavrov 1998b). (These *ad hoc* withholding attempts are an entirely separate matter from the preferential tax-sharing deals negotiated with the federal government by Tatarstan, Bashkortostan, Sakha and possibly Karelia.)

So far as governmental priorities are concerned, regional policy has usually not loomed large. For example, the government decree of 30 May 1997, listing the spheres of responsibility of the various deputy prime ministers, does not refer to regional policy. However, in 1998, fiscal-federal issues were identified specifically as part of the portfolio of Deputy Prime Minister Viktor Khristenko (*Jamestown Foundation Monitor*, 30 April 1998).

The government department for relations with federal subjects is supposed to monitor regional implementation of presidential edicts, government degrees and federal legislation. In part, at least, its work therefore overlaps with that of the Presidential Administration's Territorial Department.

In the Ministry of the Economy (MinEkon) the three departments listed in Box 5.1 all come under one deputy minister. The first of the three is concerned with strategic issues such as the federal regional sharing-out of state property, the principles of local self-government and the determination of regional governments' foreign trade role. The second is concerned with current matters, including the provision of central investment funds and other assistance to regions. The third department, as its name indicates, prepares regional development programmes.

Officials in these – and indeed other – departments of MinEkon have worked on the design of central transfers and subsidies from the federal budget (see Samokhvalov 1996; Khursevich 1998; Laykam 1998; Samokhvalov in early 1999 became a first deputy minister). In this, they overlap with work done in the Ministry of Finance (MinFin), including that Ministry's Economic Expert Group (see the latter's website, http://www.eeg.ru). When Sergey Kirienko's government was replaced by that of Yevgeniy Primakov, in August–September 1998, Viktor Khristenko dropped in rank from deputy prime minister to deputy finance minister – but took the fiscal-federal portfolio with him. That is not the end of departmental overlaps on this issue: the Tax Ministry, which has disagreed in public with MinFin over tax reform, is also likely to have an input of its own. Finally, economists in the government's Working Centre for Economic Reform (including one of the authors of this chapter) have worked on detailed proposals for the reform of federal regional budget transfers, along with MinEkon and MinFin specialists.

One rather different channel for the making of regional policy should also be noted: regular consultation between the cabinet (usually the Prime Minister or one of his deputies) and the chairmen of the eight macro-regional economic associations (MREAs). Yevgenii Primakov, when he became Prime Minister, even spoke of those eight representatives having *ex officio* cabinet seats, though nothing much seems to have come of this. From at least early 1997, however, under the government of Viktor Chernomyrdin, federal government consultation with the MREA leaders was becoming a regular event. Whether it achieved anything is another matter. The macro-regional associations have shown little ability to act collectively on behalf of their constituent administrative regions. The latter typically have long lists of grievances against their fellow association members.

So far as the national legislature is concerned, the Federation Council (the upper house) is the assembly that is designed to represent the regions. Each of the 89 federal subjects has two seats in it. However, it meets only two days a month, and the regions are represented by their executive and legislative leaders. They are typically rather busy back on their own home turf. Leaders of comparatively strong regions such as Tatarstan and Samara began in 1998–9 to form electoral blocs that would fight the 1999 elections to the lower house, or Duma. Unlike Moscow mayor Yurii Luzhkov and his Otechestvo movement, they did not do this to create vehicles for their own presidential campaigns. They appear to believe they can create centrist groupings in the new Duma that would reduce the influence of the communists and agrarians (*RFE/RL Newsletter,* 10 March 1999), without being identified with the discredited parties of reform, such as Pravoe delo, or of central executive power, such as Nash Dom Rossiya.

Pending the development of groupings led by powerful regional bosses, regional points of view have typically been represented in the lower house by deputies elected as independents, who have sometimes affiliated to parliamentary fractions with 'regions' in their titles. With one or two exceptions, these have not been weighty figures in national politics. The recent show of interest in the formation of Duma blocs, on the part of powerful governors, reflects a belief that the lower house can be a more effective channel for lobbying and for shaping legislation. Their interests are in keeping a larger share of the main taxes that at present feed their budgets (value added tax, profits tax and income tax); in greater freedom to develop natural resource projects on their territories without having to seek federal approval; and in a similar freedom of initiative in raising money on international markets (at present, federal approval is needed for the issue of Eurobonds, for example). They see the Duma as an effective forum for pursuing this agenda (*Russia Journal*, 17–23 June 1999).

In commentaries on centre–region relations in Russia, the role of the judiciary has been somewhat neglected. Any functioning federation will be subject chronically to friction over which level is responsible for what and has which powers; an independent judiciary that can credibly rule on such matters is necessary. Brynjulf Risnes (1998) has listed the requirements for a law-based federation:

- constitutional protection of federalism;
- a legal framework for the distribution of powers between levels;
- democratically elected legislatures and executives at both federal and sub-national levels;
- an independent judiciary.

Noting that in Russia the framework for the distribution of powers has been unclear (too many functions vaguely defined as 'joint', for a start), Risnes argues that since 1994 the Constitutional Court has at least begun to act constructively. The 1991–3 Constitutional Court volunteered its own solutions to all the issues put to it, exceeding its brief and failing to establish its own credibility. Its successor has not tried to fill gaps in the constitution but has pointed to the places where additional legislation is needed. For example, in the vexed question of the relationship between the Khanti-Mansy and Yamal-Nenets autonomous okrugs, on the one hand, and Tyumen' oblast, on the other, the court ruled that the constitution says only that the former are 'part' of the latter and gives no further guidance; therefore new legislation is needed to define their respective competences.

These, then, are the channels through which the economic functions and powers, revenues and expenditures of Russia's regions can be determined 'from above'. The main federal actor at present, given the weakness of the presidency in early 1999, is the federal government. But it is not the only federal actor, and it is itself internally ill-coordinated, with multiple agencies whose roles *vis-à-vis* the regions overlap and often conflict.

5.2 THE FEDERALIZATION OF RUSSIA

Russia has been a unitary state in the past. That was true of the USSR as well as of tsarist Russia. The Soviet Union's federalism was a legal fiction. The development of a federation in Russia therefore entails the building of institutions and procedures with no history or tradition to back them. It is not surprising that Russia's federal arrangements are messy, that many well-informed Russians continue to believe the country *should be* a unitary state, and that in many respects the centre has more formal power than is normal in federations.

Of the four legal requirements of a federation listed by Risnes, it might be said that the first and third (constitutional protection of federalism and direct election of executives and legislatures at both national and sub-national levels) are present, now that regional executive leaders are all elected. (In early 1997 most still were not.) The second – a clear legal framework delineating the powers of both federation and 'federal subjects' – has a long way to go. The last – an independent judiciary – is also not safely installed.

So far as government decisions on the allocation of resources are concerned, two other considerations matter a great deal. First, the economy has – on official GDP measures and barring a brief respite in 1997 – been shrinking for a decade, and the machinery of government at all levels is weak and corrupt. All Russia's governments, national and sub-national, have been struggling desperately to cope with everyday responsibilities: paying public employees; keeping schools and hospitals functioning; maintaining (at the federal level) something with a passing resemblance to an army. Possibly the only government in Russia that has had resources with which to do anything to improve the conditions of life within its jurisdiction has been the city of Moscow – and that freedom of action may have ended in 1998.

The second consideration is that the centre, while in no shape to do anything to help the regions, can and does limit quite drastically their ability to help themselves. Tax bases and tax rates for all the main revenue-raising taxes are centrally determined. This applies above all to VAT and profits tax, which are critical to regional budget revenues. In addition, like any state with only rudimentary revenue-raising capabilities, Russia relies heavily on duties on foreign trade (both exports and imports); these are federally controlled levies. In early

1999 they accounted for a third or more of federal revenues – equivalent in April 1999 to 4.8 per cent of GDP (Economic Experts Group, MinFin, http://www.eeg.ru, update of 11 June 1999).

The federal Tax Ministry collects revenue throughout the country. The quantities collected in each region from a number of core taxes are then 'shared upwards': in other words, a fixed percentage is transmitted to the federal budget. In 1996 this was 75 per cent of VAT, 34.3 per cent of profits tax and 10 per cent of personal income tax.[1] That, at least, was the principle. In practice, as has already been described, a few economically strong republics negotiated preferential sharing deals in the early 1990s. Also, when the federal budget was accepting revenue only in money (not barter or money surrogates), regional administrations had an incentive to encourage non-monetary settlements on their territory, because these could not be passed upwards (Lavrov 1998b). The Federal Fund for Support of the Regions (FFPR) has, from 1994, been used to channel funds back from the centre to the regions – in principle, on some basis of need. These amounts have been small (see below), and the working of the revenue allocation mechanism as a whole has been the subject of controversy – academic in the West, and urgent in Russia. Chapter 7 gives some of the flavour of regional officials' feelings on the subject.

One part of the picture is especially obscure: the off-budget funds. Such funds exist at federal, regional and local levels, and those controlled at sub-national levels are poorly documented. It appears that sub-national off-budget funds do not add a great deal to the resources available to most regions but probably are substantial for a handful of the richer regions. In Moscow, their amounts and usage have been well-guarded secrets – including from members of the city council (private communication from a councillor, 1996).

The state, though weak and ineffective, retains too large a weight in the Russian economy. The overall scale of government revenue and spending (budgets at all levels plus off-budget funds at all levels) was in 1995–8 of the following order: expenditure 37–41 per cent of GDP, revenue 31–33 per cent of GDP (EBRD 1998, p. 225). The spending figure is too high because it cannot be supported for long in a non-inflationary way. Russia has neither the capacity to raise enough tax and other revenue nor access to low-cost borrowing.

---

1. With effect from May 1999 the federal share of VAT rose to 85 per cent.

After the rouble devaluation and partial debt default of August 1998, this sad state of affairs has become clear. The federal government has been unable to service all its debt – both rouble and foreign – and is at the time of writing in partial default. A number of regions have defaulted on rouble bonds and sought rescheduling of foreign bank borrowing (consortium loans) and eurobonds (in the cases of the handful of Russian regions that had got as far as issuing eurobonds by early 1998). The credit ratings of municipalities and regions, as of the country as a whole now (June 1999) reflect this. Western attention has naturally been focused chiefly on federal-level sovereign debt. But this is a *de facto* bankrupt country composed of mostly bankrupt regions. In 1997 all federal subjects except Moscow city and the Nenets autonomous okrug ran budget deficits (information from the Working Centre of Economic Reform). Now none of them is able to borrow at less than penal rates.

In these current circumstances, the rules governing regions' access to credit are of merely academic interest. Nobody is about to lend to them. But the rules have been important and should become so again. In a nutshell, the centre allows regions on their own initiative to borrow domestically but has required them to have federal approval for the issue of (for example) eurobonds. At the same time, the July 1998 federal law 'On characteristics of the issue of and trade in municipal securities' makes no mention of federal guarantees of sub-national borrowing. It sets ceilings on the scale of borrowing by administrative regions: a region must not in the course of a year issue bonds to a value in excess of 30 per cent of its budget revenue excluding federal transfers, and it must not incur interest obligations exceeding 15 per cent of its annual budget expenditure. The federal government, having breached both those limits in its own borrowing, now knows that its instructions are wise.

The upshot is that regions have little fiscal autonomy. They can tinker with the minor property and other tax rates and bases that are at their discretion; they can perhaps find a few novel ways of feeding off-budget funds, but these will not amount to much unless the region houses a major commercial and financial centre (Moscow city, perhaps St Petersburg, Samara and Sverdlovsk); they can borrow, but their borrowing powers are circumscribed from above and their borrowing is not guaranteed from above; and they can lobby the centre. They do a lot of lobbying.

So far as responsibilities are concerned, the centre at the start of the reforms passed downwards a great deal of social spending: large parts of health, education and social-benefit provision. These areas are partly covered, in principle, by federal off-budget funds, but levels of provision across regions do depend heavily on local resources and are correspondingly uneven.

Orthodox public-finance theory provides some guidance to the appropriate division of responsibilities between national and sub-national governments (Musgrave 1959; Oates 1972). The starting-point is that the prime economic functions of government in a market economy are to provide macro-economic stability and, where the balance of advantage favours intervention, to act to promote efficient resource allocation (for example, by providing public goods that would be underprovided by the market). To this might be added a third function: that of reducing inequality of personal incomes according to some consensus on what is desirable.

The first of these functions must be performed by the central authorities: price stability and low unemployment are national public goods. The second probably requires central provision of an array of public goods, such as national defence and the courts. But there are local public goods (parks and fire services, for example) and there may be regional differences in voters' preferences about the trade-off between public-goods provision and taxation. Elected sub-national authorities have both motive and means to be more sensitive than national authorities to local wishes, and it is advantageous that they have the proper incentives to raise taxes and spend taxpayers' money efficiently in the light of those wishes. Taxpayers can influence local governments either by voice (voting) or by exit (moving to other localities with lower taxes or better provision, or even both). The third function is probably best handled by the central authorities: there is much inequality within most regions (see Chapter 3 on the Russian case).[2]

These general guidelines leave lots of room for interpretation so far as the allocation of functions between levels of government in any particular country is concerned. But they provide a viewpoint from

---

2. This compressed account leaves aside ideas about the merits of competitive suppliers of money, defence, law and order, and so on, in a minimal-government society. It does however cover the sort of rationale that is supposed to lie behind most Western practice.

which to inspect region–centre issues in Russia. It follows from these guidelines that a clear division of responsibilities should as far as possible be matched by a corresponding division of revenue-raising powers. This should enhance the accountability of sub-national governments as well as strengthen their incentives to raise revenue efficiently. The central government should be responsible for any highly progressive taxes, for taxing mobile tax bases and for taxing any tax base that happens to be geographically very unevenly distributed – such as Sakha's diamonds or Tyumen's oil and gas.

It also follows that the prime reason for transfers from national to sub-national budgets should be to assist regions with poor tax bases to reach at least a minimum desirable level of provision of public goods. Beyond that, the reduction of inequalities should be a function of central government (for example, via a national system of personal taxation and social benefits). It follows that such transfers, intended as they are to allow the provision of specific public goods and not to undermine the incentives of sub-national governments to tax and spend efficiently, should be earmarked and conditional on matching funds being added.

Russia's public finances are far from being based on these principles. At the same time, much of the discussion about them has shown an awareness of several of these ideas: the need to maintain the incentives of regional governments to tax and spend efficiently, for example. However, the sharing of core tax revenues and the association of federal transfers with reducing regional deficits are cumbersome and inefficient arrangements. Moreover, the lurching-from-crisis-to-crisis character of Russian federal finances makes the state of regional finances unpredictable and the trust between levels of government minimal.

5.3 RESOURCE FLOWS BETWEEN CENTRE AND REGIONS

Regional leaders often complain that the centre has passed down spending responsibilities but not the necessary revenue or revenue-raising powers. There is a good deal of truth in this, but during the macro-economic stabilization or pseudo-stabilization of 1995–8, the regions tended to gain marginally in revenue and spending shares from the centre. This is illustrated in Table 5.1. Row 9 is a reminder that the shares concerned are shares of a shrinking total.

Table 5.1   Russia: budgets and transfers as % GDP, 1994–8

	1994	1995	1996	1997	1998
Federal budget					
1. Revenue		13.0	11.8	12.3	10.2
2. Expenditure		18.6	19.9	19.6	15.2
3. O/w planned transfers to regions	4.3	1.9	2.7	2.7	1.9
4. Actual transfers[a]	3.3	1.7	2.2	1.7	
5. Planned FFPR	1.9	1.0	1.8	2.1	
6. Actual FFPR	0.9	1.3	1.1	1.3	
Sum regional budgets					
7. revenue	18.9	15.5	15.0	16.3	14.7
8. expenditure		16.0	16.0	17.7	15.2
9. FFPR/reg. revenue, %	4.9	8.1	7.3	8.0	
10. Memorandum item: GDP 1994 = 100	100	95.9	92.5	93.4	89.1
11. Number donor regions[b]	—	14	12	8	7

Notes: [a] The coverage of row 4 is not comparable with that of row 3. It is in fact wider, since it also includes mutual settlements (budget offsets) and budget loan balances.
[b] Regions not planned to receive any FFPR transfers in a given year.

Sources: Derived from *Russian Economic Trends Monthly Update,* June 1999 (rows 1, 2, 7, 8); ibid. plus EBRD (1998) (row 10); Tabata (1998) (rows 3 and 5); Khursevich (1998) (row 6; original gives 6 as % 5); row 9 is derived from the original rouble series behind rows 5 and 7; IEPPP (1998) and Marchenko and Machul'skaya (1997) (row 4).

Several important elements in the Russian fiscal-federal game can be seen in this table. In the period covered, both regions and centre were running deficits. This had not been true of the sum of regions in 1992–3. That was when a large slice of spending responsibilities was pushed downwards by the early reform governments. It may be that in 1992–3 the federal policy-makers trusted that sub-national budgets would be subject to quite hard constraints and that this would help to contain the overall level of government spending. After all, the regions, unlike the federal authorities, could not print money. (Here and elsewhere, unless otherwise specified, we use the term 'regional budgets' to denote the regions' consolidated regional-plus-local budgets; the latter are heavily dependent on the former.)

Over time, however, the regions have learnt how to spend above their incomes. They have done this not simply by orthodox borrowing (bond issues and bank credits), but by various undocumented combinations of transfers from off-budget funds, issuing bills of exchange (in Russian, *veksels*, from the German name), tax offsets and the like.

However, the deficits have been much smaller at the sub-national than at the national level. From Table 5.1 it can be seen that they would have been smaller even if there had been no FFPR transfers from the federal budget. At around 1 per cent of GDP, the actual FFPR transfers have had a limited role. It is possible that the regions have been able to maintain revenues within a modest margin of their spending levels by, among other things, extracting more revenue 'from above' quite separately from the FFPR transfers. At all events, their share of general government spending converged, over this period, on the federal share, without the relative size of their combined deficit changing much.

The table also shows planned transfers other than the FFPR. These are hard to document, but those that have been identified by Tabata (1998) in the federal budget data are a motley and dwindling set of minor flows. There are funds to support the transfer of enterprise housing and other enterprise amenities to the balances of municipalities (1994–7; zero in 1998); grants to closed cities and to the federal resort area of Sochi (continuing but small amounts); federal funds for special regional development programmes (small amounts; see Chapter 7 for the non-arrival of such funds in Krasnodar); the special subvention (an earmarked subsidy) to Moscow to perform its functions as a capital city (again, a modest amount on a national scale); support for the subsidized supply of food to Far North regions (the largest continuing item, but still far smaller than the FFPR); and some very small, one-off items. This is a list of planned, not actual, flows; on the basis of planned flows, the FFPR was almost 80 per cent of the total in 1998. In addition there have been so-called budget loans and inter-budgetary settlements (offsets).

What can be deduced from all this about regional policy? Our interpretation of the available evidence is that in the 1990s, for practical purposes, the Russian federal government's regional policies mostly boiled down to the year-to-year juggling with the FFPR transfers. Certainly, there are other large flows between the national budget and the regions. But a large part of those other flows is not connected with regional policy as we have defined it: the maintenance of the regional networks of federal agencies; the purchase of goods and services for federal government use, and so on. Some other elements, such as the special federal funding of closed cities, of Moscow as federal capital and of the 'federal' resort of Sochi, are of a similar nature. As for the federal programmes for regional development, these have been grandiose in concept, modest in earmarked funding and even more modest – to the point of being negligible – in actual financing (see Chapter 7, for the case of Krasnodar).[3]

The one other substantial ingredient in regional policy has been the subsidies to food supplies to the Far North – a relic of Soviet times and of the Soviet planners' absurd decisions on location. Given the Soviet inheritance, there have been obvious humanitarian grounds for continuing to subsidize these settlements pending an orderly retreat from most of them. But this assistance is notoriously subject to embezzlement, and even the planned amounts are small (about 7 per cent of the planned FFPR , or 0.1 per cent of GDP, in 1998).

Accordingly, we focus in the rest of this chapter on issues surrounding tax sharing and the Federal Fund for Support of the Regions. This emphasis conforms with the preoccupation of both federal and regional policy-makers with the subject. It appears, for example, to have been the main item in Viktor Khristenko's portfolio in 1998–9 (see section 5.1 above).

---

3. One other sort of regional policy not considered here is the establishment of special economic zones or free trade zones. There are a number of these in Russia. In Chapter 9, one of them is discussed in detail. The substance of special economic zone policy as an issue in federal policy-making is best indicated by the OECD's 1997 *Economic Survey of Russia*: 'most of these zones are currently believed not to function at all. Interestingly enough, no single agency in the Russian government appears able to confirm exactly which zones function, and to what degree' (p. 192). As Chapter 9 shows, the arrangements in Kaliningrad have been of some importance, but they are surrounded by damaging uncertainty.

5.4   TAX-SHARING, BUDGET TRANSFERS AND THEIR REFORM

Table 5.1 shows one standard feature of Russian budgets: spending on the FFPR was usually well below the planned amount – in other words, below what was legislated for. Khursevich (1998) shows for 1994 to 1997 the proportional fulfilment of the FFPR obligations region by region. The average is low and the variance is striking. In any one year shortfalls to a particular region could be as much as 60 per cent. This is one clue to the frustration and distrust with which regional officials regard the centre. It also goes a long way to explain the large amounts of time that many of them spend in Moscow to 'extract' (*vybivat'*) money.

It can be calculated from Khursevich's figures for 79 federal subjects (including autonomous okrugs but excluding Moscow city and a few oblasts not receiving FFPR transfers – so called 'donor' regions) that in 1997 the unweighted arithmetic mean of fulfilment of FFPR plans was 65.5 per cent and the coefficient of variation around that mean was 0.216, or more than one-fifth. The picture across all four years is somewhat better: a mean of 76.5 per cent and a coefficient of variation of 0.118. The higher mean reflects the presence of a rogue year (1995) when actual transfers exceeded plan. The lower coefficient of variation suggests that some of the cross-regional discrepancies in the delivery of transfers in any one year are perhaps corrected in the next. In other words, the process is probably less arbitrary and chaotic than an inspection of one year's figures alone would suggest. Even so, the experience of those years is unlikely to make federal government credible in the eyes of regional governments: you could expect to get three-quarters of the amount earmarked for you in the federal budget, subject to a large margin of error in any one year.

What is the combination of tax sharing and FFPR transfers officially intended to achieve? Russia's 1993 constitution contains a commitment to provide all citizens with common minimum social provision, regardless of place of residence. This is not the same as 'equalization' and is compatible with conventional Western *desiderata* for fiscal-federal arrangements (see section 5.2 above). Another commitment is to facilitate full and effective utilization of all resources; that is, efficient resource allocation. The latter would as a minimum require the absence of inter-regional barriers to flows of goods, labour and capital. In discussion of federal transfers some Russian commentators refer also to a need to ensure 'social justice' and even 'territorial justice'. Notoriously, the first of these does not readily yield a widely agreed operational definition; the latter is pure verbiage. The Russian debate also refers frequently to the need to preserve social stability in Russia as a whole and the country's territorial integrity. These are obviously and necessarily part of the rationale of any federal system.

It is of course acknowledged that there are trade-offs between these objectives. The difficulty, not surprisingly, is in agreeing on the dimensions of the trade-offs and where a balance should be struck between competing goals. In all countries that are not single-cell creations (Luxembourg?), negotiation over such trade-offs can be expected to continue indefinitely. The fragility of Russian arrangements, compared with those of more established federations, stems from the weak and unreliable functioning of almost all forms of government, the lack of established routines of consultation, and perhaps also (and marginally) from the lack of resort even in specialist discussion to some useful analytical concepts – public goods, local public goods and the like – that might help to clarify some of the issues.

Both Aleksei Lavrov (1997a, 1997b) and Darrell Slider (1997a) have offered their lists of the desirable economic properties of a well-functioning federation and of budget transfers between levels. Their two lists have much in common. Amalgamating and slightly modifying them, we offer the following amended list:

- The responsibilities of each level should be clearly delineated.
- Sub-national governments should have the means for primary control over economic matters within their jurisdiction.
- The budgets of sub-national governments should be substantially independent of those at higher levels.
- Transfers between levels should be based on stable, transparent, public-domain formulae.

None of these conditions has been met in 1990s' Russia. Slider contrasts this situation with that prevailing in China, where substantial provincial and commune autonomy is clear. It is only fair to add, however, that China had long had a high degree of regional autarky even before market reform began in the late 1970s. It is our contention that federalization, like the establishment of any set of human institutions, takes time.

In the absence of established procedures and criteria for the centre's regional reallocation of resources, what have been the main factors determining the transfers that have in fact been taking place? We concentrate here on what we have called 'Lavrov balances' as the key indicator. These, following Lavrov's series of studies, especially Lavrov (1997a), are made up as follows: all tax revenue remitted from a region to the federal budget *less* transfers from the federal budget to the region's budget, divided by the region's population: per capita net transfers, in other words. These will be positive if remittances to the centre exceed transfers, and negative otherwise. Most regions have had positive Lavrov balances – remitting more to the centre than is transferred back.

It is this that makes the widely used term 'donor region' (see Table 5.1) so misleading. In common Russian media parlance, a donor region is simply one that is scheduled to receive no FFPR transfers. This is a small and dwindling category, as the table shows. To put it another way: the small (1 per cent of GDP) FFPR transfers have been spread ever more thinly across an ever-wider range of federal subjects.

As a source of understanding of what has been going on, the Lavrov balance has its own minuses and pluses. On the one hand, it does not represent flows directly intended to target horizontal inequality or territorial integrity, or whatever has been driving the transfers. On the other hand, it does incorporate informal adjustments to the tax-remittance shares that have probably in fact been used to achieve the same end. In practice, much of the discussion of Russia's fiscal-federal arrangements has revolved around these net balances, often (because of the available data) treating the federal to-regional transfers as direct FFPR transfers plus the *ad hoc* adjustments of the percentage of VAT shared upwards that have been used as a short cut to making FFPR transfers, cutting out the financial cross-hauls (see Treisman 1996b, 1997, 1998; McAuley, A. 1997; Stewart 1997; Kirkow and Hanson 1998).

It seems fair to interpret these net transfers as centrally determined, notwithstanding the weakness of the Russian federal government and the extent of regional lobbying. Lavrov (1998b) makes a convincing case for the robustness of federal control of tax collection, the federal treasury and the tax accounts in federally authorized banks. As has already been noted, the main qualifications to this are the special tax-sharing deals negotiated by three or four republics and (at some periods) the sly use of in-kind settlement of tax bills when only cash or bank money could be remitted to the centre.

The FFPR transfer formulae used in the mid-1990s are set out and reviewed in the appendix to this chapter. Three conclusions can be drawn about them. First, the scope for non-transparent tinkering by the centre, in determining the eventual transfer amount to any region, is large. Second, the formulae dictate a wide and thin spread of transfers across regions. Third, the emphasis on plugging gaps between regions' 'own' revenue and expenditure leaves a substantial moral hazard problem: a weakening of incentives to curb spending and collect revenue efficiently.

In any multi-level budget system, the third problem is hard to get round. Continual formula tinkering seems to be common around the world. The first two weaknesses are more distinctly Russian.

Assessments of the process in Russia should address three questions: What has been driving the pattern of transfers so far? Have the outcomes helped to even up the regional distribution of public-goods provision? Has the process tended to assist market reform?

The first of these questions has attracted a lot of attention. Have the net-transfer outcomes been driven by 'power' or by 'need'? Has it been chiefly a matter, as Treisman has argued, of the centre buying off those regions that have stridently threatened secession or in other ways withheld support from the central authorities? Or can the transfers be quite well accounted for, as Alistair McAuley, Stewart, and Kirkow and Hanson have contended, by a roughly redistributive pattern of net transfers, with the regions that are neediest tending to benefit? (Predictions based on these two hypotheses might be hard to distinguish.) We have reviewed this debate at length elsewhere (Kouznetsova *et al.* 1999). Here we simply repeat our calculations for 1996 outcomes.

Using budgetary data from Lavrov (1997), we get the following OLS regression result:

Lavrov balance 96 = –1.579 + 1.143 real y 95 – 0.303 rep
(–7.53) (11.72)   (–1.83)

$n = 76$; adj $R^2 = 0.673$

where Lavrov balance 96 is the per capita balance described above, in 1996, standardized to the average for all regions = 1; real y 95 is per capita regional personal money income divided by the local cost of the 19-item food basket; and rep is a dummy for republic status (republic 1, oblast or kray 0). The real y 95 coefficient is significant at 1 per cent and the republic dummy only at 10 per cent. If the republic dummy is dropped, the adjusted R^2 declines only very slightly, to 0.663, and the coefficient on real y changes very little (to 1.18) and remains highly significant. (It should be remembered that the Lavrov balances are positive if more goes to the centre than comes back from it, so expected signs of explanatory variables are the opposite of what they would be if FFPR transfers were the dependent variable.)

This simple but apparently robust result (similar calculations for the previous year produce similar results) leaves the burden of proof on those who contend that the pattern of transfers is driven by 'power' considerations *that do not overlap with 'need' considerations.* To that extent, we regard fiscal redistribution across Russian regions to have been not flagrantly at variance with the desirable properties of such transfers.

Have the transfers been strongly redistributive in their effects? Le Huerou and Rutkowski (1996), using 1994 and 1995 data, addressed this question. They asked how much such transfers had altered the cross-region dispersion of regional public spending per capita and of per capita personal incomes. They concluded that the effects were equalizing, but only very weakly so. This is hardly surprising: the dispersion of per capita budgetary revenues and of real incomes across Russian regions is high (see Chapter 3 on the latter); the scale of FFPR transfers is small (see Table 5.1), and those transfers are spread across the great majority of federal subjects (see the appendix to this chapter). This weakness is well understood by Russian specialists (see below and the chapter appendix).

Have fiscal-federal arrangements been used (and could they be used) to promote reform? If international financial institutions can impose policy conditions on their disbursement of assistance to countries, could a reformist federal government in Russia use the same approach in disbursing regional transfers?

One obvious candidate for such conditionality is regional and municipal reform of housing subsidies. These are now the largest iden-tifiable form of direct, overt subsidy in Russia. Local authority subsidization of housing maintenance and housing utilities (water, sewerage, heating, power supply) takes as much as a half of many cities' budgets, crowding out education and health spending. These subsidies are not targeted on poorer households but go indiscriminately to all, including people occupying privatized housing. The Chernomyrdin government backed a programme of reform of housing subsidies, aimed at bringing maintenance and utilities charges up to cost-recovery levels by 2003, while promoting competitive tendering for the provision of those services in order to create downward pressure on the costs in question.

Freinkman and Haney (1997) showed that regional spending on subsidies was sensitive to variations in transfers from the centre. In other words, more transfers were associated, other things being equal, with more spending on subsidies. Similar findings have been made for some Western countries (Oates 1991). On the face of it, this would seem to make it sensible to attach reform conditions to transfers. That, indeed, was what Freinkman and Haney recommended.

There are, however, some grounds for being cautious about attaching reform conditions to federal transfers. Some subsidies are more identifiable than others. Russian regional governments are deeply enmeshed in the provision of implicit subsidies to 'their' (often privatized) local manufacturing via the use of non-monetary settlements (especially of tax bills but also of electricity bills from regional electricity companies and of those companies' gas bills to Gazprom) (Commander and Mummsen 1999). Conditions attached to explicit subsidies might simply induce a shift towards larger implicit subsidies. Also, the greatest difficulty in reducing housing subsidies will be met in the poorest regions. Attaching housing-reform conditionality to transfers might have the side effect of widening regional inequality of provision. Finally, the administrative capacity to target subsidies on the poorest households may be lacking.

One idea, therefore, that has emerged in the Russian discussion of reform of regional transfers is that conditionality might be introduced, but attached chiefly to performance in reducing the share of non-monetary settlement in tax collection. This device would on the face of it be immune to the concerns about housing-subsidy conditionality but would at the same time address a critical problem.

All deployment of conditionality in federal transfers, however, is vulnerable to a different objection: that the transfers are so small and thinly spread across so many regions that the effects of variations in them are likely to be small. There is a need to target regional transfers more narrowly on the most needy regions. But that in turn may make it politically more difficult to apply the conditions strictly.

In 1998 the reform of FFPR formulae was debated amongst government advisers. Much of the detail of this debate is relegated to the chapter appendix, along with a simulation of the application of some proposed formulae. See also *Kontseptsiya...* (1998).

One key issue was how to arrive at reliable criteria for assessing both a region's revenue base and its 'needs'. This is necessary if regional administrations are to have stronger incentives to deploy tax effort and to curb spending. Another related issue was how to go about concentrating transfers on a narrower group of regions. Figures A5.1– A5.4 in the appendix illustrate in a stylized way the impacts on the spread of regional budget balances of different modifications of the formulae. One choice was between a formula that reduced the deficit (as a proportion of budget revenue) of all transfer-receiving regions to a common minimum, and one that provided a minimum or floor deficit only for the neediest regions.

Kontseptsiya... (1998) was the first outcome of this discussion. It was adopted by the Russian government in July 1998, before the default and rouble devaluation of 17 August. Much of this document remained general, leaving specific formulae still to be agreed. The intention was (and remains) that expenditure norms (in principle, objective measures of needs for public provision) for regions would be worked out by the year 2000, when spending needs would be based on these norms. Meanwhile, existing budget revenue would remain a guide, but with adjustments for major (for example, climatic) differences in regions' circumstances, including those reflected in differences in cost of living. Given that, the variant adopted was the one that would bring all transfer recipients' budget deficits up to a common floor (as a proportion of their revenue). Some elaboration was contained in a second government decree, *O plane-grafike...* (1998), adopted five months later.

The adoption of variant 2 (Figure A5.2) leaves a large incentive problem unsolved. If many regions are going to have their deficits brought up to a common floor level (relative to their means), there is no pressure on them to improve revenue raising. At the same time, a broader problem also remains: Russia has (at the time of writing) a shrinking economy; it also has a high regional variance in per capita production, personal incomes and public provision. The subsidization of poorer regions by wealthier regions – nowhere a simple matter – is bound to be more difficult and contentious when resources are declining for almost everyone.

Meanwhile there have been proposals to move away from the cross-hauls involved in tax-sharing upwards followed by transfers downwards. Thus, Laykam (1998) advocates increasing the original regional tax shares, fixing them for 3–5 years at a time, to give more budgetary independence to regions. Unfortunately for that project, the exigencies of meeting IMF demands on the 1999 federal budget have produced a change in the opposite direction: the federal centre's share of VAT revenue has been raised from 75 to 85 per cent.

5.5   CONCLUSIONS

The Russian federal authorities cannot at present do a great deal to influence the economic fortunes of Russia's regions. Or, more precisely, they cannot do very much that is positive. This is not surprising when one considers the legacy from Soviet times. Federal institutions are still in the process of being developed from scratch. Location of economic activity by 1990 was grossly distorted, especially by the massively subsidized over-development of the Far North and of a Far East region that was not open to its Asian neighbours. A shrinking national economy has hardly made assistance to particular regions abundant or politically easy.

At the same time, there are other weaknesses that might have been avoided. Data on public-goods requirements and their provision, region by region, were still too poor, at the end of the decade, to be used to guide federal transfers. The central authorities' machinery for developing any sort of coherent regional policy is impeded by overlap and conflict amongst agencies. The constitutional delineation of responsibilities between centre and regions is still blurred. The provinces' powers to tax and spend have been kept small. The federal government has failed to honour spending commitments to which it has been pledged by budget laws, including grandiose development programmes for particular regions. It would have been better for

Moscow's credibility in the provinces if such grand plans had been skipped in favour of an ability to deliver on lesser promises. The combination of power-sharing agreements with unpublished protocols on tax-sharing, on the one hand, and opaque formulae for federal budget transfers, on the other, has made it impossible to achieve any useful amount of trust and agreement between regions and the centre.

Beneath these 'avoidable' weaknesses there are deeper problems with the transformation in Russia: the sources (whatever they are) that have made for weak and corrupt government at all levels. One characteristic trait of regional governments, to judge from our case-studies, is that their leaders are often very closely linked with a dominant group of managers of large enterprises in their regions. Part of the failure in 1995–8 to translate aggregate monetary tightening into a hardening of budget constraints on all producers is attributable to this. Regional leaders have often – perhaps universally – connived in the extension of hidden subsidies to large manufacturing enterprises, especially via non-monetary settlements and a growth of arrears – in both tax payments and energy payments.

This pattern of behaviour is blamed by some observers on cronyism, by others simply on a fear of the political consequences of allowing large-scale enforced redundancies to occur. It may also have much to do with the type of mass, large-scale privatization in Russia, ahead of the development of capital markets, that has left the country with a particularly damaging version of the divorce of ownership and control. These questions will be taken up, along with others in the concluding chapter.

At all events, this characteristic of the economic behaviour of Russia's regional elites has much to do with the persistence of the economic crisis. It should make us pause before blaming all the defects in centre–region relations on the centre.

APPENDIX: THE FEDERAL FUND FOR SUPPORT TO THE REGIONS: FORMULAE AND REFORMS

Transfer Formulae

The FFPR formula worked in 1994 and 1995 as follows (modified from Stewart 1997).

FFPR formula in 1994 and 1995
Step 1   A region qualifies for some assistance from the FFPR if

$$rev_{reg} < rev_{rf}{}^* 0.95$$

where rev denotes per capita budget revenue in 1993 and the subscripts reg and rf denote region and Russian average, respectively.

Step 2   How much will be transferred, in the first round of calculations, to a region that qualifies, is determined as a rouble total as follows:

$$trans_1 = adj\ popn_{reg}{}^*(rev_{reg} - rev_{rf}){}^*(exp_{mr}/exp_{rf})$$

where adj $popn_{reg}$ is the region's population excluding residents of closed cities (which are directly funded from the federal budget); exp denotes per capita budgetary expenditure excluding capital spending; and the subscript mr denotes the macro-region in which the administrative region is located (Urals, Volga, East Siberia, and so on). The expenditure figures were taken from 1993 but 'adjusted for current conditions'.

Step 3   A second round of calculations identifies regions 'in need of considerable support' if

$$trans_1 + (adj\ popn_{reg}{}^*rev_{reg}) < exp_{reg}$$

where exp has the same meaning as in step 2, but the subscript denotes that it is the adjusted 1993 spending of the region in question. In other words, if the transfer calculated in step 2 does not bring the region's total budget revenue up to the level of its (adjusted) 1993 spending, it qualifies for additional support. It is possible for a region that did not qualify for any assistance under step 1 to qualify none the less under step 3. According to Le Houerou and Rutkowski (1996), in 1994 seven regions with per capita revenues above the Russian average qualified for assistance under this heading.

Step 4 The additional transfer for regions that qualify under step 3 is calculated as

$$\text{trans}_2 = \text{exp}_{reg} - (\text{trans}_1 + \text{adj popn}_{reg}{}^*\text{rev}_{reg})$$

In other words, the notional shortfall from the adjusted base-year expenditure is, subject to step 5, simply to be made up.

Step 5 Finally, the two notional calculations of transfers are adjusted to fit into the total funds assigned for transfers (the FFPR) in the federal budget, as follows:

$$\text{Actual trans}_1 = \text{total funds}_1{}^*(\text{trans}_1/\textstyle\sum \text{trans}_1)$$
$$\text{Actual trans}_2 = \text{total funds}_2{}^*(\text{trans}_2/\textstyle\sum \text{trans}_2)$$

In other words, the actual transfers are adjusted *pro rata* for each region to the sums allocated (apparently as two sub-sets) to the FFPR.

The scope for federal-level tinkering is considerable. The centre can simply vary the amount available in total in the FFPR, determining the final budgeted transfers. That, at least, will be a transparent process. How the two sub-divisions of the FFPR are determined, however, is less clear. That determination seems to leave scope for opaque adjustments *ad hoc*. Adjustment for current conditions in step 2 also gives room for opacity.

There are also doubts about the efficacy of the targeting involved. Step 1 sets a very generous threshold for receiving some assistance. Step 3 allows assistance even to some regions whose per capita budget revenue in a base year may be equal to, or even above, the Russian average. These considerations, especially if combined with reductions of the total FFPR, affecting step 5, suggest that a wide scattering of small amounts is possible.

Moreover, moral hazard problems are obviously present. If regional decision-makers anticipate periodic adjustments of the base year or 'helpful' use of the step 2 adjustment for current conditions or both, the formula does little to provide incentives to locate new sources of regional tax revenue, collect taxes efficiently and monitor and economize on expenditure. These concerns were all, apparently, voiced at a January 1998 conference of regional leaders and representatives of the federal government (*Finansovye izvestiya*, 15 January 1998, p. 2). The desirability of a reform of the formula was already being argued in early 1996 by an official directly involved in its administration – Arkadii Samokhvalov, then head of the Ministry of the Economy's department of the economics of federal relations (*otdel ekonomiki federativnykh otnoshenii* – see Samokhvalov 1996 and Samokhvalov's views as cited in *Finansovye izvestiya*, 20 January 1996, p. 2).

FFPR Reform

The question how to improve the FFPR formula has been at the centre of policy debates on fiscal federalism in Russia. At mid-1998 there had been proposals about the FFPR formula from the Institute of the Economy in Transition (IEPPP), the Ministry of the Economy and the Ministry of Finance.

The proposals centre on two issues: what data should be used, on both the income and the expenditure side, and the extent and manner of equalization: what this financial assistance should provide to the regions that receive it. We shall review these two issues in turn.

So far as the data are concerned, the first question is whether regional budget expenditures should be included, in some way, in the calculations or whether it is sufficient to use revenue data alone. It is obvious that to use a region's actual spending in a base year would allow into the calculations of 'needs' elements of waste, inefficiency and misappropriation of funds that are of unknown size, and doubtless not equiproportional across regions. Therefore, those specialists who advocate the inclusion of some expenditure data in FFPR formulae mostly advocate the use of expenditure 'norms' (*normativy*), incorporating (in principle) best-practice resource-costs per unit of service delivered in health, education, housing, and so on.

Various ministries have attempted to advocate such norms (IEPPP 1998). They include: norms for financing the teaching of one student per year in the system of general education, calculated by type of educational establishment (Ministry of Education); a federal standard for the maximum cost of provision of housing and communal services (water, heating, sewerage, electricity) per square metre of floorspace, differentiated by the 12 macro-economic regions of Russia and the territories of the Far North (Russian government decree number 621 of 26 May 1997); norms for allowable budget subsidies, region by region, to housing and communal services in 1998–9, calculated by the Institute of Urban Economics (*Institut ekonomiki goroda*); 'discomfort' indexes, without a formal methodology, by the Ministry of Finance in setting FFPR transfers in 1997, according to climatic conditions and the local cost of the 'subsistence minimum' basket of goods; indexes derived by the Ministry of the Economy (MinEkon, 1998), based on 1991 norms for health care, education and housing expenditure; a summary indicator of the severity of living conditions by region, developed by the Central Economic Research Institute of the Ministry of the Economy – again, without a rigorous method of calculation.

None of these indices or indicators is comprehensive in coverage or capable of being applied directly to the calculations of transfer. In general, such norm-based methods are preferable to base-year material spending as a term in a transfer formula. But, first, calculating them is complicated, and based on weak data; and, second, the specification and weighting of the determinants of such indicators is irreducibly arbitrary.

For these reasons it is now widely believed that FFPR transfer calculations should be based entirely on calculations relating to regional budget revenue. The per capita revenue data cannot be used unadjusted; climatic and socio-economic differences amongst Russian regions are too large. Correction coefficients are needed, and many specialists judge that these should be applied region by region, rather than simply to groups of regions such as the 12 macro-regions. The regional cost of the subsistence minimum is one convenient, ready-made indicator that can be used for this purpose. It is not perfect: a low-cost figure for a particular region, for example, may reflect local price controls rather than local opportunity costs. But it appears to be the best indicator available.

Even with a satisfactory adjustment coefficient for regional per capita budget revenues, there are still some difficulties to be resolved before the income data can be used in a transfer formula. Current legislation allows regional governments some autonomy in setting the rates of regional taxes and of the regions' retained parts of the federal regulating tax on profits, and also provides some tax privileges for certain regions. These special arrangements are not allowed for in the present formula. This weakens the incentive for regional governments to collect more taxes (for example, by raising the regional profit-tax rate). By the same token, the formula does not encourage them to reduce arrears in tax collection.

One solution to this problem might be to use in the formula a measure of a region's tax potential, such as its gross regional product (GRP). This would be practicable, however, only if GRP data were included in the official set of data that are published regularly and reasonably swiftly by Goskomstat. At present they are not, and the last published GRP data (published at the national level for all regions) are for 1996. It would also be necessary to devise adjustment factors relating GRP to tax potential, taking account of differences in regional economic structure.

An alternative to the use of GRP would be to assess a region's tax potential from its financial balances (a regional flow of funds). That, however, would require the implementation of a single method for calculating these balances; at present there is no uniformity across regions in the methods used.

As has already been said, there is another cluster of issues to do with the character of the equalization that is undertaken. This is considered more fully in IEPPP (1998). The first option would be a method similar to the one used at present. This entails the measurement for each region of a 'shortfall', whether calculated as a gap between revenue and normative-based 'needs' or between revenue and adjusted revenue; the share of each region in the transfers from the FFPR is then determined as its share in the sum of these shortfalls. The pattern of redistribution along these lines is illustrated in Figure A5.1, which is based on actual data but is somewhat stylized – the autonomous okrugs, for example, are excluded. (The deficits are expressed as percentages of own revenue in this and the following figures.) Using this method leaves the weakest regions with very high deficits, and this tends to lead to additional financial assistance being provided to such regions through other, less transparent channels, where the possibility of cronyism or political threats determining the outcome is increased.

A second possible approach would be to ensure the same (proportional) level of deficit for all or almost all regions receiving transfers.

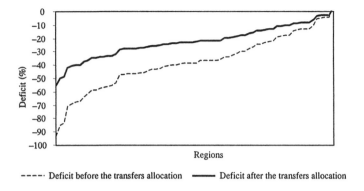

Figure A5.1 Russian federal–regional budget transfers: imposing a minimum deficit (variant 1)

This is illustrated in Figure A5.2. It avoids the drawbacks of the first approach, but has its own 'minuses'. First, it reduces the incentives for regions to reduce their shortfalls, since the federal budget will bring their finances up to a tolerable balance anyway. Second, it can be implemented, given the funds available in the FFPR, only with a reduced number of recipient regions. Thus, regions with modest budgetary shortfalls lose out, and this could cause political problems.

A third and final variant would be a compromise between the first two. This is illustrated in Figure A5.3. This brings only the very weakest regions up to a common floor level of their deficit, while others receive transfers in proportion to their shortfalls. This approach seems to combine the advantages of the first two.

In the document endorsed in April 1998 by the Russian government (*Kontseptsiya...*, 1998), the formula favoured for the FFPR works as follows (we have somewhat compressed the presentation in the official source). In stage 1, an adjustment coefficient is worked out for each region, to allow comparison of their actual and their desirable revenue levels per capita. Initially, this would be based on the local cost of the minimum subsistence basket:

$$K_i = MS_i/MS_{rf}$$

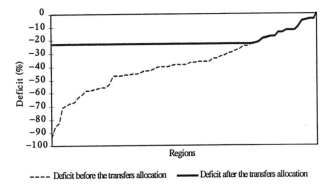

Figure A5.2   Russian federal–regional budget transfers: imposing a minimum deficit (variant 2)

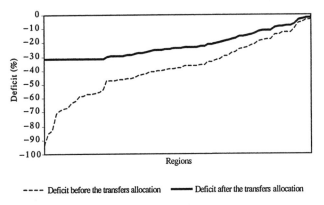

Figure A5.3   Russian federal–regional budget transfers: compromise scheme (variant 3)

where K is the adjustment coefficient, the subscripts denote the ith region (in the sense of a province) and the Russian Federation average, and MS is the cost of the minimum subsistence basket. At a later stage, regionally adjusted 'normative' costings for a bundle of health, education and housing services would be substituted for the minimum subsistence basket. The data and calculations for these are not yet available.

In stage 2, the desirable amount of transfer would be worked out by reference to the difference between average Russian per capita regional budget revenue and that of the ith region.

$$T_i = (R_p - R_{pi})^* K_i^* N_i$$

where T is the desirable level of transfer, R is per capita own-budget revenue, the subscript p denotes that the revenue figure has been adjusted by the coefficient K (and R_p is the population-weighted average of all the adjusted per capita Rs for all regions), and N is population.

In stage 3 the actual transfer (that is to say, the transfer to each region planned in the federal budget) is determined in an iterative procedure, adjusting the size of all Ts and the number of recipient regions until the total funds available in the FFPR are exhausted. That, at any rate, is how the procedure is described in the official document. How the average size of transfer was traded off against the number of recipient regions would presumably be determined by a prior decision on the distribution principle, between a range of variants represented by variants 1–3 above.

In order to explore the potential effects of variant 3 a small experiment is conducted to illustrate the effects introducing this measure using 1996 data. Although this would be impossible in practice (as tax collection would be unavailable contemporaneously for transfer decision-making) this is to serve illustrative purposes only.

The first step is to calculate the adjustment coefficient (K) and some measure of the desirable level of transfer based on the formula $(R_p - R_{pi})*K*N$. Several problems are apparent in that the figures we have for transfers include all types of federal transfers: support transfers; grants; and Moscow's subvention for the upkeep of federal property located in the capital. As a result the sum of the transfers is greater than would be available in the fund, but we use these figures both because they are the only available data and to investigate the potential effects of channelling all funds available for transfers through the fund.

We initially assume that the actual transfers in 1996, adjusted by the adjustment coefficient K, indicate a minimum level of desirable transfers. This reveals Ingushetia as the baseline region, and that an additional four regions would need transfers to bring their income from tax and transfers up to this minimum level. One other adjustment is that the 17 regions with negative transfer indicators are excluded from receiving transfers. In addition to the resource-rich and wealthy regions, Ul'yanovsk oblast' is also ineligible for transfers as a result of the low adjustment coefficient. For the remaining regions the residual funds (after raising the five regions in most need to the baseline) are distributed in proportion to their calculated indicators.

However, by assuming that the total amount of transfers is available (excluding the transfers to Moscow city) it can be seen that sufficient funds were available to raise all regions to the desired level of tax and transfer income in 1996, thus collapsing variant 3 into variant 2. Figure A5.4 illustrates this.

Given that there were sufficient funds transferred to cover the requirements of the regions based on variant 3, how much larger could

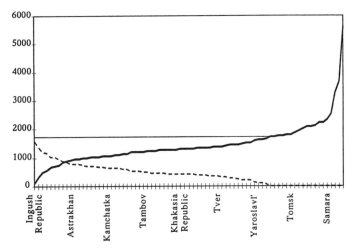

Figure A5.4   Variant 3 effects on 1996 income

the transfers be? To investigate this the value of the desirable level of per capita transfers is raised until it exhausts the total transfers in 1996 (see Kouznetsova *et al.* 1999). It is found that the desirable national level in per capita transfers could be raised 6 per cent, taking into account the weighting for the regions' differentials in living costs, while reducing to 13 the number of regions ineligible for transfers.

A final test of the effects of the transfers is to see just how much more 'equalizing' they would be. Regressions are run with the per capita transfers as the dependent variable and a measure of regional per capita income – either real monthly monetary income or gross regional product per capita – as the independent variable. What these tests reveal is that the implied transfers from variant 3 (or indeed variant 2) would have twice as large an effect on 'equalizing' per capita income in the regions as the actual pattern of transfers seen in 1996. Results (below) show that the negative coefficient on the real monetary income indicator is far more negative for the implied transfers, indicating a larger 'equalizing' effect:

$$\text{Actual transfer} = 6.35 - 1.02 * \text{Real income} \quad \bar{R}^2 = 0.13$$
$$(44.24)\ (-3.30)$$

$$\text{Implied transfer} = 6.90 - 1.94 * \text{Real Income} \quad \bar{R}^2 = 0.24$$
$$(50.82)\ (-5.02)$$

Those regions for which the federal budget provides half or more of their revenue merit – by common consent amongst Russian policy analysts – special attention. It seems appropriate to have special arrangements for them. (This subject is addressed in *Proekt sredne-srochnoi...* 1998; IEPPP 1998; and *Kontseptsiya...* 1998.) These regions could be categorized as regions in financial crisis, using criteria that would need to be rigorously defined and embodied in legislation. Such criteria might be the *n* regions with the lowest per capita budget revenue, or the lowest per capita GRP, for example. A category comprising 10–15 regions is envisaged.

Their special status would entail assistance from the centre that was more than proportional to the size of their budget deficits (or revenue shortfalls from target levels, depending on the formula applied).

Something along the lines of the previous sub-section's variant 3 (see Figure A5.3 above) might serve this purpose. But the view now being widely canvassed is that there should be conditions attached to this special treatment: a review of the regional governments' spending powers to prevent the misuse of resources, with the federal government perhaps taking over some of these regional authorities' powers and administering such spending directly. Alternative arrangements might be the use of additional conditionality (over and above that applied to other regions) or a targeting of a larger part of the transfers than elsewhere to specified federal programmes. This would require appropriate legislation.

Strengthening the incentives for regional governments to implement reforms is one of the aims of the reform of interbudgetary relations. The changes already discussed in the FFPR transfer mechanisms should help in this. But additional incentive arrangements for provincial and local authorities are also being considered.

The lines along which this might be done are indicated in *Proekt srednesrochnoi...* (1998), and *Kontseptsiya...* (1998). However, the details have yet to be worked out, and for this reason there are some internal inconsistencies in the proposals made so far. Here we offer a further development of the proposals, drawing on both these documents and making some additional suggestions.

The first problem here is that there is no generally accepted set of indicators for comparing progress in reforms across regions. A synthetic index should cover the extent of subsidization of housing and housing services (electricity, gas, water, centralized heat supply), the extent of subsidization of public transport, the rate of restructuring of agricultural enterprises, and perhaps some other indicators of a similar kind. It is also possible to compare provinces' per capita spending with national guidelines for a number of budget headings. Adjustments would have to be made to take account of inter-province differences in climatic, socio-economic and ecological conditions. The adjustment coefficients used in the calculation of FFPR transfers might be appropriate.

Given an assessment of how different regions stand with respect to reform implementation, there seem to be two main ways of influencing them. First, conditions could be attached to the FFPR transfers from the federal budget which would apply to specific spending heads in province budgets. As with conditionality for financial crisis regions, this would require appropriate legislation. One advantage of this approach is that no additional budget finance would be needed for strengthening reform incentives.

The other approach would be to offer transfers from a separate fund, outside the FFPR, aimed at financing measures that would allow the province's spending to be cut in future, by cutting housing subsidies or some forms of health-care spending, for instance. This new fund might be called a Fund for the Development of Regional Finances (FRRF); that, in fact, is the name proposed in the *Kontseptsiya...* (1998). The FRRF might be built up from savings from the main transfer fund, the FFPR – though, with the latter dwindling in size, this does not look very promising. Additionally or alternatively, there could be funds from other sources, such as World Bank and EBRD loans, though this of course would require coordination with the original lenders. The transfers do not have to be grants; they could be loans.

6. St Petersburg and Kostroma

Douglas Sutherland, Vladimir Gel'man, Andrey Treyvish and Dmitri Zimine

INTRODUCTION

St Petersburg and Kostroma have very few things in common. Not only are the economy and geography radically different, but the initial expectations for these regions were also radically different. In particular the regions in the Central economic macro-region were expected to be some of those which would experience the greatest downturns in economic performance during the period of economic transformation.

St Petersburg was the culmination of Peter the Great's struggle against the Swedes, at the turn of the eighteenth century, for access to the Baltic Sea, and it therefore served as the 'cradle' of the Russian fleet. Construction of the city started in 1703, and by 1712 St Petersburg became the new capital of the Russian Empire and developed rapidly under Petrine rule. Defence production was quickly set up, as were educational establishments. At the beginning of the 1990s these two specializations were still to the fore in the economic structure of the city. As a result of the naval presence St Petersburg also became one of the most important trading centres for the Russian Empire. In addition, it flourished as a cultural centre, where, as Lebedev (1996, p. 49) states: 'The highest achievements in all possible spheres (from geodesy to ballet) were purposefully and constantly being performed...'.

Although St Petersburg is renowned around the world as a cultural centre, Kostroma also has an important history, stretching back to 1152 when Yurii Dolgorukii ordered the construction of the city on the banks of the Volga. In 1613 Mikhail Romanov, the first Romanov tsar, took refuge from the Polish invaders in the Ipat'ev monastery; the Boyars travelled there from Moscow to offer Mikhail the throne. Hence the claim that Kostroma is the 'cradle' of the Romanov dynasty. Legend also states that the peasant leader Ivan Susanin sacrificed himself for Mikhail Romanov by deceiving the marauding Poles.

St Petersburg has the reputation of being a reformist region, whereas little is ever published about events in Kostroma. The post-communist mayors of St Petersburg, Anatolii Sobchak and Vladimir Yakovlev, have had national prominence thrust upon them. Kostroma, on the other hand, is rather like Belgium: nobody can name three famous people who come from it. During a visit by President Yeltsin the region was characterized by his then press spokesman, Sergei Yastrzhembskii, as 'one of the typical problematic regions of Central Russia' (*Moscow Times*, 20 June 1998). By one definition, Kostroma oblast sat astride the dividing line, the Volga, between the centre and periphery in Soviet times (Gritsay *et al.* 1991, p. 21). Little has changed.

6.1   INHERITED ECONOMIC STRUCTURE

The initial conditions of St Petersburg would be regarded as generally favourable for the city. Although it was slightly more industrialized than the Russian average, some of the production was in comparatively advanced products. The real strength of the city, however, would have been assumed to lie in the strength of its human capital. The higher education sector was particularly renowned, as were its scientific research establishments, and the cultural side of the city also enhanced its reputation.

Although enterprises such as LOMO, Arsenal and Elektrosila were relatively well developed, the high share of military production did present several problems. Much of it was not in particularly advanced products, and the civilian output of these enterprises was in goods, such as televisions, that stood little chance of competing with higher-quality imported products. Although these factors were recognized as constraints it was also felt by many observers that restructuring would be able to meet the challenge. Certainly, this was a city in which Jacobs externalities (see Chapter 3) should have facilitated the growth of new economic activity.

The very location of St Petersburg should also confer certain advantages, as it is the largest sea port in present-day Russia. The transportation infrastructure has also been relatively well developed, making St Petersburg a potential hub for the North-West of Russia, and linking the city and the region to the heart of European Russia. The size of the city in Soviet times also drew consumers from the wider surrounding macro-region. Thus, certain advantages from size and the attendant greater choice of products would also be expected to maintain a certain level of economic activity above those of surrounding regions (see Map 6.1).

The cultural heritage of the city is something that might be expected to confer certain advantages through the development of tourism. A United Nations ranking places St Petersburg as the eighth most popular and attractive city in the world (Karelina *et al.* 1998, p. 13). However, one legacy of Soviet development is the manner in which the cities grew; this poses several problems for residents and policy-makers in larger cities. The peculiar use of land has resulted in cities having inner industrial belts and high population densities on the outskirts (Bertaud and Renaud 1997). This places heavy costs on the city authorities as a more developed transportation infrastructure is needed to move people the greater distances from place of residence to place of work than would be found in many Western cities. A related issue is that, once car ownership increases, traffic congestion will become an unanticipated problem for much the same reason.

A summary of the inherited economic structure at the beginning of 1992 would have been relatively favourable. The population of the city was one of its major advantages, and whereas the enterprises were a mixed bag, some of them were producing advanced products. The geographical location and the cultural heritage of St Petersburg were also potentially major assets during transformation.

Whereas St Petersburg had the advantages of economic diversity that come with being a major city, the region of Kostroma was highly dependent on a limited range of activities that were already in decline by the late 1980s: flax and textile production, the capital stock of which was already showing its age. Comparing employment shares in 1990 with the national average (see appendix to this book), it can be seen that Kostroma, at this aggregate level, was almost the average Russian region.

However, as already indicated, the output of the region, with one exception, did not bode well for the future. The fairly basic

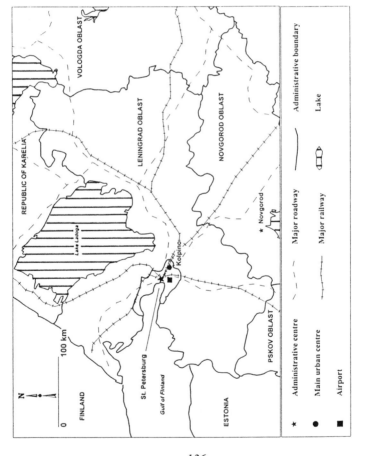

Map 6.1 St Petersburg and Leningrad oblast

manufacturing that did occur was not expected to survive, at least not in anything like its original form. Such orientation as it had towards military orders, such as for military clothing, was particularly susceptible to the cuts in military procurement announced by the Gaidar government in 1992. Only one enterprise stood out as having a more secure future: the Kostroma power station at Volgorechensk.

Kostroma also suffered in terms of geography. The raw materials that Kostroma does possess, particularly timber, suffer from their distance from the market. Hopes that they could provide some succour for the region are dashed by considerations of transport costs. Major consumers in the European market for timber are predominantly based in Nordic countries close to the major timber stands in the North and North-West of Russia.

Although Kostroma does have 24,000 students in the three colleges and 19 technical schools, the neighbouring region of Yaroslavl' is more developed in this respect. The competition from surrounding regions is a general problem for Kostroma' oblast, compounded by the poor transport links conecting the oblast. The strong pull of Moscow and the main east–west transportation axes in other regions leave Kostroma in a relatively isolated position (see Map 6.2).

The distribution of the population in the oblast, with around half of the population in the region around Kostroma city and the remaining residents widely scattered across the large remaining area, presents particular problems for the local authorities, especially in providing assistance to the poor.

In terms of the potential for a culture-led development of the city, the situation was worse than would be suggested by considerations of its position in the 'golden ring', popularity with Soviet film makers, and historical importance, mainly as a result of being very run down. In sum, the handicaps of the economic inheritance of Kostroma oblast suggest that the process of economic transformation would be particularly difficult there.

The contrasts between the two regions' inherited economic structures are, unsurprisingly, more striking than any similarities. St Petersburg had advantages in a diversified employment structure, a broader array of comparatively good enterprises, a highly educated labour force, and the blessing of a good location. The most obvious advantage that Kostroma had over St Petersburg, namely raw materials, amounted to very little once transportation costs were taken into account. A

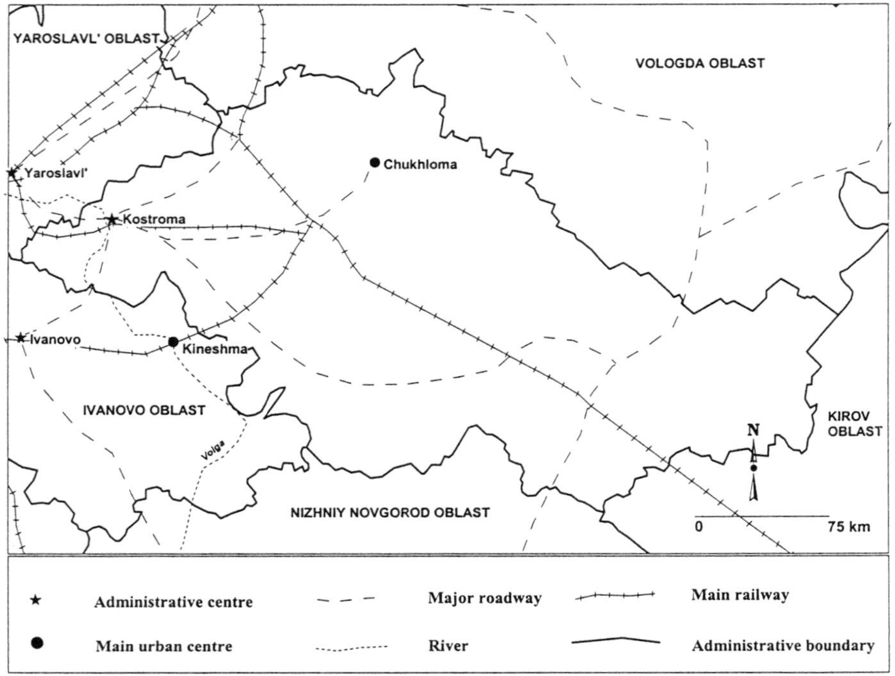

Map 6.2 Kostroma oblast

slightly more obscure similarity that potentially conferred benefits, in slightly different ways, was water.

6.2 LINKS BETWEEN INITIAL CONDITIONS AND SUBSEQUENT DEVELOPMENTS

From section 6.1 it is obvious that during economic transformation the two regions would be expected to follow completely different trajectories of economic change. It is worthwhile spelling out more clearly how the forces stemming from the increasing liberalization of the economy might be expected to interact with the inherited economic structure.

If one of the principal aims of economic transformation is to impose hard budget constraints over enterprises, then owing to the state of the enterprises in the two regions there was a distinct possibility that Kostroma would suffer to a far greater extent than St Petersburg: much of the capital stock was in a far worse condition. The impact of enterprise closure would be cushioned to a larger extent in St Petersburg, partly due to the size of the city. Greater aggregate demand in a large city and the highly educated workforce would be expected to compensate for closures by facilitating the establishment of new economic activity. The opposite is true in Kostroma: large-scale closure coupled with low aggregate demand, even though the latter meant low wages and therefore cheap labour, would not compensate in the short run for the loss of employment for a large proportion of the population.

To understand why this may be the case it is necessary to examine the forces that would lead to new employment creation. These all tend to arise from considerations of economic geography. One part, as mentioned above, is the catchment area of the region. Because of its poor infrastructure linking it to other regions and very severe competition from regions such as Moscow, Nizhegorod and even Yaroslavl' on the one hand and bordering very depressed areas such as Ivanovo on the other Kostroma lacks the advantages of size that St Petersburg enjoys.

A second factor is that greater liberalization of foreign trade results in a reallocation of economic activity across space. As reference markets for regions change as international trade is liberalized, the loci of economic activity would be expected to change to take advantage of the new opportunities. Again Kostroma's location in the European heartland, far from a gateway, is a constraint. St Petersburg should benefit from the through traffic as the largest sea gateway to the outside world and to Europe in particular. Gravity models of international trade suggest that Europe would be the principal trading partner for Russia, and St Petersburg was poised to reap the benefits from these trade flows. The port facilities in the Baltic States would not have been expected to provide serious competition, given that the very act of crossing a border is usually considered to entail a non-trivial cost. An additional benefit that should have accrued to St Petersburg as a result of increasing trade liberalization was the reallocation of economic activity to take advantage of proximity to the gateway. In the Russian case this is not only new types of economic activity, but also the possibility of smaller declines in existing economic activities, particularly of certain branches of industry that were overdeveloped in the Soviet economy but had export opportunities.

A final consideration is the liberal and democratic nature of St Petersburg. This led many to believe that policy would be radically different in St Petersburg, with perhaps broader-based support for the necessary policies. Given the rural and small-town character of Kostroma, it could be assumed that its political elite was not as pro-reform as that of St Petersburg.

6.3   ADJUSTMENT IN THE 1990s

Having established some of the priors concerning the expected outcomes at the start of reform, in this section we review some of the actual outcomes. Table 6.1 presents a few headline indicators with which economic change can be gauged.

The expected ranking of St Petersburg *vis-à-vis* Kostroma is apparent in Table 6.1. St Petersburg has, at least during the first half-decade of economic transformation, outperformed or, more precisely, performed less badly than Kostroma. The surprise is that in relation to the rest of Russia the city has performed so poorly in relation to the indicators for productivity, financial sector development and real

Table 6.1   *St Petersburg and Kostroma: key indicators, 1997 (per capita, Russia = 1 or 100, except as indicated)*

Indicator	St Petersburg	Kostroma	Russia
GRP per capita 1997	117.0	81.0	100.0
SE employment 1997 (% all employment)	22.7	6.7	10.1
Bank credits 1997	0.30	0.15	1.0
Foreign investment 1997	1.18	0.0	1.0
Real income 1997	0.97	0.79	1.0
Net migration 1989–97 (% initial population)	–0.4	3.0	1.7
Federal funds in budget 1997 (% budget revenue)	4.1	35.0	11.7
Industrial employment change, 1990–5 (%)	–7.7	–4.3	–4.2

Source: Derived from Goskomstat Rossii (1999a).

income. The indicators which show that St Petersburg is above the average of Russian regions in per capita gross regional product, foreign investment and small-firm employment are only what one would expect of a big city. In the cases of GRP and foreign investment, moreover, these indicators have been above the national average only since 1997. Generally far more positive outcomes for St Petersburg would have been expected. An indication of why this may be the case is the far more severe contraction of industrial employment experienced by St Petersburg than by either Kostroma or Russia as a whole.

For Kostroma the picture is much as might be expected, with most indicators somewhat below the Russian average and with a heavy dependence on federal transfers in its budget[1]. One of the complaints of local politicians is that they should have received far more federal money, but the very low population density, which was used in the calculation of inter-governmental transfers, counted against them.[2] The

1. In 1996 35 per cent of Kostroma's budget revenue came from transfers from the centre (Lavrov 1997a).
2. Whether it should have done so is another matter. Low population density raises the costs of health-care and education provision, and is usually treated as a factor increasing 'needs' in Western grant equalization formulae.

surprise is that industrial employment did not fall further. If the industrial composition of the oblast was so bad one would expect this figure to be somewhat larger. Why this was the case will be explored below. The second surprise is the movement out of agricultural employment. Partly, it would be expected as a result of increasingly unprofitable flax production being scaled back, but this is during a period when for Russia in general there was a net movement into agriculture, partly as a subsistence measure.

In St Petersburg, although there has been marked development of new economic activity, this has on the whole failed to compensate for the severe structural difficulties the city's economy faces. Much as economic analysts and theorists are trying to understand why the output fall in the countries of the former Soviet Union was so much greater than in Central and Eastern Europe, so a re-evaluation of St Petersburg is taking place. In part, it seems that the structural problems facing the city were far larger than anticipated. By the less than perfect indicator of physical output of certain branches of industry the effect of transformation can be seen across various sectors. Some engineering products declined by between one-third to one-half since the beginning of the decade, but many branches of industry have virtually disappeared. Tyres, most consumer electronics and textiles all belong to the latter group (Sankt-Peterburg GorKomStat). The problems of local industry and restructuring were particularly severe in military-related enterprises. Conversion as a simple programme was insufficient to deal with the specific constraints and challenges in this sector.

6.4   POLICIES AND ADAPTATION IN ST PETERSBURG AND KOSTROMA

Structural factors may help to explain why economic developments in St Petersburg were not as favourable as initially anticipated, but they do not seem to be the whole story. Consideration of the policies pursued at the local level can also help to explain why some of the expected results failed to materialize. To facilitate comparison, attention is paid to the general policy orientation and the outcomes (intended or otherwise) rather than to addressing specific details.

The leadership of St Petersburg is renowned for its liberal orientation. Several of the liberal economic policy-makers at the national level, notably Anatolii Chubais, have come from positions in St Petersburg. As a result St Petersburg gained certain advantages in pursuing a somewhat independent policy path: for example, in the realm of privatization. The down side is that the region also lost many capable policy-makers to Moscow. The two mayors of St Petersburg since the start of economic transformation, Anatolii Sobchak and Vladimir Yakovlev, however, have been somewhat less liberal or democratic once in office.

Sobchak's relations with Lensovet, the local legislature, were fraught during the early period of his office, and eventually led to its dissolution by an order from Moscow in 1993, allowing Sobchak to rule by decree until the 1994 elections for the city Duma. St Petersburg is also unusual for European Russia in that it has a declining population, a result of the unconstitutional adherence to the *propiska*, or resident permit, system.

Yakovlev, the present mayor, has never had the reformist reputation of Sobchak; he previously served under Sobchak as the deputy mayor in charge of the city's infrastructure. Since Yakovlev's election as mayor he has also had uneasy relations with the local legislature, resulting from his plans to raise charges for housing, energy and public services towards cost-recovery levels. This was national policy in 1997 under the Chernomyrdin government and was pushed strongly by Boris Nemtsov. However, St Petersburg initially tried to move ahead of the national reform.

There has been some continuity in the two administrations, but the loss of prominent liberals to posts in Moscow, such as the former deputy mayor, Aleksei Kudrin, reduced the reformist orientation of the administration as a whole. What really distinguishes the two mayors is the ordering of economic priorities for the city. These differences may not be large, but they go some way to explain why developments in the early 1990s were not as positive as expected.

Under the mayoralty of Sobchak the most obvious advantages of the city acting as an entrepot were played down. Although trade promotion was a stated policy aim, little attention was paid to it in comparison with attempts to develop local financial markets and tourism and to promote inward investment and the conversion of the city's defence plants.

Rivalry with Moscow's financial markets was always going to be difficult, as it was the Moscow banks that earned the huge rents available by acting as the 'authorized' banks for federal budgets and funds. The appearance of BNP-Dresdner Bank and Lionskii kredit (Crédit Lyonnaise) in St Petersburg did give some early confidence that a credible challenge to the might of the Moscow banks could be mounted. However, the advantages of the Moscow financial markets and the tendency for financial markets to be geographically concentrated were sufficient to undermine the St Petersburg challenge. After considerable frustration at the sluggish development of a sector that was initially felt to offer such hope, St Petersburg did manage to develop a financial market niche in bond trading, much of it subnational. The events of August 1998, although possibly not unduly affecting local banks in comparison with the large Moscow-based banks, underlined the weakness of the city's broader ambitions in capital market development.[3] (See Chapter 5 for a brief discussion of the collapse of the Russian sub-national bond market.)

For Yakovlev, local financial markets (in the sense of indigenous) were less important. Authorized accounts of the city administration were withdrawn from local banks and, recognizing that the majority of assets were in the Moscow banks, the administration encouraged them to participate in the local market. Following the collapse of the Russian financial markets in August 1998, the Yakovlev administration has taken equity stakes in four of the largest local banks (Balt-Uneximbank, Petrovskii bank, Promstroibank, and Bank Sankt-Peterburg), suggesting a reversal of its previous policy.[4] In return for the transfer of these shares to the city authorities the banks expect the local authorities to place their accounts with them, in a fashion reminiscent of the relationships between the federal authorities and the Moscow banks in the early to mid-1990s. In one sense this would secure the liquidity of these banks, but at the same time it risks establishing patronage relationships that can undermine the functioning of the local financial market.

3. *Finansovye Izvestiya* (21 August 1997) predicted that St Petersburg would develop more strongly as speculative profit-taking in financial markets declined and Moscow banks started looking for opportunities to invest in the real economy. The basis for this expectation was the city's scientific, technical and industrial potential.

4. One version of this was forcible nationalization of the banks by Yakovlev (*St Petersburg Times* 3 November 1998).

The development of tourism has proceeded only gradually, and the infrastructure for broader-based tourism is not in place. Pulkovo-2, the new international terminal at St Petersburg airport, which was built with the assistance of the EBRD, does give the visitor a friendlier welcome than Moscow's Sheremetevo, but more fundamental problems remain. New hotels have been constructed and some old ones renovated, but in general these hotels are aimed at the top end of the market, and more for business clients than for tourists. Tourism is also a source of a substantial amount of informal activity: handcrafts, gambling, restaurants and so on. Outside the hotels, however, the business environment is far from encouraging.

One of the general observations about Sobchak's mayoralty is that although he acted in an autocratic manner the surrounding elite was very divided. Mary McAuley (1997), discussing privatization in the city, argues that this led to an expansion of the state apparatus 'as an attempt to manage and regulate a lucrative process.' The same development can be seen with respect to inward investment as competencies fragmented in the search for rents. Inward investment as a result faced considerable obstacles in the labyrinthine procedures of overlapping committees and agencies. The failure to simplify and make transparent the investment process in St Petersburg may have profound longer-term consequences as ground is ceded to neighbouring regions. Even though one would expect to see relocation of new economic activity to gateways, the rising prominence of Novgorod, a region that possesses few advantages other than a favourable investment climate, and Leningrad oblast highlight the problems of inward investment into the city. The importance of these developments is that St Petersburg may find it difficult to recapture these flows of inward investment once the developing infrastructure in neighbouring regions is taken into account.[5]

The treatment of large-scale direct investment by various parts of the local authorities serves to underline the problems facing even large investors, and gives one indication why neighbouring regions are seen

5. The concept of 'putty clay' geography is useful in this context. Initially there is great flexibility in where particular activities are located, but once spatial differentiation takes shape they become quite rigid. Thus, over time as the economy begins to grow and input costs rise (wages and energy will be of particular importance to Russia), older vintages of capital become too costly to operate given current requirements and they are either mothballed or scrapped (Ottaviano and Puga 1997).

in such a positive light. The construction of three factories (Coca Cola, Wrigley's and Gillette) was jeopardized by the local fire inspectorate's demands for US$1 million from the municipality to construct a new fire station closer to the factories (IEWS *Russian Regional Report* 2 (15), 24 April 1997). The Wrigley plant eventually opened in 1999 (*Finansovye Izvestiya* 29 June 1999: III). In another case, equipment for Mitsui to open an oven plant in St Petersburg was held in customs for over a year. Customs officials were demanding US$4 million in duties, while Mitsui had been granted a five-year import fee holiday (IEWS *Russian Regional Report* 2 (30), 11 September 1997). Comparison with other regions that facilitate inward investment is not favourable.

When foreign investors have overcome the barriers, their participation in the economy has made a significant impact. Firms with foreign participation have generally performed better than the rest of the local economy. Of course, there is a selection bias in this, as foreign investors would in any case not be interested in firms that could not be turned around. Joint ventures have been a major entry vehicle to the St Petersburg market; whether this is merely a result of local participation being necessary to navigate the legislative swamp is harder to say. Baltika, the very successful beverage company, is the most prominent example.[6]

Even if inward investment did face considerable obstacles, one would still expect the advantages conferred by the major sea port to benefit the city. Unfortunately, extensive corruption in the local economy, seen in the process of privatization and in the problems associated with inward investment, is also present in the city's docks. Even given the additional costs of crossing two borders instead of one, and even when the Russian authorities have tried to make it even more costly, St Petersburg has lost its pre-eminence as the entry and exit port for Russia as much freight is diverted to neighbouring countries. The Baltic States and Finnish ports are, individually, nearing the point where they will have more through volume than St Petersburg: something that was

6. The policy initiative to establish free economic zones in order to encourage inward investment (the initiation of this idea is associated with Chubais while he was still in St Petersburg) has been far from smooth. A single zone failed to form, possibly not helped by Sobchak's unilateral decree that Kronshtadt should be taken from the military to serve as one. Instead of the grand plan of having a single large zone, several micro-zones with particular foci of economic activity have been developed. On some of the problems of free or special economic zones in other regions, see also Chapter 9 on Kaliningrad.

unthinkable at the beginning of the 1990s. The costs of using St Petersburg as an entry point into Russia are simply too great.

Industry, despite being the largest section of the local economy, was far less of a priority in the early stages of economic transformation. Industrial output and employment fell severely from 1992 to 1994, forcing Sobchak to redress this situation to a certain extent by granting tax breaks to those enterprises in real distress. The *de novo* private sector did develop quite strongly, reflecting the high levels of human capital in the city, but the development of that sector and other prioritized developments were unable to compensate for the problems in the rest of the economy.

Finding sufficient resources to finance the new policy agenda presents the current leadership with considerable challenges. Improving the port facilities has concentrated on providing supplementary facilities outside the existing docks (which have also seen some expansion), perhaps indicative of the existing problems within the St Petersburg docks. The project for a dry-goods dock at Ust-Luga was halted when funds ran out. This project was developed by Leningrad oblast when Gustov was the Governor; St Petersburg did not approve of the development. In order to attract sufficient finances the collaboration of the city and the surrounding Leningrad oblast now appears increasingly attractive: not least to overcome some of the problems of bureaucratic coordination.[7] Whether unification would alleviate financing and coordination is harder to judge; but calls for the two administrations to coexist in the unified region suggest that the coordination problems may remain. Financing for other projects is also uncertain. The proposed high-speed railway to Moscow and a third terminal at Pulkovo airport are two such schemes. A proposal to build a toll ring road based on the Helsinki model, which would help to alleviate congestion and pollution at the same time as it raises revenue for the city authorities, is under consideration. This project, however, will take up to ten years to complete and the sources of revenue for construction are unclear.

The Yakovlev administration realized that something needed to be done about eliminating opportunities for rent seeking, but it now faces some very entrenched opposition. An attempt was made to streamline

---

7. The relations of these regions have not been smooth, even as talk of unification intensified. In the past leverage was applied by the city authorities on enterprises in Leningrad oblast to re-register in St Petersburg (IEWS *Russian Regional Report* 2 (17), 15 May 1997).

the procedure for granting planning permission in allocating land for investment. Now construction sites on the city's outskirts are distributed through open auctions where bureaucratic interference is minimal. However, serious problems remain in the city centre, where it is extremely difficult to obtain permission for construction or reconstruction. This is because numerous technical and legal obstacles remain in place. The previous fragmented system was to be replaced by a single department which would be obliged to reach a decision within two and a half months. Opposition, however, has effectively blocked the implementation of this policy.

At the end of the Sobchak period the main gains to the city were a new airport terminal at Pulkovo and some prestigious real-estate development. The failure to take account of the real needs of the city is a damning legacy of Sobchak's tenure. Under Yakovlev attention swung back to a more traditional concern for local industry, while another major change in policy direction was that more effort was put into trade promotion (Karelina *et al.* 1998). Yakovlev's concentration on the existing economic infrastructure of the city and the prospects for its development, though not framed by any coherent strategy (though a strategic plan has been created on paper), would perhaps have been the appropriate priorities at the beginning of the decade. Thus, the reversal is overdue, but the previous misguided policies, together with the loss of control over many aspects of the city's economy, present a severe challenge to Sobchak's successor.

What the opportunities were for Kostroma oblast is uncertain. The sheer scale of economic restructuring required in the region was, and is, immense. The region has limited opportunities to act as a supply region or transportation hub once transportation charges move to cost-recovery levels. The agglomeration shadow of Moscow's buoyant economy spreads quite extensively in the Central macro-economic region, and also limits access to surrounding markets. The inherited economic structure, with the exception of electricity generation, were in no state to compete with imports, and although there are pockets of developments within Kostroma which are successfully carving a niche for themselves, the remaining economic structure continues to depreciate. Unlike other regions, Kostroma also lacked fire-sale commodities that could have helped to cushion the severe shock at the start of the 1990s.

At the end of 1996 gubernatorial elections were held in the oblast;

they do not appear to have led to any marked shift in policy orientation. The previous governor Valerii Arbuzov, who relied on rural support, was replaced by the communist-backed Shershunov. Arbuzov had been a rural resident in the oblast before taking up a party post in Soviet times, but prior to the election a report prepared by the administration warned of the complex socio-economic position in the region, and particularly the discontent associated with problems in paying pensions, something that the communist campaign was highlighting.[8] In the event this proved an accurate prediction. The 'democratic' forces in the regions had enjoyed support in the past, but the mood of the population had turned against them prior to the elections and the favoured liberal candidate, Romanov, fared poorly, gaining just 21 per cent of votes in the first round. In addition, leading local liberals had either become disenchanted with the local political process or had left politics to become entrepreneurs.[9]

The general thrust of the Kostroma administrations' policies towards the regional economy has been to support the traditional sectors, such as flax, dairy products and timber. The region, however, lacks any real financial resources to pursue such a strategy actively (Treyvish 1994). In this light, Treyvish (1998b) notes that in terms of measures of anti-market activities by local authorities (such as price controls) the region is relatively liberal: *laissez-faire à la Russe*. As we shall see in a moment, however, this liberalism is not applied consistently across all spheres of economic policy.

Timber and light industry have been in long-term decline, offset since the 1970s only by growth in electricity generation and some engineering (Kostroma Oblkomstat 1994). Since the start of the 1990s the situation has deteriorated, accelerating the emergence of the underlying problems in much of the economy. Much of the military-related output in the region was very severely affected by declines in procurement; most textiles proved uncompetitive in the face of import competition; and although plywood exports have performed relatively well (*Severnaya pravda* 6 April 1995), the timber industry as a whole has not. Competition in agricultural produce from neighbouring regions

8. The situation with regard to pensions did not change, and by mid-1997 pensioners were demonstrating as well as textile workers complaining about wage arrears.
9. The local head, Pavel Romanets, of the GKAP (State Committee for Anti-monopoly Policy) complained that Arbutzuv ignored the functions of the GKAP, forcing them to lobby Moscow for support in upholding their decisions.

also illuminates Kostroma's problems (Wegren 1997). The region has attracted almost no inward investment.

Although Kostroma oblast is close to the average Russian region in many respects, it tends to be slightly worse off than the majority of its neighbours (Vologda, Yaroslavl', Nizhnii Novgorod and Kirov). In 1995, it was classified as a region 'in particular need of support', indicating that it had had a large fiscal deficit the preceding year. Per capita tax collection has been some 30 per cent lower than the Russian average, while per capita budgetary expenditures are 16 per cent lower.[10] The problem facing the local policy-makers is how to cope in such a situation. Kostroma in this sense is like an EU objective 1 region in being underdeveloped and not strictly peripheral, but it lacks the associated EU grants. Further complicating the position for the local authorities is the presence of military establishments that fail to pay their bills. The particular problems the region faces are no doubt intensified by lack of correspondence between expenditure obligations and the very weak tax base in the region.

The fiscal position of the local authorities is indeed perilous. Electricity has been turned off in the past due to the local authorities' failure to pay their bills. The local authorities in turn do not pressurize local firms too strongly. Enterprises that face going under, and that probably means most of them, are granted tax forgiveness by the local authorities; one deputy governor, Yurii Tsikunov, justified this by saying that 'it is harmful to give up smoking all at once' (*Reuters* 3 August 1998). The question is whether the Kostroma authorities want to give up smoking at all.

In this cash-strapped region, control over the local firms is probably more effective than in relatively rich St Petersburg. The differential application of tax policy is one means of exercising such control, helping to support enterprises that in other circumstances would be forced to cease operations. In addition to granting tax forgiveness the oblast authorities can also make use of the major asset in the region. The hydroelectric power station at Volgorechensk does to a large extent cross-subsidize the rest of the oblast. The local authorities in Volgorechensk complain that they receive only a fraction of the tax revenue collected that they are due from the operation of the power

10. RPEC no. 139, 20 August 1997, cites a local press report of the contribution of fines on local dog owners to the local budget. It is unlikely that a similar announcement would make the St Petersburg press.

station, but even so the town is visibly better off than neighbouring towns. The non-payment for electricity has also had repercussions in the past, when the threat of cutting off the power station's supply of gas[11] was averted only by Arbuzov's intervention.

Such *de facto* redistribution of tax burdens is one means of cross-subsidization in the region; it is augmented by the officially tolerated non-payment for energy. The control exercised by the regional administration over the hydroelectric power station is not complete, as attested by the periodic threats to cut off supplies from various enterprises and organizations, but the chronic problem of non-payments reveals that power does not reside with the power station alone.

Another factor in the control of various levels of the local authorities over the economy is the gradual process of renationalization of enterprises. Wegren (1996) notes that the city of Kostroma took an equity stake in a local farm in order to secure milk supplies for the city. The city authorities, reportedly, were so happy with this arrangement that they considered extending it. Yet direct equity participation is only one way of controlling local enterprises. Wegren also notes that a local flour mill was told by the city administration to continue selling to local bakeries despite their chronic non-payments, even though other customers were willing to pay cash. Here again is a form of cross-subsidization: in this case of the bakeries at the expense of the flour mill and perhaps also of potential new entrants to the bakery business.

The outcome of the implicit cross-subsidization of the weakest parts of the economy is to delay the necessary restructuring. Existing local enterprises are supported, and this gives very little incentive for restructuring within enterprises or the entry of *de novo* enterprises. The figures in Table 6.1 (and in the appendix to this book) reveal the expected outcome. Although industrial output has collapsed by over two-thirds from the beginning of the 1990s, industrial employment has declined only modestly. In addition, if small enterprise development in the region is taken as a proxy for *de novo* activity it is clear that this sector is still very retarded in comparison with other regions. An associated outcome of this policy of cross-subsidization is the relative lack of cash in the region. The indicators of banking activity in the region (see appendix to this book) certainly paint a very poor picture of

11. Even though it is a hydroelectric power station, supply of gas is still required.

Kostroma oblast in comparison with the rest of Russia. The share of non-monetary forms of tax payments in the regional budget is also high at over 50 per cent in 1997 (Lavrov 1998a). Once the share of non-monetary forms of payment together with the already comparatively low per capita tax revenues are taken into account, the picture of a severely distressed region is clear. Another indicator of the problems in the region is the ratio of wage arrears to the monthly wage bill: at the end of 1998 this was 3:1 in Kostroma, slightly above the Russian average (Goskomstat Rossii 1999a).

If many of the problems in the region can be traced to the fiscal strains, the emerging pattern of policy adaptation is, at the same time, one that will tend to ossify the existing economic structure. The attempts to preserve existing economic activity are among the reasons why industrial employment has fallen less than in St Petersburg, though both regions suffered the same fall in industrial output. These efforts to preserve existing enterprises also undermine the incentives for new entrants (the implicit subsidization will put a new entrant at a disadvantage) and damp the incentives to mobilize the resources available for new uses (Berkowitz 1996). The very low indicators for *de novo* activity in Kostroma tend to illustrate this outcome.

6.5   CONCLUSIONS

The comparison of St Petersburg and Kostroma oblast highlights the dangers of two radically different approaches to economic transformation in Russia in the 1990s. St Petersburg initially had opportunities for successful adjustment to the new environment. The authorities there, however, pursued a set of policies inconsistent with those opportunities. Too much attention was paid to high-profile and high-prestige developments and insufficient attention to the pressing needs of the city. The mismatch between these policies and the constraints on the city became ever more apparent. During this period valuable time was lost. The eventual reorientation to more sensible local policies came at a time when the effort to put things right was costlier. Still, the early optimism about the prospects for St Petersburg is understandable. It became apparent only later that the share of military industrial production placed an excessive burden on the city; the cost of adapting this industrial and scientific capability to the new conditions had been underestimated.

In Kostroma oblast the options available for pursuing any coherent set of policies were severely hampered by the economic structure of the region at the beginning of the 1990s. The outcome was an attempt to preserve existing economic activity with whatever resources were available. The very poverty of the region and uncertainty about federal support, at the beginning of the 1990s, may well have influenced the policies that were pursued. The unfortunate result was that the region was locked into an increasingly ossified condition with little prospect for future development.

One similarity in the outcomes has been the heavy impact of state organs on the functioning of the economy. While attention was focused on the grand projects in St Petersburg, proliferating bureaucratization of decision-making in other areas had a negative impact on the functioning of the economy. For different reasons, but again partly as a direct consequence of policy, the grip of the administrations on Kostroma oblast intensified.

In both cases the outcomes of policies pursued tend to support the argument that local economic policy has little capacity to improve the trajectories of economic development in a region. These two cases, indeed, suggest that local economic policy can more easily have a negative effect. At the same time, initial conditions in these regions seem to have determined to a large extent the outcomes that are observed. Policy may have been misdirected in St Petersburg, but not sufficiently to undermine the natural advantages conferred by size, location and human resources. In Kostroma, economic transformation has had a particularly severe impact, reflecting above all the lack of opportunities available. Misguided policy in this region has served only to accentuate the problems.

The August crisis of 1998 has affected both regions. Surprisingly, given the almost complete absence of a financial sector, Kostroma appears to have suffered the more. The International Red Cross identified that the region was facing one of the most severe winter food-supply crises in Russia, while the deputy head of the administration claimed that 67 per cent of the population, mainly rural, had fallen below the poverty line in the wake of the crisis and that the regional authorities no longer had sufficient resources to organize food deliveries (*The Financial Times* 12 November 1998). For St Petersburg, the sharp devaluation of the rouble will help some local industry, especially food processing; meanwhile higher defence spending in the federal budget is also likely to benefit the city. The increased strain of servicing the city's foreign debt, however, will place its finances under great pressure.

7. Samara and Krasnodar

Philip Hanson, Arbakhan Magomedov, Andrei Tatarinov, Irina Tartakovskaya and Pavel Romanov

INTRODUCTION

Samara oblast and Krasnodar kray have a few things in common; they also differ in a number of ways that have been important for their economic fortunes in the 1990s.[1] Both are considerably larger than the average Russian administrative region. Both are in European Russia, south of Moscow. Both are populated predominantly by ethnic Russians. Both feature quite prominently in domestic Russian news and could be said to be in that sense important regions. Both contain major transport hubs. And both have, of course, like every Russian region, suffered the extreme social and economic dislocation that has accompanied post-communist change in Russia.

By the late 1990s, however, they represented two very different sorts of adaptation to the new circumstances. Samara is considered an economically strong region. In various 'ratings' of Russian regions, intended to rank their attractiveness to investors, Samara comes at or near the top (see, for instance, 'Reyting...' 1997; 'Reyting...' 1999; Tikhomirova 1997). The region has acquired a reputation for comparatively successful adjustment to the new world. The governor, Konstantin Titov, plays a prominent part in national politics. Until 1997 he was a leading member of the 'government party', *Nash dom Rossiya* (Russia is our Home). In 1997, according to the regional statistical office, gross regional product rose by 6 per cent (Samara Oblkomstat

---

1. Reference to economic and social statistics has been kept to a minimum in this chapter. Relevant background statistics are grouped in the Statistical Appendix to the book.

1997), making the region one of only a handful that were beginning to show a clear output recovery.[2] The fact that, uniquely among Russian administrative regions, Samara contains two large cities[3] may have something to do with this comparative success, if our surmise about the role of Jacobs externalities (see the Introduction) has anything in it (see Map 7.1).

Krasnodar, in contrast, is a region that was in acute difficulties even in the period (late 1996 to early 1998) when the collapse of Russian output showed signs of bottoming out. A heavily agricultural region, its prosperity has been severely damaged by the steep decline since 1991 of the farm sector's terms of trade with the rest of the economy, while its Black Sea resort sector has at the same time been hammered by the polarization of the Russian income distribution: many Russians can no longer afford holidays, while many richer Russians have taken to holidaying abroad.

As the last paragraph suggests, Krasnodar kray also has something unusual about its economic geography: it contains two sharply differentiated sub-regional economies – the rural heartland that has traditionally been Russia's strongest agricultural region and the coastal strip that contains two substantial ports, Novorossiysk and Tuapse, and the Sochi-Adler resort area (see Map 7.2). The coastal strip is in many ways more 'modern', and certainly more connected with the outside world (including Moscow), and it has in its own way suffered badly in the 1990s, just like the rural Kuban'.[4]

To be a gateway region, as Krasnodar is, in the newly open Russian economy should in general be an advantage in adjusting to the post-communist world. But Russia's Black Sea gateway has suffered from three handicaps. First, the part of the world on which it opens – the Middle East, Turkey and the Balkans – has less gravitational pull in trade and investment than Europe or the Pacific Rim. Indeed, 70 per

---

2. Gross regional product is calculated by regional offices of Goskomstat according to a single methodology. However, the difficulty, compared with less aggregated series, of checking each region's calculations has led central Goskomstat to refrain so far from publishing these data systematically. It has done so only for the years 1994 and 1995.
3. Samara city with a population currently of about 1.3 million; Tol'yatti, with a population of 0.7 million. They account between them for about two-thirds of the region's population and, though not forming a single conurbation, are not far apart.
4. The Kuban' is a traditional name, often applied to the *krai* as a whole, but primarily designating the agricultural heartland of the region.

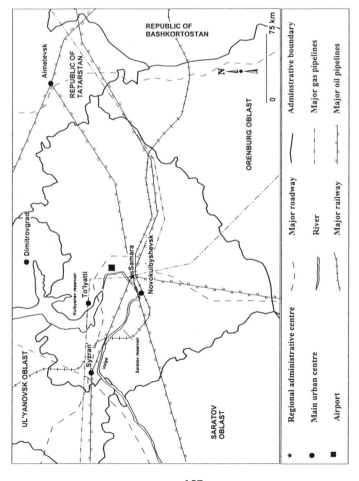

Map 7.1 Samara oblast

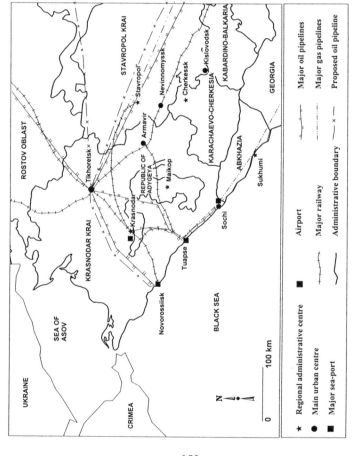

Map 7.2 Krasnodar kray

cent of the region's trade in 1997 was reported to be with Europe (*Kuban'-Biznes* 10 February 1998, p. 27); this percentage is probably of merchandise transactions conducted by Krasnodar producers, rather than being the share of shipments through the region's ports). Second, the North Caucasus macro-region, of which Krasnodar forms a part, has, together with neighbouring Georgia, been a battle-zone in the 1990s, even though there has been no fighting in Krasnodar itself. Finally, much of the development of Novorossiysk as an oil terminal is vulnerable to the uncertainties of the new Great Game that is being played around Caspian and Central Asian oil and of world oil prices.

In the rest of this chapter, we first describe the two regions' inherited economic structures, and then make some conjectures as to how their subsequent development might have been expected *a priori* to differ. The fourth section summarizes their economic status in 1995–8. Then there is a brief account of leading actors and policies and their bearing on the outcomes. We end with some tentative conclusions about the factors that seem likely to have generated the two rather different outcomes.

7.1 INHERITED ECONOMIC STRUCTURE

Soviet-era specialization differed markedly between the two regions. Krasnodar was noted for farm output, its crops ripening earlier than in most of Russia. Within Soviet-era Russia it was a major producer of winter wheat, maize, sugar-beet, sunflower-seeds and even (on a smaller scale) rice and tea. The federally designated spa (*kurort*) zones were also nationally important, covering about a quarter of the territory of the kray. In 1990 Sochi alone received 2,130,000 visitors, who stayed for an average of almost 16 days (Tatarinov 1998).

Samara housed the Soviet Union's biggest car-making complex, the VAZ works at Tol'yatti, and one of the country's largest defence complexes based in Samara city and with a strong aerospace specialization. Most of the defence complex was installed when plants were moved away from central European Russia in the face of the German advance in 1941. Thus a huge industrial district was tacked on to the old city of Samara (named Kuybyshevsk between 1935 and 1991), and it was, until the collapse of communism, a closed city.

The employment data for 1990, showing regional workforce allocation between nine sectors, indicate the most obvious differences between the economic structures of Samara and Krasnodar at the end of the communist era. The farm sector occupied about a fifth of the Kuban' workforce and less than a tenth of Samara's; the Russian average came between the two. The employment roles of the two regions' industrial sectors showed the converse picture: 36.4 per cent in Samara, against 23.1 per cent in Krasnodar, with the two figures again bracketing the Russian average (Goskomstat 1997a, pp. 430–31).

Across the other seven sectors, structural differences were proportionally less striking, except that Krasnodar's employment share in 'health services, physical education and social welfare' was well above the national average. This reflects (though it does not fully capture) the importance of spas and tourism in the coastal strip. Under the Soviet spa system, much organized holiday-making, typically at sanatoriums controlled by particular ministries or workplaces, was treated officially as part of medical provision. (See Tatarinov 1998 on the data definitions, and Goskomstat Rossii 1997a, p. 199.) Both regions had a slightly larger than Russian average share of employment in transport and communications, reflecting the fact that both contain substantial transport hubs – chiefly sea ports, resorts and connecting services in the case of Krasnodar, and major junctions of rail, air, river, road and pipeline networks in the case of Samara.

This 'hub' characteristic is especially important for Samara. The extent to which it has developed as a financial hub is discussed below. In 1998, 21 Russian regional airlines proposed that its airport be developed as a hub for at least intra-CIS flights, in place of one or more Moscow airports (*Kommersant"-Daily* 16 October 1998, p. 4).

The less-developed character of the Kuban' economy is apparent also from the branch structure of gross output in the industrial sector at the end of the communist period. In 1991, at the then-established prices, the engineering branches occupied, by Soviet standards, a low share of Krasnodar's industrial output: 12.2 per cent against a Russian average of 23.9 per cent, whereas Samara's engineering share was well above the national average at 42.3 per cent. Krasnodar was similarly light on the energy branches, metals and chemicals – in the last of which the branch share in Samara was above the national average. In so-called 'light' industry (textiles, clothing and footwear), Krasnodar was close to the Russian average and Samara far below. The food-processing industry accounted for almost half of Krasnodar's gross industrial output, but only just over a sixth of Samara's, against a Russian average of 20.4 per cent. The only other branch that loomed comparatively large (within a rather small industrial sector) in the Kuban' was building materials – an industry that was widely dispersed in Russia, in what were by Soviet standards relatively small units (Goskomstat Rossii 1992, pp. 91–4).

Neither region is particularly rich in natural resources, by Russia's high standards, apart from Krasnodar's fertile soil and sunny beaches. Both have hydrocarbon deposits, and some oil and gas are extracted in Samara, but neither region is important for oil, gas or coal.

To call the Samara region of 1990–91 more developed than Krasnodar is to beg a number of questions. Samara housed a number of activities that were in Soviet terms at the leading edge of technology; but Soviet terms were peculiar. The VAZ car-making complex was held up as an example of advanced organization for the whole of the domestic civilian engineering sector, but the technologies were those of Fiat and major Fiat suppliers of the late 1960s, and had not been significantly upgraded (Hanson 1981). The aerospace plants, design bureaux and research and training centres in Samara city were no doubt more impressive in a purely technological sense; but there was no guarantee that they could make aircraft and rockets, or major sub-systems for them, that were internationally competitive in cost and quality.

7.2 LINKS BETWEEN INITIAL CONDITIONS AND SUBSEQUENT DEVELOPMENT

In general, if the Russian economy was full of value-subtracting manufacture, it was not obvious that a more 'advanced' region was better placed to adapt to international competition than a more rural and agricultural region. If the development of an open and competitive Russian economy was destined to lead to the closure of many, perhaps most, of the giant Soviet-era manufacturing enterprises and their replacement by a crop of new firms started from scratch, then a region with a higher ratio of green- to brown-field sites might in fact have an advantage: it would have less of a rust-belt and fewer of the social stresses and strains of adjustment associated with steep industrial decline. If the skills of the Samara workforce proved in fact to be mainly specific to the dinosaur enterprises in which (it might be assumed) they had worked, then training in skills appropriate to the new era might be as easily carried out in Krasnodar.

In addition, the dependence of so much activity in Samara on defence production would make the region especially vulnerable to the massive cut in defence hardware procurement imposed by the Gaidar government in 1992. In principle, the demands of civil aviation and the business of commercial space satellites might quite readily be substituted for military end-use, but there was no guarantee that the region's inherited capacities and skills in aerospace would prove competitive when surviving and prospering depended on criteria like cost, product performance, reliability and delivery times.

The *a priori* arguments in favour of the more 'Soviet-advanced' region adapting better to the post-Soviet world were of a quite different character. Human capital was stronger in Samara: higher average educational levels suggest more transferable skills. In addition, the scope for recombining labour and capital in new activities could be greater in large conurbations where 'Jacobs externalities' are likely to be substantial, and the largest city in the Kuban', Krasnodar city, is somewhat smaller than Samara's second city, Tol'yatti.

City size, together with location in transport and communication networks, also suggested that Samara city had the potential to become a major regional hub for the generally strong Volga region, whereas Krasnodar's gateway potential might be insufficient for development as a regional hub for the reasons already given.

At the same time, the shock of huge defence cuts, forcing many educated and skilled people to look for new ways of making a living, would be a factor pushing adjustment in Samara but not having much of an effect in Krasnodar. And there is an element of political economy involved as well: the mainly rural Kuban' had an electorate which, on the evidence of Russian elections from 1989, was likely to be comparatively traditionalist, tending to vote for Communists and Agrarians, and therefore installing regional and local assemblies and (when voting for regional executives was allowed) governments that would resist structural change.

Finally, if existing contact with the outside world was likely to be helpful, Samara had an advantage there, as well. The region was a major exporter (by Russian standards), most notably of cars and of oil products from local refineries. (The region contains about one-tenth of Russian refinery capacity.) On 1997-dollar data from Russian customs, Samara region is one of the largest originators of merchandise exports.[5] With the domestic economy collapsing, any region that derived significant revenues from foreign markets had a built-in advantage. If human capital, agglomeration and hub effects were in fact significant, they would favour a concentration of foreign direct investment in the region in addition.

These conjectures are all about the effects on post-communist economic adaptation of a region's initial starting-point. But other things might not be equal. There are four other factors that could intervene to alter the post-communist economic trajectory of either of these regions: federal policies; regional policies; changes on world markets; and changes in Russian institutions connecting regional economies.

During 1992–8 federal economic policies included price, trade and currency liberalization, privatization and (from late 1994) monetary stringency; they stopped short of a systematic imposition of hard budget constraints on existing enterprises. Given those general policies, the federal authorities might have affected the fortunes of Samara or Krasnodar in a number of ways: in particular, by protecting the farm sector more strongly from import competition; by reviving military hardware orders; or by transferring resources to very large investment projects in one or the other region. In fact, Moscow did none of those things within the period under review. There was supposed to be a special strategic plan for the development of Krasnodar kray but the funds never materialized (Magomedov 1998; see also *Vol'naya Kuban'* 28 August 1998). As Chapter 5 shows, the federal government's efforts at redistributing resources regionally were small and got smaller.

Regional policies could have been, and in fact were, different in the degree of liberalization espoused. Konstantin Titov presided in Samara over broadly reformist policies. Successive leaders in the Kuban', after D'yakonov in 1991–2, did not. The current leadership is rather noisily traditionalist (see below). These differences between the two regions may have been mitigated by sub-regional policy deviations from the

5. Seventh equal, with Chelyabinsk, after (in descending order) Moscow city, Tyumen', Krasnoyarsk, Sverdlovsk, Kemerovo and Irkutsk. Its exports were estimated at $2030 million, against Krasnodar's $376 million (Goskomstat Rossii 1998d, table 25.2).

gubernatorial line in Krasnodar – both Krasnodar city and Sochi have more reform-oriented leaders – but in general there could be differences in regional implementation of reform. Those differences in turn might, as we have suggested above, be themselves strongly influenced by the initial economic structure of the region. But it seems reasonable to credit regional elites with some modicum of free will.

Changes on international markets can have an obvious influence. Rises and falls in real farm or energy prices on world markets affect different Russian regions differently. Similarly, a collapse in investors' confidence in emerging markets, such as occurred in 1997–8, will be more damaging to a region that has been attracting significant foreign direct investment or credits than to one that has not.

Finally, the connections between Russian regions can be affected by institutional change in the country at large. If capital markets initially operate highly imperfectly between regions, regional savings and investment rates will correspond more closely than they might with a more developed capital market, if savings and investment potential do not happen to be closely matched across regions. Similarly with foreign currency markets: if they function poorly across regional boundaries, overseas spending and earning are likely to match more closely, region by region, than they will do as currency markets develop. We suggested in Chapter 3 that an improvement of this sort may well have occurred in 1994–5.

What, then, were the outcomes in the two regions by the late 1990s? The next section provides a broad summary.

7.3   ADJUSTMENT IN THE 1990s

Table 7.1 is an assembly of a few indicators of the state of the two regions' economies in the mid- to late 1990s. More details are provided in the statistical appendix to this book. Unfortunately, for most of these indicators (gross regional product or real personal incomes, for example) a direct comparison with the situation at the end of the communist period in 1989–1 is not possible.

These indicators support for the most part the received opinion about these two regions. In the mid- to late 1990s, Samara appeared in the official record as having labour productivity levels well above the

Table 7.1 Samara and Krasnodar regions: selected economic indicators in 1995–8

Indicator	Samara	Krasnodar	Russia
Per capita GRP, 1995, RF = 1[a]	1.24	0.56	1.0
Change in industrial gross output 1990–98 (%)	–34.0	–62.0	–54.0
% employed in small firms, 1997[b]	9.0	11.8	10.1
Per capita foreign I stock, end-96, RF = 1[c]	0.51	0.19	1.0
Per capita forex inflow, 1995 ($)[d]	442.0	98.0	437.0
Per capita real y 1997, RF = 1[e]	1.17	0.90	1.0
% loss-making enterprises in industry, 1997	45.9	48.3	50.1
% farm output from private sector, 1997[f]	58.0	39.1	50.1

Notes: The most recent available data are used. All are from Russian official (Goskomstat) sources.

[a] GRP denotes gross regional product. The figure for Russia is for the sum of GRPs. This is less than GDP since some of GDP is not regionally allocated.

[b] Percentage of recorded employment that is in small private firms.

[c] Foreign I denotes the cumulative stock of foreign direct investment, which shows a high concentration in Moscow.

[d] Forex inflow is *valyutnye postupleniya*, which reportedly means flows into bank accounts in a region, whether from export receipts or other sources such as foreign credits. Export earnings retained abroad would be excluded.

[e] Real y denotes per capita disposable household money income divided by the local cost of the subsistence minimum and expressed as a multiple of the Russian average.

[f] Output from household plots plus *fermy* as % of total gross farm output. The balance is output from 'agricultural enterprises'. Most of these are now, formally, non-state joint-stock companies. They are however basically the old state and collective farms, unreconstructed.

Sources:
Row 1:   Derived from Goskomstat Rossii (1997a, Table 1.2)
Row 2:   Derived from ibid. vol. 2, table 11.1; Goskomstat Rossii (1997d, pp. 313–14); *Samarskie izvestiya* 21 September 1998 (extrapolating first nine months to whole year, for 1998); *Kubanskie novosti* 14 February 1999
Row 3:   Derived from Goskomstat Rossii (1998d, tables 7.3 and 13.7)
Row 4:   Bylov and Sutherland (1998)
Row 5:   Derived from Goskomstat Rossii (1996, pp. 936–7)
Row 6:   Derived from Gosmkomstat Rossi (1998d, tables 8.14 and 8.25)
Row 7:   ibid., table 22.32
Row 8:   ibid., table 15.7

Russian average while Krasnodar appears well below.[6] Industrial output, though admittedly of less importance to the economy in Krasnodar than in Samara, had fallen far more precipitously in the former. Foreign investment (FI) had favoured Samara over Krasnodar (and more than the Russian average if the Moscow FI and population figures are taken out).[7] A similar picture, including the comparison with a Moscow-free Russia, applies to foreign-exchange inflows. Personal real income levels fit the broad picture: above the Russian average in Samara and below it in Krasnodar – though the omission of subsistence food production means that the difference in real incomes between the two regions is exaggerated by this measure. To all this could be added the fiscal dimension: for what it is worth, in a land of destitute governments, the Samara regional budget was one of the few not supported by transfers from the federal budget (through 1997: see Chapter 5 above).

Two indicators appear to be the odd ones out: Samara had a very similar proportion of loss-making enterprises and a lower proportion of employment in small firms. The first of these observations is in one respect not surprising: the region contains a comparatively large share of defence plants, most of them in a very poor state (see below). On the other hand, the comparatively modest fall in industrial output might suggest an industrial situation that was marginally healthier (or rather, less unhealthy) than the national average, rather than the reverse. A little more (rather dim) light is shed on this in the next section.

The second observation is at first sight odd in view of the received view of Samara as a region of comparatively dynamic adjustment. In fact, the region did have a density of small firms that was higher than that of Krasnodar or the Russian average (that is to say, it had a smaller number of residents per firm). It seems that lower employment per small firm offset this. Also, Samara in 1998 had four times as many

6. In fact, these are GRP per head of population, not of workforce, but this makes no difference to the orders of magnitude.
7. The regional data available for 1997 are for all foreign investment (FI). At national level, the FI data are split into direct and portfolio (FDI and FPI) and credits, but this split is not replicated for the regional level. Moscow city accounts for 69 per cent of all recorded FI in 1997, but that amount (FI into Moscow) is far larger than the total given for all FDI into Russia (Goskomstat Rossii 1998d, tables 23.19 and 23.21). It would be a reasonable working assumption that FI into regions outside Moscow roughly corresponds to FDI, while FI into Moscow greatly exceeds FDI into Moscow.

registered but unincorporated sole traders as it had small firms (the two reporting categories appear to be separate). And reported small-firm employment was rising very rapidly from 1996 to 1998 – reportedly at 24 per cent a year (IEWS, *Russian Regional Report* 11 February 1999). In contrast, Krasnodar at mid-1998 had fewer unincorporated sole traders than it had small firms at end-1997 (*Vol'naya Kuban'* 31 October 1998).

That, then, is how late 1990s outcomes, superficially, compare. In the next section, we look at the differences in the processes behind these outcomes.

7.5 POLICIES AND ADAPTATION IN KRASNODAR AND SAMARA

In Krasnodar the regional leadership has been traditionalist and nationalist in character. The only exception was the short and erratic gubernatorial reign of D'yakonov (1991-2). He tried to implement reforms in the teeth of opposition from the regional elites, and failed (McAuley, M. 1997). Since then the region has had three governors: Nikolai Yegorov, Yevgeniy Kharitonov and Nikolay Kondratenko. Yegorov served for a time as head of Yeltsin's presidential apparatus. In that capacity, he was one of the more influential people at the centre of federal political life who pushed for the disastrous invasion of Chechnya. Kondratenko, who is governor at the time of writing and has been in post since December 1996, is one of the more extreme nationalists and anti-Semites in Russian political life. His pronouncements have been extreme to the point of dottiness.

Our interviews with members of the political and business elite in the kray in 1996–8 showed, however, that the region's political office-holders were far from uniformly traditionalist. Three groupings stand out: an anti-reform and xenophobic cluster around the regional leadership; moderate or reform-minded people in the city administrations of Krasnodar city and Sochi; and more moderate or reform-minded people representing the coastal strip (for example, in the federal Duma).[8]

8. Magomedov interviews in Krasnodar city, 1996, 1997, 1998; Hanson interviews in Sochi, 1998.

The anti-reform character of the regional government seems characteristic of predominantly rural Russian regions. Attitudes towards land privatization were demonstrated early. In 1994 there was a campaign to take land back from the new private farmers (*fermery*). Reportedly, some 10,000 hectares were taken back into the collective farms through legal actions in which the courts received instructions, apparently from the regional leadership, to 'save our collective farms' (*Argumenty i fakty* 1994 (16), p. 5). The region now has its own special land law, specifying that land cannot be bought and sold, though lifetime, inheritable private leases are allowed. This law, passed in 1995, was allegedly facilitated by a provision of the power-sharing agreement with the federal government, under which the kray could introduce its own land legislation pending the passing of federal legislation on land (that, at least, is the interpretation of Vladimir Beketov, chairman of the regional assembly, in an interview in *NG-Regiony*: 1998 (9), p. 4). Private freehold ownership of farmland is restricted to a maximum of two-fifths of a hectare (Magomedov 1998). This is contrary to the Russian constitution – as if anybody cared. As in other Russian regions, privatization and liberalization none the less went ahead in the early 1990s at federal instigation, at any rate in most sectors of the economy. That did not, however, prevent a highly interventionist, *étatiste* approach continuing to prevail in the region's economic policies – as indeed it did in the great majority of Russian regions.

At the same time, a Soviet-style patron–client relationship dominated economic transactions with the centre. The report of a meeting in February 1996 between the then governor Yevgeniy Kharitonov and the then Prime Minister Viktor Chernomyrdin has a completely Soviet character: the occasion for the meeting was that Chernomyrdin was holidaying in the region (a standard Soviet opportunity for a regional satrap to lobby the all-powerful centre); the main items of business, according to the report, were all requests from the region: for a 40 km gas pipeline to be laid to Tuapse; for more funding of the spring sowing campaign; and for alleged deficiencies in the buying of Kuban' farm produce by the Ministry of Agriculture to be rectified (*Vol'naya Kuban'* 21 February 1996, p. 1). Not long afterwards, a power-sharing agreement between the kray and the federal government was signed, and – closely connected with this – a federal programme of socio-economic development for Krasnodar in 1996–2000 was unveiled. Magomedov (1998) has shown how this grandiose plan came to naught. Little or none of the planned investment, which was supposed to be federally funded, has taken place.

In a gubernatorial decree of June 1997, Kondratenko launched a remarkable attack on past privatization in the region and called for the reconsideration of a number of cases.[9] The examples cited in the decree may or may not have included instances of malfeasance. The messy state of Russian commercial law, law enforcement and business ethics makes the identification of wrongdoing in business transactions highly problematic. What several of them exemplified was restructuring: steep reductions in the workforce; acquisition by 'commercial structures' from Moscow and, even worse, from abroad; the conversion of the bus station in Sochi into a trading centre (a thriving trading area in early 1998), and so on. All of these developments were cited as self-evidently unwholesome. One factory was described as having been sold at an 'illegally low price'.

The measures to be taken included a review of past privatizations (6,553 of which had been completed by the beginning of April); the unravelling of sales deemed illegal; the creation of a regional government commission to manage blocks of equity still in the hands of the kray; and the transfer of federal state shares in enterprises 'socially significant' for the region into regional (state) hands.

The tone of the decree was one of hostility: not to privatization in the abstract, but to what might be called the 'really existing privatization', and also to ownership by Moscow banks and ownership by foreigners. The underlying concern that was expressed was less easy to lampoon: output, employment and tax revenue in the region had fallen drastically, and the governor evidently wished to be seen to be doing something energetic about it – and to be finding scapegoats.

One influence on the choice of scapegoats in Kuban' politics is the influx of migrants from other CIS countries. Often these are forced migrants fleeing from wars in the Transcaucasus. In this respect, Krasnodar is one of the ethnically Russian regions that is a kind of front-line state. In 1994 the regional government required visas for such

---

9. Decree no. 228 of 10 June 1997, *O negativnykh posledstviyakh privatizatsii nekotorykh predpriyatii Krasnodarskogo kraya, vskrytykh v khode proverki obrashchenii grazhdan k glave administratsii kraya, i merakh po ikh ustraneniya* [On negative consequences of the privatisation of a number of enterprises of Krasnodar *kray*, revealed in the course of investigation of citizens' petitions to the head of the *kray* administration, and on measures for dealing with them'], *Kuban' segodnya*, 21 June 1997, p. 2.

migrants to enter the Kuban' and a daily charge of 20 per cent of the monthly minimum wage was supposed to be levied on foreign visitors doing business in the kray (*Izvestiya*, 4 May 1994, p. 1). By 1997 (and perhaps earlier) a Krasnodar residence permit (*propiska*) was required for employment or for the receipt of medical care in the kray (*Izvestiya*, 21 August 1997, p. 5).

No influx of migrants justifies the bizarre rhetoric employed by Governor Kondratenko. It probably helps, however, to account for it. In early August 1997, he told a meeting of Kuban' dignitaries that poisoned food was being sent to the region. The poisons were produced in the USA and the organization of the food supplies was undertaken by 'world Zionism'.[10] According to the account in *Izvestiya*, the President's representative had been reporting such outbursts to Moscow, but no action had been taken to curb what *Izvestiya* described as 'swastika politics' (*Izvestiya*, 21 September 1997, p. 5).

Interviews in the region during 1996–8 with members of the political and business elites suggested that others high up in the regional administration had something of the same blend of populist, statist and nationalist views. Here are some excerpts:

> Privatization has divided people… [and] destroyed workers' morale. It has led to foreign control. [Cites Crédit Suisse First Boston at the Novolipetsk Metallurgical Combine and 'a Georgian citizen' (presumably Kakha Bendukidze, who is ethnically Georgian but may well be a Russian citizen, for what it is worth) at Uralmashzavod.] (Member of kray government and adviser to the Governor, July 1997)

> Privatization has been part of a strategy for weakening Russia. (A deputy governor, July 1997)

> Privatization had to happen… But privatization *à la* Chubais has little to recommend it. Its biggest defect is that it hasn't led to a mass layer of

10. Kondratenko covered himself against verification by saying that the effects of the poisons might not show up for one or two generations. In all this there are echoes of the controversy in the European Union over so-called 'mad-cow disease' (bovine spongiform encephalopathy, or BSE, thought to cause Creutzfeldt-Jakob's disease (CJD) in humans through the consumption of beef from infected animals). Kondratenko referred constantly to 'authoritative' and 'high-level' sources for his information. It is conceivable that shipments of unsafe British beef might provide a particle of reality that could be hidden somewhere in all this nonsense. If so, the British Ministry of Agriculture, Fisheries and Food was evidently deemed too dreary to be named as a conspirator.

owners. [All the enterprise survey evidence shows that it has, in the form of employees, a typical holding being around 40 per cent of equity in privatized concerns. But they are passive.] It has just produced rip-off artists... (An inspector in the kray's administrative control and analysis division, July 1997.)

Attitudes towards the federal government (then headed by Viktor Chernomyrdin and containing both Boris Nemtsov and Anatolii Chubais as deputy prime ministers) are what might be expected from these sentiments. The first of the interviewees cited above characterized Kondratenko's position *vis-à-vis* the federal authorities as follows: 'His position is a normal, patriotic one: he criticizes the centre.' Seen from another angle, this is a source of trouble for the region. A liberal adviser to a Nash Dom Rossiya Duma deputy from the coastal region, when asked what problems there were between the region and the centre, replied (July 1997): 'There aren't any, but the new governor will create them.'

Asked what was the main subject of negotiation between the region and the centre, the deputy governor, in the interview quoted above, replied: 'Money, money, money. ...Why have the Federal Fund for Assistance to the Regions? If we were allowed to keep what we earned, we wouldn't need transfers.' In the same vein, a divisional head in the kray administration said: 'The only point of our contacts with Moscow is to get our money back. Moscow gives us only problems' (July 1997).

The same complaint, it must be said, is levelled at the regional administration by the administration of Krasnodar city (Sochi is in a different situation: as a federal spa area, it has direct funding from the federal budget). Valerii Samoilenko, the mayor of Krasnodar, speaking at the March 1997 conference of Cities of the South of Russia, described the flow to the kray budget of revenue raised in the city as 'robbery' (interview with Samoilenko's press secretary, July 1997).

The same informant differed strikingly, however, from interviewees in the regional administration in his assessment of the impact of foreign investment. He cited:

the example of the former Krasnodar tobacco works, which has changed its name and is now foreign-owned. ...this [foreign investment] has allowed the workers there to get a very decent wage, the works pensioners to get a good pension and the city budget to get a solid monthly [tax] revenue amounting to 5–7 per cent of the total tax collection in the city. If we had five or six such enterprises, we could solve all our problems.

This attitude on the part of city officials is understandable. According to local press reports, Philip Morris invested $150 million in the cigarette factory in question, Krasnodartabakprom, in 1993–8; in January–September 1998 the factory's production was recorded as 5.2 per cent of regional gross industrial output and it provided 20 per cent of the revenue of the city budget (*Kubanskie novosti* 26 July 1998).

In contrast, the gubernatorial adviser and the deputy governor, in the interviews cited above, spoke suspiciously of foreign investment, implying that economic activity was a zero-sum game: if foreign investors benefited, it was necessarily at the expense of Russians. The local level of government, closer to the ground than the regional authorities, may simply have less opportunity to indulge in evidence-free editorializing. Certainly the same favourable attitude to foreign investment was expressed in separate interviews by two deputy mayors of Sochi (March 1998).

Whether the levels of government differ much in their propensity to micro-manage economic activity on their territory is more doubtful. The director of a company marketing pharmaceuticals and perfumery in Krasnodar city had this to say (July 1997):

> We have long avoided contacts with the local administration... We don't depend on them. We lease premises and transport from private sources. We did some sponsoring of children's institutions. We helped local sport organizations. Then the administration noticed us. They wrote and asked us to help fund the Invalid Society, help the poor, etc. They started wanting to know about our labour safety arrangements. The tax office and the tax police started showing an interest in us. But lately they've given up and left us in peace because we've shown we have everything in order.

The quasi-Soviet tone of the political authorities when they are dealing with business on their patch is epitomized by this observation by the mayor of Krasnodar, interviewed in July 1997: 'Soon I am going to have to induce our bankers to make an interest-free loan of 50 billion roubles to the city. And if one of them isn't prepared to meet the city half-way, we're not going to meet him half-way. That I can promise.'

At the same time, members of the business community had some confidence (in early 1998) that the logic of economic change would itself affect the politicians: 'Even governors who start off by opposing change, learn from experience. Kondratenko has been changing over the past year' (Director of the Sochi branch of a Moscow-based bank, March 1998). Indeed, later that year the kray administration was reported to be negotiating seriously with the American company Global over the terms of a deal to build a new power station (*Vol'naya Kuban'* 17 December 1998).

Our suspicion is that most of the ingredients in this set of attitudes in various regional elites in Krasnodar would be replicated across Russia, both in 'retrograde' and in 'progressive' regions. What seems to be distinctive about Krasnodar is that the regional government has a clear and strong antipathy to change and foreign investment in general, rather than a pragmatic, opportunistic approach that would be more open to new developments, even if it was accompanied by the same reflex tendency to intervene at the drop of a hat. This probably amounts to a serious impediment to economic adjustment compared with the situation in Samara.

Examples of interventionism by the Kondratenko regime in 1997–9 are numerous and often extreme. In August 1998 the kray administration reportedly issued a decree (not published) on the 'passportization' of firms in the region. This required all registered businesses to give the authorities information about their balance sheets, physical assets, securities issued, sales and the banks servicing their accounts. The requirement that all registered firms must do this was said by the weekly *Kuban'-Biznes* (28 August 1998, p. 44) to be contrary to federal law.

A gubernatorial decree of 9 September 1998 aimed to limit the shipment of food out of the province. This was criticized by the federal authorities as contravening federal law. It was annulled in October, but replaced by an agreement between the kray administration and local producers that the latter would not ship products out of the region – the inducement being that otherwise their output would be impounded in settlement of tax debts. Meanwhile a commission was established to control wholesale and retail food prices (*Kommersant"-Daily* 21 October 1998, p. 2; *Kubanskie novosti* 28 October 1998). None of this is necessarily to be seen as a response to the August 1998 financial crisis; Kondratenko had tried the same measures in 1997 (*Vol'naya Kuban'* 24 June 1998). None of these measures was judged to have worked, in the sense of keeping local food prices low and supplies plentiful to the population. In November 1998 retail food prices rose 30 per cent (*Vol'naya Kuban'* 1 December 1998).

What such measures probably do achieve is rich pickings in economic rents: bribes to officials or arbitrage profits between controlled and free prices, or both.

In the sphere of investment finance, faced with banks unwilling to lend to non-bank companies in the region and the disappearance of federal funding, the regional administration has also acted in a completely Soviet fashion. In mid-1998 they tried to get local banks to finance a list of 200 'priority' investment projects. According to one account, these 'priorities' covered 'everything' (*Vol'naya Kuban'* 16 June 1998). The credibility of regional public finances, however, was such that the banks refused to finance any of these projects, even with the supposed inducement of a financial guarantee from the kray budget (*Kuban'-Biznes* 17 July 1998, p. 26).

Criticism of the region's leadership must, however, be kept in perspective. The region certainly has problems. However, the underlying difficulties themselves cannot simply be blamed on the traditionalist attitudes of the leadership. As the previous section indicated, the Kuban' has very large structural adjustment problems because of the kind of region it is. A speech in June 1997 by the chairman of the kray government, V. A. Mel'nikov, rehearsed all the symptoms: falling output (continuing to fall in 1997, unlike Samara); dwindling budgetary revenue; dwindling support from Moscow; growing payment arrears; a growing share of loss-making enterprises; and new small firms which were contributing little to the budget (*Kuban' segodnya*, 27 June 1997, p. 2). In the end, however, the deficit in the regional budget in 1997 was, as a percentage of expenditure, well below the average for Russian regions (1.5, against 7.2 per cent; Lavrov 1998).

A reasonable judgement on the policies of the Kondratenko regime, none the less, is that they impede an adjustment process that is difficult enough as it is.

At the same time, it is hard, with respect to Krasnodar, to avoid a conclusion that de Melo and Ofer (1999, p. 16) suggest in their study of ten cities along the Volga: namely, that 'policies normally follow the political orientation of the local population'. Mary McAuley (1997) noted the strong traditionalism of the local elites in the region in the early 1990s. In the elections to the regional assembly on 22 November 1998, 38 out of 50 seats were won by candidates professing allegiance to Kondratenko's umbrella organization, Otechestvo (separate from and predating the movement of the same name launched by Moscow mayor Yuriy Luzhkov). Kondratenko's Otechestvo unites the Communist Party of Russia, the Agrarian Union, veterans' and Cossack organizations, and the like. Of the remaining seats, one went to a professedly liberal party, Yabloko, and the rest were won by independents (*Kubanskie novosti* 27 November 1998). That is hardly a setting for market-friendly policies.

Nevertheless, foreign investment was not being kept out. Apart from the cigarette factory referred to earlier, there have been a number of quite large developments which depend on foreign investment: a large new hotel in Sochi; a planned Hyundai assembly plant;[11] and the planned construction of a new oil terminal at Novorossiisk, extending the port's capacity from 15 to 30 million tons per annum, by a consortium including the French company Bouygues, and finance from the Banque Nationale de Paris (Interfax 3 September 1998). It can be calculated that in 1997 about one-fifth of all gross fixed investment in the kray was by foreign companies (derived from ruble and dollar figures in *Kubanskie novosti* 28 August 1998, using the exchange rate, not a purchasing power parity).

In Samara Konstantin Titov has headed the regional administration from August 1991 to the time of writing. He has been seen throughout as a Yeltsin loyalist and moderate reformer. In the gubernational elections of 1 December 1996 he won comfortably, with 60 per cent of the vote. His main opponent, representing the communists, obtained only 30 per cent (*Jamestown Foundation Monitor* 2 December 1996).

Titov's career and pronouncements suggest a canny, centrist politician. In 1991 he left the Communist Party (he had been a member of the Kuibyshevsk city party committee) for the short-lived Movement for Democratic Reforms. In 1994–5 he was on the Council of Russia's Democratic Choice, whence he moved to become deputy chairman of the 'party of power', NDR (Romanov and Tartakovskaya 1998). He has described himself as a disciple of Keynes (he trained in engineering, but worked in economic institutes in the 1970s and 1980s). One of his aims, he has said, is to make Samara a 'Chicago on the Volga' (IEWS *Russian Regional Report* 25 September 1997). He

11. Institute of East–West Studies, *Russian Regional Report* 2, p. 22 (25 September 1997).

has not used nationalist rhetoric or made sweeping criticisms of Russian privatization; he publicly supported Chubais at a tricky time in mid-1997 (interview on NTV, 10 June 1997).

In 1998–9 Titov distanced himself from NDR without entirely breaking off relations with the former 'party of power'. In January 1999 he launched a political movement, Golos Rossii (Voice of Russia) with the professed aims of presenting views from outside Moscow and forming a pragmatic, centrist grouping in the Duma that would reduce the parliamentary strength of the communists and their close allies. Launched too late to put its own candidates on the proportional representation slate for the 1999 Duma elections, Golos Rossii was seen by some commentators as chiefly a step towards a Titov presidential candidacy in 2000.

Titov has developed a reputation for running a region that is stable. His team of deputy governors and department heads, many recruited from local research institutes or universities, has itself been comparatively stable in composition (Romanov and Tartakovskaya 1998).

Certainly, several of the measures taken in the region have been of a pro-market kind. Regional legislation is said to support the private buying and selling of land. The region was slow to introduce the institution of authorized or plenipotentiary (*upolnomochennye*) banks acting for the administration – a common vehicle for embezzlement of public funds (Hanson 1997b). The arrangement was then abolished – ahead of most Russian practice – in early 1998 (*Delo* [Samara] 11 March 1998). Pressure from petrochemical producers to subsidize them, by intervening to cut electricity charges, has been resisted by the administration (*Samarskoe obozreniye* 3 June 1996, pp. 6 and 10). In interviews with Western journalists, Titov presents himself as a free marketeer. He has claimed, for example, to be pressing for settlements both amongst enterprises and of tax bills to be exclusively in cash.

At the same time, Titov has been actively involved in detailed ways in the regional economy, in a fashion that is reminiscent of Russian and Soviet traditional practice, not of free-market ideology. He is, or at any rate was in 1997, on the boards of the car firm AvtoVAZ, the aerospace company Aviakor and the oil company Yukos (part of the Menatep group) (Romanov and Tartakovskaya 1998). For a regional political leader to hold such posts with firms that are major local employers would be seen in many other countries, quite rightly, as producing a conflict of interests. As governor, he has pressed for

AvtoVAZ to continue to keep Yukos as its main supplier of oil products; he claims to have helped protect AvtoVAZ, which is a large tax debtor. And he has sought to have the tax debt (in the region in general) converted to shares held by the regional administration – a form of renationalization (OMRI *Russian Regional Report* 20 March 1997). The deals that formed part of the region's 1 August 1997 power-sharing agreement with Moscow indicated the same interest in share ownership by the region (IEWS *Russian Regional Reporter* 6 September 1997).

In a similar, traditionalist vein, Titov criticized the Chernomyrdin government in March 1997 for not doing more to help producers (ibid.). At that time he called on the NDR to support Lebed' rather than Chernomyrdin. (Later, in the autumn of 1998, he initially supported Chernomyrdin's reappointment as Prime Minster, and then switched to backing either Luzhkov or Stroev: *RFE/RL Newsline* 7 September 1998.) Reports of a meeting, summoned by Titov, of district heads of administration to discuss the spring sowing plans for 1998 reveal a thoroughly traditional, purely Soviet arrangement (*Delo* 7 June 1998).

Charges of cronyism and corruption are levelled at all Russian politicians, usually with good reason. Whether Titov is unusual in this respect is hard to say. His 24-year-old son Aleksei's appointment as president of the region's third largest bank, Gazbank, in May 1998 (*Russkiy telegraf* 28 May 1998), an appointment made by the bank, not the governor, seems little different from (say) export marketing by the son of a British Prime Minister while the latter was in office.

One element in Titov's economic poiicy activities has been neutral with respect to market reform: standing up for his region against the federal government. As leader of one of the seven or eight regions that receive no transfers from the centre (the so-called 'donor regions'), as a leading member of NDR and as chairman of the Federation Council's budget and finance committee, Titov is well placed to do this. With the leaders of other donor regions, he has called for those regions to retain, not about 50 per cent, but 60–65 per cent of the tax revenue collected on their territories (*Moscow Times* 6–12 November 1996, p. 3). A year or so later he was criticizing the 'tough' draft 1998 budget for harming the regions (*RFE/RL Newsline* 17 December 1997). His administration also arranged for a number of their specialists to be seconded to work in federal ministries (*Samarskoye obozreniye* 4 June 1996, p. 5), presumably as a fifth column that would press the region's interests.

Against this mixed policy background, the development of market institutions in Samara along with the decline of established state and privatized large enterprises look like adaptations that owe rather little to local policy. The brief summary of these adjustments that follows is drawn mostly from Hanson (1997) and Romanov and Tartakovskaya (1998), where more detail is provided.

The financial services sector has developed strongly in Samara. In 1994 the city of Samara contained one of only eight foreign exchange bourses in the country. When on-line securities trading on the Russian Trading System was extended beyond Moscow in 1996, Samara was again one of eight trading centres on the network. A few new share issues began to be made in the region in 1996–7, though only a handful of locally based companies (including Samaraenergo and Volgotanker) had liquid markets in their shares. Moscow-based banks established a strong presence in the region relatively early, but some locally based banks survived and did relatively well up to 1998; the largest of them, Rosestbank, was among those Russian banks with foreign-currency debt-service obligations whose payments abroad were halted by the Kirienko government's 'moratorium', imposed on 17 August 1998.

The regions saw the development of a number of new businesses that grew to substantial size during the 1990s: *Intensivnyi Korm*, *Zakhar* and *Dovgan* among others (details in Hanson 1997b). Foreign trade and inward foreign investment have been by Russian standards substantial. In early 1998 the regional electricity company, Samara-energo, was 22 per cent foreign owned and was planning an American Depository Receipt (ADR) issue that would have raised that share (*Russkiy telegraf* 3 March 1998). The 1995 purchase of the leading confectionery company, Rossiya, by Nestlé, appears to have been a successful venture, at least into 1998. Employment and output at Rossiya have been raised; some re-equipping has been undertaken; wages are high by local standards, and regularly paid.

At the same time, AvtoVAZ, the giant car works in Tol'yatti and a major regional exporter, has been making losses. This is important. VAZ has been reported as contributing 40 per cent of the region's gross industrial output (Tartakovskaya 1998) and providing 25 per cent of regional tax revenue (*Wall Street Journal Europe* 19 September 1998). However, its output has been stable by the standards of the Russian engineering sector in the 1990s. In 1998 it produced 600,000 cars (*Kommersant"-Daily* 20 January 1999). That is 82 per cent of the 1990 level. If the reported weight of VAZ in regional industrial output is treated as fixed, the implication of that modest decline would be that the production of the rest of the region's industry fell by 45 per cent over the same period. Without VAZ, in other words, Samara's rate of industrial decline would be much closer to the national average.

Meanwhile, the cluster of large defence plants and research organizations in Samara city has been declining in a fashion familiar in many Russian regions.

Sameko, a large producer of aluminium sheet, saw its output fall from 600,000 tons a year in 1990 to 60,000 in 1996. Originally under the Ministry of the Aviation Industry, and therefore in an administrative sense part of the Soviet military-industrial sector, Sameko was privatized early. By 1996 it was 60 per cent owned by Inkombank.[12] More recently, it has been reported to be owned by Sibirskii alyuminii (Tartakovskaya 1998).

The giant bearings factory, Shar, privatized in 1992, saw its workforce decline from 35,000 in the mid-1980s to 10,000 in 1995. The non-ferrous metals fabricating works, ZiM, is still state-owned. It is required by the federal authorities to maintain so-called 'mobilization capacities'. It has had a similar fall in its labour force: from 33,000 in the mid-1980s to 11,000 in 1995. The aerospace factory Aviakor, which used to make as many as 50 Tu-154 aircraft a year, was expected to sell five in 1998 (Itar-Tass 16 November 1998).

The pattern of change – decline of most of the large, Soviet-era enterprises and the rise of new financial and trading businesses, alongside successful adjustment by some older production units such as the Rossiya chocolate factory and some new business development – is not in itself distinctively Samaran. What seems specific to Samara and a handful of other regions is that the scale of the more successful adaptation has been (until the crisis of 1998) relatively large. The administration appears not to have blocked this sort of development at any rate. The region's initial conditions seem most important in producing this outcome. They include its housing two large cities, with the potential for recombining production inputs that the notion of Jacobs externalities indicates should be easier in large conurbations;

12. In this and the following paragraph, information comes, unless otherwise indicated, from case-studies carried out by Irina Tartakovskaya and Pavel Romanov. For some scandalous details on earlier adventures with some of these giant defence plants, see Hanson (1997b).

and the initial possession of substantial exporting capabilities. The large share of highly trained people displaced from a collapsing defence sector seems to have been a key ingredient.

7.6   CONCLUSIONS

Two main conclusions come out of these narratives. First, the evidence of the case-studies supports the conjecture that a comparatively advanced region with large cities would on balance adapt more successfully than a rural region. In other words, the beneficial agglomeration effects connected (probably) to Jacobs externalities seem in these two regions to have outweighed the disadvantages of rust-belt effects arising from the presence of a large amount of moribund heavy industry.

Second, the influence of regional policy-makers seems to be limited. Our impression – and it can only be an impression – is that the sort of economy each region had in 1990 was more important to their subsequent adaptation than decisions made by regional leaders. Perhaps the influence of regional policies is best seen as negative: regional leaders can impede adjustment; but they may be capable of exerting only very limited positive influence on events. Much of Titov's activity in Samara is not readily distinguishable from much of what was done by regional leaders in Krasnodar, except that Titov did not make strong anti-reform pronouncements calling into question previous privatizations, and he has not been surrounded by officials openly sceptical about foreign investment. At the very least, the public stance of successive regional leaders in Krasnodar has not been encouraging to the development of new business.

One question we have not pursued is whether local city leaders may be capable of influencing economic development more than their regional counterparts. De Melo and Ofer (1999) in a study of ten cities along the Volga, suggest that city administrations can make a difference. They consider that Samara city had both comparatively favourable initial conditions and comparatively reformist policies – though these attributes were not necessarily conducive to favourable outcomes in the 1990s.

The view that city administrations matter seems to be shared by residents of the Samara region. Survey evidence in the region shows that, in the perceptions of the population, the mayor of a city is credited with more influence on people's economic circumstances than the more distant regional leadership (even in Samara city, where the regional leadership is based) (Romanov and Tartakovskaya 1998). Whether that perception matches reality, however, is something we have not investigated. De Melo and Ofer do not address it.

Did the financial crisis of August 1998 alter the comparative prospects of the two regions? It is conceivable that adaptation to the crisis might have been easier in a more 'backward' region. After all, the crisis originated in financial markets, and its earliest impact on the real economy showed up in a drastic decline in imports, including food imports. A food-surplus region like Krasnodar, and particularly one with an interventionist regime, might well cope better with shocks to the banking and foreign-trade systems. (It should, however, be noted that both regions, and not just Krasnodar, placed controls on the shipment of food from their territories (Latynina 1998), though Titov has denied doing so: *Kommersant"-Daily* 23 October 1998.)

The governor of Samara also claimed in that October 1998 interview that the region's automobile and food producers were responding to the opportunities for import-substitution created by the rouble devaluation of 17 August. Perhaps this is really the case. None the less, over the year as a whole VAZ produced 20 per cent fewer cars than in 1997, and its 1999 target of 675,000 cars is below its target for 1998 (though above 1998 actual: *Kommersant"-Daily* 20 January 1999). One encouraging sign was the report of a memorandum of intent signed on 3 March 1999 between VAZ and General Motors to create a joint venture producing Opel Astras (*Russian Regional Investor* 18 March 1999; Oxford Analytica, *Eastern Europe Daily Brief* 5 April 1999). But it should be noted that this is only a memorandum of agreement, not a done deal; that multinationals' efforts at local car production in Russia have not yet prospered; and that 30 per cent of VAZ components are already imported (*Kommersant"-Daily* 20 January 1999). Another indication of gains from the crisis for Samara producers can be seen in reports of Sameko receiving orders to supply parts for Airbus and Audi (*Business Eastern Europe* 4 January 1999, p. 3).

One difference between the two regions is likely to be of lasting importance: financial intermediation is less problematic in Samara than in Krasnodar. Shortly before the August 1998 crisis, a conference on banking in Krasnodar was told that the already low rate of bank financing of the region's real economy had been falling since 1996; of the 35 surviving, locally based banks, only 28 were profitable, and only 14 of these (at mid-1998) were able to meet the new, nationally imposed minimum capital requirements of EUR1 million, which were to come into effect on 1 January 1999 (*Vol'naya Kuban'* 16 June 1998).

It might be thought that a region with weak local banks would not suffer greatly from a crisis in Moscow financial markets. The weakness of the Kuban's local banks, however, had led to Moscow-based banks acquiring a large share of the regional market for banking services. Of the six leading Russian banks whose depositors were advised by the Central Bank of Russia to move their deposits to the State Savings Bank (Sberbank) after the crisis, five were operating in Krasnodar (*Vol'naya Kuban'* 12 September 1998). More to the point, the Moscow-based banks held more of the region's hard-currency bank deposits than did the locally based banks: about $700 million as against about $500 million (estimated from *Kubanskie novosti* 9 September 1998).

These figures exclude Sberbank, which held more hard-currency deposits than all the other banks put together: about $2 billion. From the point of view of the finance of investment in the region, however, the regional Sberbank affiliate was every bit as inactive as the next bank. It was reported (probably for early 1998) to have 80 per cent of its assets in precisely the Treasury bills (GKOs) on which the federal government defaulted in August, and only 6 per cent in loans to entities in Krasnodar (ibid.).

The siphoning of funds out of the Kuban' by all banks except one local bank – Yugbank, owned by local businesses – has been a cause of constant complaint by local officials and commentators. To a considerable extent, it must simply reflect the well-founded reluctance of Russian banks to invest in the real economy anywhere in Russia. Precise comparison is not possible with the available data, but it also seems likely that this tendency is more pronounced for Krasnodar than it is for Samara. In so far as that is the case, it would reflect something else: that the more diverse and resilient economy of Samara offers rather more that is worth investing in.

With or without the 1998 crisis, then, Samara has apparently adapted less badly than Krasnodar to life after communism. That difference can be clearly linked to differences in initial conditions.

Differences in the policies of the two regional administrations are less sharp, when looked at closely, than mere reputation would suggest. But the doggedly traditionalist interventionism of the Krasnodar administration has probably been more damaging than the lighter, more pragmatic meddling by Konstantin Titov's regime in Samara.

8. Irkutsk and Sakhalin

Michael Bradshaw,[1] Alexandr Chernikov and Peter Kirkow

INTRODUCTION

This chapter compares developments in two 'resource-oriented' regions, one in East Siberia and the other in the Russian Far East. Irkutsk oblast is located 5042 km east of Moscow, at the heart of the Eurasian landmass (see Map 8.1). Its nearest foreign neighbours are Kazakhstan, Mongolia and China. In terms of 'economic–geographic position' Sakhalin could not be more different. Sakhalin oblast comprises the island of Sakhalin and the Kurile Islands and lies offshore of Primorskiy and Khabarovsk krays on the mainland of the Russian Far East and just to the north of Japan. Sakhalin is located 10,417 km from Moscow. At present the only permanent transport links between Sakhalin and the Russian mainland are the oil and gas pipelines that run from the north of the island to Khabarovsk kray. There is a ferry service from Vanino and the mainland to the port of Kholmsk in the south of Sakhalin, but this is now infrequent and very run down.

As we shall see later, despite their different relative locations, the two regions have much in common as resource regions whose

1. Michael Bradshaw wishes to acknowledge the support of ESRC award number L324253005, which funded the Sakhalin component of this case-study chapter. The authors would like to thank Dmitry Zimine and Jon Oldfield for their assistance with the fieldwork components of this research. Five research visits were conducted: two to Irkutsk and three to Sakhalin. Thanks are also due to all the local officials and members of the business community who gave generously of their time. Any misinterpretations and factual errors are the responsibility of the authors. The most recent visit to Sakhalin took place in December 1998 and the most recent visit to Irkutsk was in April 1999.

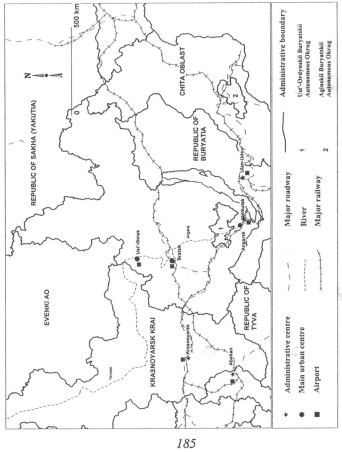

Map 8.1 Irkutsk oblast

futures are tied to their ability to revitalize their resource economies and gain access to foreign capital and international markets. However, there are also many differences between the two regions that require consideration.[2] First, there is the question of scale. Irkutsk oblast covers a territory of 767,900 sq km (about four times the Russian average) and accounts for 4.5 per cent of Russia's territory. The total population of Irkutsk oblast was 2.7 million at the beginning of 1998, 1.9 per cent of the population of Russia and 30.6 of the population of East Siberia. The oblast has a population density of 3.6 persons per square kilometre, but most of this is concentrated in the southern regions in a series of cities along the Trans-Siberian railway and its branch lines (see Map 8.1). The oblast capital, Irkutsk (population 590,500) is located at the first bridging point of the river Angara as it leaves Lake Baykal some 60 km away. Other large settlements are Angarsk (266,800), Bratsk (255,600), Ust'-Ilimsk (108,300) and Usol'e-Sibirskoye (104,300). Together these cities house about 40 per cent of the oblast's population, with a further 40 per cent living in other settlements classified as urban. The level of urbanization was 79.6 per cent at the beginning of 1998, higher than the Russian average of 73.1 per cent. In 1996 Irkutsk oblast produced 2.4 per cent of Russia's gross regional product (GRP); it accounted for 1.9 per cent of the economically active population of Russia; and for 2.2 per cent of the volume of industrial production. The level of GRP per capita in 1996 was 16,518,500 roubles, 24 per cent above the Russian average, without adjusting for regional price differences. In its regional context, Irkutsk accounts for 34.5 per cent of the total GRP of East Siberia, 30.7 per cent of economically active population and 32 per cent of the volume of industrial production.

Sakhalin oblast occupies a territory of 87,100 sq km (less than half the Russian average), 0.5 per cent of Russian territory. The total population of the oblast was 620,200 at the beginning of 1998, 0.4 per cent of the population of the Russian Federation and 1.4 per cent of the population of the Russian Far East. The oblast has a population density of 7.1 persons per square kilometre. The largest city is the capital Yuzhno-Sakhalinsk, with a population of 177,000 (Map 8.2). The other cities of any size are the southern ports of Kholmsk (42,000) and

---

2. All the statistics reported in the following section were obtained from Goskomstat Rossii (1998a and b).

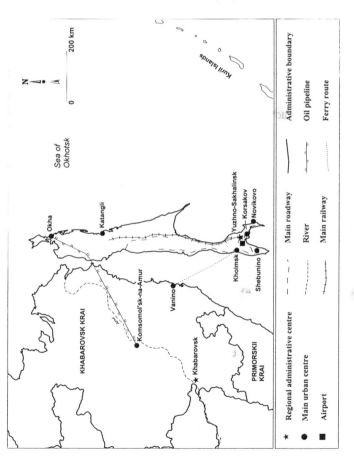

Map 8.2 Sakhalin oblast

Korsakov (39,700) and the northern oil and gas centre of Okha (30,000). Together these four settlements account for 46.5 per cent of the oblast's population. The level of urbanization is 86.3 per cent, considerably higher than the national average: a factor explained by a harsh environment and the resource-based nature of the economy. In 1996 Sakhalin oblast produced 0.5 per cent of the total GRP of Russia; it accounted for 0.4 per cent of the economically active population and 0.4 per cent of the volume of industrial production. Sakhalin accounts for 8.6 per cent of the total GRP of the Russian Far East, 8.6 of the economically active population and 8.5 per cent of industrial production.

From this brief comparison of vital statistics it is clear that Irkutsk oblast is a much larger undertaking than Sakhalin oblast, in terms both of the relative scale of settlement and economic activity and of their relative standing within the national economy and within their respective regions. Neither region can be considered to have a large, concentrated local market; furthermore, a combination of climatic conditions and economic structure means that both regions are wholly dependent on outside supplies of agricultural and consumer goods.

The second major difference between the two regions is their relative importance during the Soviet period. Irkutsk oblast was at the heart of the planned exploitation of the hydroelectric potential of the Angara–Yenisey river system. A series of large hydroelectric stations (HEP) were constructed, first at Irkutsk and later at Bratsk and Ust'-Ilimsk. These HEP stations formed the basis for the construction of large energy intensive industrial complexes focusing on aluminium smelting, pulp and paper production, and chemicals and petrochemicals. The aluminium and petrochemicals industries are dependent on external supplies of raw materials, while the forestry and chemicals industries, initially at least, used mainly local resources. The logic of schemes such as the Bratsk–Ust'-Ilimsk Territorial Production Complex (TPC) was that the planned combination of energy-intensive industries around a source of cheap energy would result in more cost-effective development. However, as elsewhere in the Soviet Union, the planners failed to take into account the true cost of transporting raw materials to these complexes and then delivering their products to market. They also restricted the level of processing, and therefore value-added, within the TPC. The construction of these huge complexes had a negative effect upon the natural environment and the construction of a pulp mill at Baykal'sk on the shores of Lake Baykal became the focal point for the emergence of an environmental movement in the 1960s (Pryde 1991, pp. 84–5).

During the 1970s the Irkutsk region was again a focus of attention as the starting-off point for the Baykal–Amur Mainline (BAM). The BAM was to parallel the Trans-Siberian railway and allow the opening-up of the vast resource wealth of the Trans-Baykal region (Shabad and Mote 1977); instead it became the largest monument to the Brezhnev period of stagnation. None the less, the development of Irkutsk oblast was a priority project during the Soviet period, even though the level of military industrial activity within the region was modest. Irkutsk was open to foreigners and was on the Intourist itinerary; foreign tourists were able to visit the HEP station at Bratsk as well as take in the beauty of Lake Baykal.

Sakhalin was a closed garrison region during the Soviet period; not even Soviet citizens could visit the island without special permission. Economic development was secondary to strategic concerns. Military installations on Sakhalin safeguarded Soviet interests in the Sea of Okhotsk and guarded the entrance to the Sea of Japan. It was over Sakhalin that a Korean Airlines 747 jet was shot down in 1983, killing 269 people. The economy of Sakhalin owes as much to the period of Japanese occupation of the southern half of the island between 1905 and 1945 as it does the Soviet Union. The island's coal and oil industry were initially developed by the Japanese, as was the pulp and paper industry. Japanese companies working concessions on Soviet territory carried out much of this development (Stephan 1971; Vysokov 1996).

During the Soviet period the economic development of Sakhalin was subsidized by the central authorities for strategic and ideological as much as economic reasons. The Soviet Union set about removing all vestiges of Japanese occupation and Sakhalin's urban landscape soon became much like anywhere else in the Soviet Union. Stephan (1971, pp. 177–85) noted that, following the Soviet takeover of southern Sakhalin in 1945, the island's population increased from 200,000 in 1945 to 660,000 in 1957. During this period the island experienced rapid industrial growth based on the exploitation of the offshore fishery and the development of energy resources and timber onshore. In the early 1970s Stephan (1971, p. 185) noted that 'Sakhalin plays a role in the USSR economy out of proportion to its population and area. While its inhabitants comprise only 0.3 per cent of the Soviet Union's population, the Oblast supplies 7 per cent of the country's fish, pulp and paper'. Much of this production was delivered in unprocessed form to industries on the mainland. During the mid-1960s Sakhalin was formally drawn into Soviet plans to promote increased economic cooperation between the Far East and Japan. The region then became the subject of a compensation agreement to explore and develop offshore oil and gas potential. Despite its relative economic obscurity, the standard of living on Sakhalin was probably above the national average.

Today the visitor to Yuzhno-Sakhalinsk is struck by the variety of run-down civic facilities, the ski hill that no longer functions, the theatres and shops that seem unchanged since the Soviet period. The local population speaks of the Soviet period as a time when life on Sakhalin was much better. As a closed military region and as a region designated part of the 'Soviet North' Sakhalin benefited from various subsidies, wage supplements and privileges. Today, Sakhalin can no longer sustain this standard of living. The island's infrastructure is falling into disrepair and many people have left. Since 1989 the oblast's population has fallen by 12.7 per cent; during the same period the population of Irkutsk oblast fell by 2.0 per cent (Russia's population declined by 0.2 per cent).

8.1   INHERITED ECONOMIC STRUCTURES

Because of their relative locations, harsh environment and the emphasis placed upon resource development, both regions exhibit rather unusual economic structures. In 1990 industry accounted for 30 per cent of total employment in Irkutsk oblast and 26.8 per cent on Sakhalin, compared to a national average of 30.3 per cent.[3] But agriculture accounted for only 7.7 of employment in Irkutsk and 4.6 per cent on Sakhalin, compared to a national average of 15 per cent. The service sector accounted for the remaining 62.4 per cent in Irkutsk and 68.6 per cent on Sakhalin, compared to the national average of 56.8 per cent. In both cases the relatively high share of the services was due to higher than

---

3. These data on employment structure are taken from Goskomstat Rossii (1995, pp. 29–32).

average levels of activity within the transportation and construction sectors. Across Russia transitional recession and economic restructuring have brought about a shift in the relative importance of industry and services (see Chapter 3). By 1997 the share of the workforce employed in industry had fallen to 26.7 per cent in Irkutsk and 22.8 per cent on Sakhalin, while at the national level it had declined to 23.0 per cent. At the same time both regions experienced a growth in employment in the trade and consumer goods sector that was close to the national average. In Irkutsk the construction industry suffered a higher than average decline in its share of employment; while on Sakhalin the transport sector suffered a higher than average level of decline.

In both regions employment data suggest that the level of de-industrialization is below the national average. Data on the decline in the volume of industrial production also show that both regions have fared slightly better than Russia as a whole (Figure 8.1), with Irkutsk doing better than Sakhalin. Within the industrial sector there has been marked variation in performance and this has had a distinct spatial impact on economic activity within each oblast. Table 8.1 shows the branch structure of industrial production in both regions in 1994 and 1997. While these data are subject to the distortions of differential price

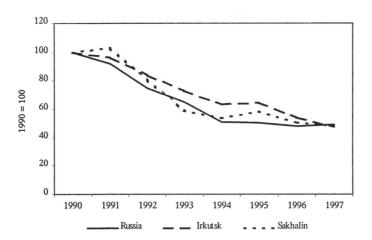

Source: Goskomstat, 1998d, pp. 380–81

Figure 8.1 Dynamics of industrial production, 1990–97

Table 8.1   Branch structure of industrial production, 1994 and 1997

	Russia		Irkutsk		Sakhalin	
	1994	1997	1994	1997	1994	1997
Electricity	13.4	17.1	12.6	17.5	11.7	21.7
Fuels	15.1	17.4	25.6	12.3	17.2	34.7
Ferrous metals	8.3	7.9	2.2	2.3	0.0	0.1
Non-ferrous metals	6.6	5.5	16.4	20.2	0.2	0.2
Chemicals	7.4	7.2	4.6	5.1	0.1	0.0
MBMW	19.6	18.8	6.0	12.2	22.7	4.5
Forestry	4.6	3.7	17.8	15.4	8.9	6.5
Construction materials	4.8	4.1	4.0	3.2	3.4	1.5
Glass and ceramics	0.4	0.4	0.2	0.2	0.0	0.0
Light	3.1	1.8	0.8	0.5	0.4	0.3
Food	12.5	12.4	7.6	9.4	33.0	29.9
Flour and fodder	2.2	2.1	1.5	0.9	1.7	0.1
Other	2.0	1.6	0.7	0.8	0.7	0.5

Sources:
1994: Goskomstat Rossii (1995, pp. 62–73).
1997: Goskomstat Rossii (1998d, pp. 382–3).

increases, they do convey the industrial specialization of each region and the relative performance of each sector.

Electricity generation is important in both regions, but for different reasons. In the case of Irkutsk the generation of cheap HEP forms the basis of the regional economy. In the case of Sakhalin its relative, and increasing, importance is because Sakhalin has an independent energy grid and therefore has to generate all its own electricity (Bradshaw and Kirkow 1998). The fuels sector is also important in both regions. In both regions coal is used to generate electricity and heat. Both regions exported coal in the past. In Irkutsk between 1990 and 1998 coal production fell by 41.7 per cent, but electricity generation fell only 21.9 per cent. Irkutskenergo has 36 facilities, including 13 thermal power stations; it also has three very large HEP stations which provide about 70 per cent of generating capacity: Irkutsk (660,000 kW), Bratsk (4.5 million kW) and Ust'-Ilimsk (3.84 million kW). Irkutskenergo is one of only two power utility companies that remain independent of the national energy company RAO 'EES Rossii'. This means that it can set its own energy tariffs locally, a factor that has been critical to maintaining the region's energy-intensive economy (Chernikov 1998, p. 380).

Oil and gas are also important in both regions. In the case of Irkutsk this is related to the activities of the Angarsk Oil Refinery, which is located at the end of the pipeline carrying West Siberian crude oil. On Sakhalin the prominence of the fuel energy sector is related to the onshore production of oil and gas in the northern regions. Sakhalin lacks substantial refining capacity and the majority of its gas and most of its oil production is either exported abroad by tanker or transported by pipeline to Khabarovsk kray where the oil is refined and the gas is used for heating. The limited amount of refining that takes place on the island is confined to the activities of the Petrosakh joint venture which supplies petrol and diesel fuels for local consumption.

The importance of ferrous metals in Irkutsk is linked to the mining of iron ore, which is consumed elsewhere in Russia, rather than the presence of iron and steel smelters. The other three sectors of importance in Irkutsk are non-ferrous metals, which is dominated by aluminium smelting; chemicals, and forestry, which includes pulp and paper production. The forestry industry on Sakhalin has traditionally been of significance but, as we shall see later, has suffered a dramatic collapse. The only other sector of significance on Sakhalin is fish processing, which accounts for the majority of the food industry in the oblast.

A further characteristic of both regions is that each of the key industries is dominated by one or two very large formerly state-owned enterprises. Thus, for example, Bratsk and Ust'-Ilimsk are dominated by the aluminium and forestry industries respectively. The Bratsk aluminium plant (Bratsk AZ) is the largest in Russia and Irkutsk produces 40 per cent of Russia's aluminium. The refinery at Angarsk meets 60 per cent of demand in East Siberia and is also a key supplier of crude oil and refined products to the Russian Far East, via the Trans-Siberian railway. Not only do these enterprises dominate their local labour markets; they are also major contributors to the oblast budget. In 1996 the Angarsk Oil Refinery is reported to have produced 26.3 per cent of the total industrial output of Irkutsk and also 30 per cent of the budget revenues, while Irkutskenergo accounted for a further 15.1 per cent of total industrial output (Irkutsk Oblkomstat 1996a, p. 129; Zelent, 1997,

p. 34). The two aluminium enterprises at Bratsk and Irkutsk together contributed a further 13.6 per cent of production.

Thus, the economic fortunes of the region are tied to three or four enterprises; in fact the ten largest enterprises account for 72 per cent of the oblast's industrial production. This makes the oblast particularly vulnerable should these enterprises falter or should they fail to make their tax payments to the local budget. It also means that the major donor districts in the oblast lie outside the capital city of Irkutsk. In 1996 the city of Irkutsk accounted for 23.6 per cent of total industrial production, the Angarsk region 30.1 per cent and Bratsk 14.9 per cent (Irkutsk Oblkomstat 1996a, p. 128). However, by 1998 Irkutsk's share had risen to 30 per cent of oblast industrial production, while the share of Angarsk had fallen to 11.7 per cent, but Bratsk had increased its share to 21 per cent (Irkutsk Oblkomstat 1998, p. 132). This spatial shift in relative importance reflects the varying fortunes of the key enterprises in the different regions, namely aluminium smelting and oil refining.

8.2   THE DYNAMICS OF TRANSITIONAL RECESSION

Information on production dynamics for the key region-forming sectors in Irkutsk oblast is presented in Table 8.2. Unfortunately, a full run of data is unavailable for aluminium production and oil refining, the two most important products. Nevertheless, the data that are available suggest that all is not well. All the key sectors show significant decline and in most cases the level of decline experienced in Irkutsk is slightly worse than in Russia as a whole. Thus, for example, between 1990 and 1997 national electricity generation declined by 22.9 per cent; it fell by 26.2 per cent in Irkutsk. The difference between national levels of decline and decline in Irkutsk is not that significant; however, these industries are the core of the regional economy.

The one area of relative success is aluminium smelting. Oblast-level data on the decline in the physical volume of industrial production between 1990 and 1995 show that total production fell by 36 per cent, but non-ferrous metals production fell by only 12 per cent (Irkutsk Oblkomstat 1996b, p. 67). In 1995 production of primary aluminium is

Table 8.2 Production of major industrial products in Irkutsk, 1990–98

	1990	1991	1992	1993	1994	1995	1996	1997	1998	98 % 90
Electricity (bn kWh)	67.1	64.5	62.7	61.9	57.3	59.5	55.6	49.5	52.4	78.1
Coal (mn ton)	24.3	23.3	20.5	18.2	15.6	14.9	14	12.4	14.4	59.3
Iron ore (mn ton)	5.6	4.8	4.7	4.8	4.5	4.2	4.1	3.7	2.6	46.4
Sawn timber (mn cu m)	30.7	27.7	23.5	15.6	10.9	12	9.8	7.9	8.0	26.1
Pulp ('000 tons)	1466.8	1215.4	1168.2	945.9	798.3	1178.5	907.0	703.0	689.4	47.0
Cardboard ('000 tons)	188	174.9	156.2	128.1	110.6	141	90.5	111	121.8	64.8

Sources:
1990–95: Goskomstat Rossii (1996).
1996–7: Goskomstat Rossii (1998b).
1998: Irkutsk Oblkomstat (1998).

estimated to have been 964,400 tons. In 1998 the production of primary aluminium is reported as 1,100,600 tons, 14 per cent up on the 1995 level. Thus, it is probably safe to conclude that aluminium smelting has remained relatively stable compared to all other industrial sectors in Irkutsk. The reasons for this relative success are explained in section 8.4, on foreign trade and investment activity.

Unfortunately, the performance of the Angarsk Oil Refinery is far less satisfactory. Again local statistical handbooks provide some idea of production trends. In 1995 the level of oil processing in the oblast was 68 per cent of 1990 production. In 1995 it is reported that the volume of primary processing of oil was 16.5 million tons. In 1998 the volume processed had fallen to 7.1 million tons, 45 per cent of the 1995 level. In September 1998 it was reported that the refinery was only operating at 32 per cent of capacity and that only one of its suppliers, its parent company Sidanko, was continuing to supply it with crude oil. In fact, during the first nine months of 1998 the company failed to receive 464,000 tons of oil it was due from suppliers and amassed salary arrears of nearly 85 million roubles (IEWS *Russian Regional Reporter*, 1998, 3 (36)). In May 1998 the parent company Sidanko was declared bankrupt and the future of the refinery remains uncertain. Given the importance of the refinery to the oblast budget, this is a severe problem for the region. At present it would seem that the regional economy is being kept afloat by the generating capacity of Irkutskenergo and the aluminium smelters at Irkutsk and Bratsk.

The situation on Sakhalin is even more difficult. Physical production data are shown in Table 8.3. The performance of the region-forming sectors shows a high degree of variability; the production of oil and gas has remained relatively stable, but the forestry sector has totally collapsed. Coal production has declined far more significantly than electricity generation and the oblast has gone from being an exporter to an importer of coal. The majority of electricity is generated in coal-fired · stations and the local utility company Sakhenergo has had major problems with non-payments and has been forced to reduce generation, often due to a physical shortage of coal. Consequently, power shortages are a common occurrence on Sakhalin. Sakhalinmorneftegaz (hereafter SMNG), a subsidiary of Rosneft', dominates the oil and gas sector. The various divisions of SMNG employ around 12,800 workers and the

Table 8.3   Production of major industrial products in Sakhalin, 1990–98

	1990	1991	1992	1993	1994	1995	1996	1997	1998	98 % 90
Coal ('000 tons)	4967	4359	4510	4250	2947	2756	2815	2143	1716	34.5
Electricity (mn kWh)	3160	3256	2791	3089	2712	2623	2408	2298	2250	71.2
Oil ('000 tons)	1918	1846	1677	1584	1627	1724	1662	1720	1696	88.4
Gas (mn cu m)	1832	1888	1730	1619	1481	1637	1782	1836.2	1807	98.6
Timber ('000 cu m)	2669	2394	2242	1589	1124	1088	930	453	112	4.2
Fish catch ('000 tons)	927	856	576	491	378	414	349	383	486	52.4

Sources:
1990–95: Sakhalin Oblkomstat (1996).
1996–7: Sakhalin Oblkomstat (1998b).
1998: Sakhalin Oblkomstat (1999).

company produces 90 per cent of the Russian Far East's oil and gas. There are two major producing regions in the northern regions of Sakhalin: Okha, which produces about 750,000 tons annually, and Nogliki, which produces 700,000 tons annually (*Pacific Oil and Gas Report* 1999, 2 (1), p. 51). The damage done by the 1995 earthquake at Neftegorsk, increasing production costs and the fall in world oil prices all hit the profitability of SMNG hard. If that were not enough, the company's major domestic customer, Khabarovsk kray, has amassed a substantial debt for unpaid deliveries of oil and gas. By late 1997 the outstanding debt was 600 billion roubles (*Sovetskiy Sakhalin* 13 December 1998, p. 1). The financial problems of SMNG have a direct impact on the oblast as the company provides about 40 per cent of total budgetary revenue (Bradshaw and Kirkow 1998, p. 1082). It is also clear that most of the onshore production is nearing the end of its productive life, but the oil industry and its associated support activities remain one of the few viable economic activities on Sakhalin. The future of SMNG is directly related to the fortunes of its parent company Rosneft' and to the success of the offshore projects. These are discussed in section 8.4, on foreign trade and investment.

Neither the coal mining nor the forestry sectors, both of which are concentrated in the mid-region of the island, are profitable. Coal mining suffers from high production costs, low labour productivity, obsolete equipment and a shortage of paying customers. Prior to the economic collapse, the industry produced about 5 million tons of coal a year and was organized under the monopoly producer Sakhugol'. At its peak the industry employed between 20,000 and 24,000 people; by 1997–8 total employment had fallen to 8,000 people (Northern Economics 1998, pp. 3–4). Until recently the federal Rosugol' company owned mines on Sakhalin; these have been transferred to oblast and municipal ownership. The subsequent privatization and restructuring of the industry has already seen the closure of seven underground mines and further closures are planned. In the process outstanding debts have been left on the books of the formerly state-owned enterprises. Combined losses in the coal industry amounted to 80 billion roubles by 1998 (*Sovetskiy Sakhalin* 13 December 1997, p. 1). Emphasis is now placed on the more efficient open-cast mines, and eventual employment in the sector could fall to between 1500 and 2000 workers. At present coal is the principal fuel for electricity generation; however, the longer-term plan is to use offshore natural gas to fuel thermal power stations. It is hoped that the coal mining industry can survive by exporting to Japan and elsewhere in Pacific Asia.

Forestry is in even worse shape than coal mining. In the past this sector accounted for a quarter of economic activity on Sakhalin; in early 1998 its share had fallen to 3–4 per cent (Northern Economics 1998, pp. 3–4). Only the timber harvesting and preparation sectors are said to be profitable; the pulp and paper industry is more or less finished. One of the problems hindering the profitability of the forestry enterprises is the fact that they have to maintain the infrastructure of the workers' settlements. At the end of 1997 the total debt of AO Sakhalinlesprom was 800 billion roubles (*Sovetskiy Sakhalin* 21 February 1998, p. 2). Attempts are being made to restructure the industry; most of the assets of Sakhalinlesprom have been transferred to a locally owned company Fineko. This new company is favoured by the Sakhalin administration and won over another company, Sakhalinles, which has 75 per cent foreign equity. Like the coal industry, forestry suffers from obsolete capital stock, but faces the additional impediment of high transportation costs. To transport a cubic metre of timber from the Smirnykhovsky District to the southern port of Korsakov costs $29; whereas the same cubic metre can be delivered from Irkutsk to the Black Sea port of Novorossisk for just $19 (*Sovetskiy Sakhalin* 16 May 1998, p. 1). Furthermore, the economic downturn in Japan has depressed timber prices. Most recently, devaluation of the rouble has increased the profitability of forestry, but without substantial investment in equipment and improvements in infrastructure Sakhalin is likely to continue to export modest volumes of round wood and timber.

The fishing industry is particularly important in the southern coastal regions and the Kurile Islands. The industry is divided among numerous small companies, some of which are joint ventures, and employs some 30,000 people. In 1998 the island had 26 fish-processing factories, up from 16 in 1996. However, as elsewhere in the Far Eastern fishery, much of their catch is sold illegally out at sea and the profits, and hence tax payments, never make it to Sakhalin. By the end of 1997 the fishery had a tax debt of 200 billion roubles. In 1989 the fishing harvest was about 1 million tons but, as Table 8.3 shows, the official catch declined substantially during the 1990s. During 1997–9 the fishing and fish-processing sectors have started to show signs of recovery. In 1998 the fishing industry paid 115 million roubles in tax, but oblast officials have complained that it should be at least twice that amount. The problem for Sakhalin is that its narrow resource specialization means that, with the possible exception of SMNG, it is dependent upon region-forming enterprises that are either bankrupt or are avoiding paying taxes, and even SMNG has run up tax arrears thanks to the non-payment problem with Khabarovsk kray. In short, the regional economy is not capable of supporting its current population without substantial injections of new revenue.

8.3 POLICIES OF ADAPTATION

This section considers the political situation in both regions and focuses upon the relationship between the economic problems discussed earlier and the strategies adopted by the regional administrations. Neither Irkutsk nor Sakhalin is a high-profile region on the Russian political map. The present governor of Irkutsk, Boris Govorin, was elected in July 1997, following the resignation of the long-standing governor Yurii Nozhikov. The present governor of Sakhalin, Igor Farkutdinov, is the third person to hold office since 1991. The first governor was Valentin Fedorov, who held office from 1991 to 1993; he was followed by Yevgenii Krasnoyarov, who was forced to resign over misuse of relief funds for the Kurile Islands in 1995. The present governor was appointed by President Yeltsin in 1995 and subsequently elected governor in October 1996. However, his victory has been contested because he won with only 39.47 per cent of the vote and a second round should have been held but was not. The Moscow courts have upheld the complaint, but nothing has been done. It is probably fair to say that both governors have tended to focus their efforts on getting a better deal from the federal government and on trying to provide support to inherited economic structures, rather than embark on ambitious new programmes to promote marketization. Both have fought hard to gain control over the regions' resources, with mixed results. Both regions have signed power-sharing agreements with the federal government and have benefited from a variety of special programmes; however, both regions' leaders undoubtedly feel that the federal government has failed to deliver on most of its promises. The following sections review the key economic issues and strategies of the two regions.

The Irkutsk region was one of the last regions to agree to sign the Federal Treaty of March 1992, reserving the right for a special clause on the ownership of natural resources and revenues from the privatization of federal enterprises operating in the region, particularly the gold producer Lenzoloto. For Irkutsk the key issue has been, and remains, gaining greater control over the region's resource base and the key region-forming enterprises; or, put another way, resisting outside control of those key enterprises. The 1996 power-sharing agreement between the oblast and the federal government provided the region with a greater degree of control over the economy. Perhaps most importantly, regional officials were given the right to represent state interests in running the fuel and energy complex through control of 40 per cent of the shares of Irkutskenergo. The significance of this concession was heightened after the management of Irkutskenergo and the oblast administration took RAO EES Rossii to the Russian Constitutional Court and the former was granted structural independence. Thus, Irkutskenergo is able to set its own tariffs and the oblast administration is able to influence the cost of electricity in the region. Given the logic that the existing capacities of the regional economy are based on the availability of cheap electricity, this is a critical factor in maintaining the profitability of local enterprises. For example, in early 1999 the cost of electricity in Irkutsk was 8.58 kopeks per kilowatt-hour (kWh), compared with 30 kopeks in neighbouring Buryatia (*Vostochno-Sibirskaya Pravda* 23 February 1999, pp. 1–2). By comparison, in May 1998 the cost of electricity on Sakhalin was 70 kopeks per kWh. However, RAO EES Rossii still controls both energy transmission lines and prices for electricity sold to other Siberian regions, and the continued availability of cheap local energy has given a boost to local export producers, principally the aluminium plants.

The importance attached to this issue may also be explained by the fact that the former governor Yurii Nozhikov came from Bratsk and was the former director of Bratskgessstroi, the construction company that built the Bratsk HEP. While governor, he fought to protect the interests of key region-forming enterprises, most notably Irkutsk-energo, the Angarsk Oil Refinery and Vostsibugol'. These companies were provided with support from the regional budget and were excluded from paying district (not regional) taxes. Thus, the dominance of a handful of giant enterprises in the Irkutsk economy largely accounts for the specific features of local corporatism and state protectionism that characterized economic strategy under Nozhikov. Cross-share ownership, insider privatization, preferential tax treatment and the presence both of top politicians on the management boards of leading regional companies and of executive directors in political office were distinctive characteristics of the Irkutsk-type corporatism. Forms of direct state intervention included price control for fuel, energy and housing; the setting up of oblast funds for budgetary procurement of agricultural products based on state orders, implying targets for local producers; and also barter with neighbouring regions. Less dirigiste forms of state regulation consisted of granting tax preferences, investment credits, subsidies and budgetary financing through authorized banks.[4]

As noted above, the backbone of this type of state-controlled economic policy was the special position of the local energy producer Irkutskenergo. However, by keeping energy prices low, Irkutskenergo effectively became a major regional credit institution due to mounting debts for supplied electricity which its management was increasingly determined to swap for equity. The company took a leading stake in the chemical plants Usol'skkhimprom and Sayanskkhimprom and the oil company Sidanko and it also participated in the regional gas programme through a 12 per cent stake in the oblast share.[5] Non-payments by the regional coal producer Vostsibugol' and the fact that Irkutskenergo uses locally produced coal for 50 per cent of its coal-fired electricity generation raised the issue of a possible structural merger between the two industrial giants into one holding company (*Vostochno-Sibirskaya Pravda* 3 June 1997, p. 2). In late 1996 the regional energy commissioner offered special discounts to those large industrial enterprises which paid their electricity bills regularly in cash. But the main breakthrough of the vicious circle of non-payments was

4. Interview with the head of the economics department of the previous Irkutsk oblast administration, A. Irgl, in June 1997. One way of administratively arranged barter between neighbouring regions was the organization of local trade fairs in which the Irkutsk oblast played a particular brokerage role through its committee for trade and services (*Vostochno-Sibirskaya Pravda* 6 March 1997, p. 2).
5. Interview with the deputy director of Irkutskenergo, V. Mezhevich, June 1997. After accepting the position of deputy first governor in the new administration of Boris Govorin, Valentin Mezhevich announced in September 1997 that the entire Irkutsk industry owed Irkutskenergo 3.5 trillion roubles, a figure which exceeded the total assets of local banks. Thus, Irkutskenergo was effectively propping up the rest of the oblast's economy (*Vostochno-Sibirskaya Pravda* 20 September 1997, p. 4).

seen both in new industrial expansion, including gold mining in Sukhoi Log and a new aluminium smelter in Ust'-Ilimsk, and the export of up to 20 billion kWh of electricity per year to China, which accounts roughly for the amount of excess production that Irkutskenergo cannot sell on the domestic market (*Segodnya* 18 January 1997, p. 5).

In late 1997, the growing non-payment problem and the general decline of industrial production brought about the fall of the Nozhikov administration. Because the administration was too heavily involved in the direct running of the economy, when the oblast economy faltered it was blamed for mismanagement. According to the regional tax inspection, mutual payment settlements or write-offs between local enterprises and the oblast budget amounted to 50 per cent of tax collection in 1996, which dramatically reduced cash revenues earmarked for wage payments in budgetary organizations (Zelent 1997, p. 35). In the spring of 1997 governor Nozhikov blamed the federal authorities for not having transferred an accrued amount of 2 trillion roubles for wages in health care, education and other state-financed sectors and threatened to stop the payment of federal taxes (*Segodnya* 4 March 1997, p. 1). His anti-crisis programme, announced on 14 April 1997 in a special address to the Russian government, contained elements of state protectionism and the attempted reassertion of administrative corporate control. The programme included a call for the renationalization of leading industries, particularly the fuel and energy sector; the enforcement of anti-monopoly policy with regard to energy and transport tariffs; the administrative control of the flow of budgetary and extra-budgetary resources; the charging of rent for the use of natural resources; and an increase in import tariffs on luxury goods (*Delovoy mir* 17 April 1997, p. 1). But this desperate attempt to reassert local state control over major regional assets and leading industrial giants was more a publicity stunt driven by the implicit recognition of increasingly lost administrative influence over economic management. A week later Nozhikov was forced to resign and to call gubernatorial elections in July 1997.

One of the problems for governor Nozhikov was that the power base of the regional administration was undermined by the progress of market reform. The influx of Moscow-based and foreign capital taking control of major industrial enterprises was particularly problematic. Marketization and the opening up of the Irkutsk economy had not only blurred organizational boundaries between private and public, but the entry of new economic agents complicated the existing governance structure in industry while property rights were redefined. The Irkutsk administration's residual claim over net revenue streams was undermined by a new category of taxpayers, and state shares had to be relinquished to outsiders with more liquid assets.

Analysis of changing ownership rights provides an interesting picture of the reconfiguration of economic management and corporate governance in Irkutsk oblast. The London-based TransWorld Group now owns the Bratsk aluminium smelter, the region's major export producer. Even the flagship of the Irkutsk economy, Irkutskenergo, became increasingly owned by foreign capital.[6] The Australian company Star Mining gained a foothold in the gold mining company Lenzoloto, but soon ran into financial difficulties which were further compounded when the initial privatization of Lenzoloto was declared illegal. In addition to growing foreign ownership, there has also been an influx of Moscow-based capital. As noted earlier, in 1997 the Angarsk oil refinery came under the control of Sidanko (and implicitly ONEKSIMbank) and was immediately subjected to substantial downsizing as part of a major restructuring programme by the new owners (*Vostochno-Sibirskaya Pravda* 21 January 1998, p. 1). Sidanko had acquired 38 per cent of its share in spring 1997, but was faced with the oil refinery's debt liabilities of 2.5 trillion roubles for 1996 alone (*Finansy v Sibiri* 1997, no. 6, pp. 46–7).

The nature of institutional arrangements has so far not changed since Boris Govorin, the former mayor of Irkutsk city, was elected governor in July 1997. Before entering political office he had worked at Irkutskenergo and offered one of the company's deputy directors, Valentin Mezhevich, the post of first deputy governor. While Nozhikov's political support came from the Bratsk industrial management, the new governor could build on networks of the Irkutsk industrial elite. The only real difference in Govorin's approach is that the leading industrial enterprises are expected to pay local taxes. The combination of regional managers and technocrats in the oblast administration has changed, but

---

6. Among the main shareholders of Irkutskenergo are the Bank of Bermuda (Cayman Islands) with 10.9 per cent, Crawford Holding Ltd (10.4 per cent) and the working collective of Irkutskenergo (7.9 per cent). Another 30.9 per cent of shares are more widely dispersed among Russian and foreign shareholders while 39.9 per cent are in the ownership of tne Irkutsk oblast administration (*Izvestiya* 18 October 1997, p. 2).

the previous policies of local corporatism and state protectionism in economic management remain. For example, the governor protested at actions by the federal government to stop the internal tolling operations on which the oblast's aluminium smelters depended. However, the August 1998 financial crisis and the subsequent problems at the Angarsk oil refinery have revealed real limitations to the administration's ability to protect the key region-forming enterprises. The governor blames the problems at Angarsk on the incompetence of the ONEKSIMbank and Sidanko management (*Vostochno-Sibirskaya Pravda* 3 February 1999, p. 2). Closure of the refinery would be a major setback for the oblast's already shaky finances.

The problems that face the Sakhalin administration are rather different. The oblast is a recipient of support through the federal budget, whereas for much of the 1990s Irkutsk was not (see Chapter 5). Sakhalin also benefits, in principle, from a number of special programmes. According to the 1998 budget, 68.2 per cent of the oblast administration's budget came from federal transfers. The region benefits from the Presidential Programme on the Economic and Social Development of the Far East and TransBaykal; there is also a special programme for the development of the Kurile Islands. However, as with all such programmes, the level of federal funding provided is lower than planned (see Chapter 5 for the general failure of such programmes, and Chapter 7 for the parallel case in Krasnodar).

All forms of federal payments to the oblast seem subject to arbitrary reductions and delays. Sakhalin signed a power-sharing agreement in 1996, but has not been able to gain the level of control over resource development enjoyed by Irkutsk. This is in large part because the offshore oil and gas fields lie on the continental shelf beyond the jurisdiction of the oblast. The governor has complained that the federal government collects too much money from the oblast in the fees it charges for various services and the prices charged by the so-called natural monopolies, such as mail and transport (IEWS *Regional Profiles, Sakhalin* 1998, p. 1).

With the possible exception of the fishing industry, none of the island's major enterprises has attracted substantial outside interest. Instead, the federal authorities have handed over ownership of economic assets such as the coal mines to the oblast administration, which has then sought to rationalize and privatize enterprises to reduce the burden placed on the oblast budget. At the same time, the single most important enterprise, SMNG, remains under federal control through its parent company Rosneft'. Over the past few years the oblast's economic strategy has focused on two key issues: promoting the development of offshore oil and gas potential; and restructuring the island's fuel-energy complex, including the persistent non-payment problem and the attendant energy crisis. In the longer term the oblast administration plans to use income from oil and gas production to modernize the forestry and fish-processing industries.[7]

Unlike Irkutsk, the Sakhalin administration has limited direct influence over the key region-forming enterprises. The administration has one member on SMNG's board of directors and has some equity in the Petrosakh joint venture. Of late, the oblast administration has shown a desire to become more directly involved in the island's economy. In the aftermath of the August 1998 financial crisis, the island found itself with very few functioning banks. In an attempt to provide some stability, the oblast administration has taken a 50 per cent share of the Sakhalin-Vest bank.

The creation of the administration's own oil company, Sakhalinskaya Neftyannaya Kompaniya (Sakhalin Oil Company), is a much more significant development. The aim is for Sakhalin's oil production to provide a feedstock for Central Fuels' refineries in the Moscow region. When asked why the administration needed its own oil company, the governor pointed out that the oblast already had a 5 per cent share of Petrosakh and the company was to develop gas deposits near Yuzhno-Sakhalinsk as a means of resolving the energy crisis. However, the longer-term plan is for the company to participate in the offshore oil and gas projects.[8] As a beginning, Rosneft and SMNG have transferred a combined equity stake of 5 per cent in the Sakhalin-3 (Kirinskii block) offshore oil and gas project to the Sakhalin Oil Company (*Russia and FSU Monitor* 1999, 2 (11), p. 6). This modest start may enable the oblast to participate directly in the offshore projects, but the company will have to fund its involvement in the development stage of the project. It will also ensure a share of the profits as well as royalties and tax income. However, it raises a potential conflict of interest, as the oblast administration could potentially be both a developer and a regulator. The governor may feel that only

7. Interview with Ivan Malakhov, first vice-governor, Sakhalin oblast administration, June 1998.
8. Interview with Governor Farkutdinov, December 1998.

direct involvement can guarantee that the region will benefit from the oil and gas projects. Equally, a resolution of the island's energy crisis may provide the basis for his re-election campaign in autumn 2000.

8.4 THE ROLE OF FOREIGN TRADE AND INVESTMENT

From the discussion so far, it is apparent that foreign trade and investment play an important role in both regions. For Irkutsk, export-oriented energy-intensive industrial activity has been a key component of the region's relative success post-1991. For Sakhalin, increased foreign trade activity has compensated for the distance of the region from traditional markets and suppliers in European Russia. In both instances the attraction of foreign investors is critical for the future development of the respective regions' resource-based economies.

In terms of the current level of foreign trade activity, Irkutsk is the more important region. According to Goskomstat Rossii (1998b, p. 783), in 1997 the value of reported exports to non-CIS states attributed to Irkutsk oblast was $2242.5 million or 3.2 per cent of the total value of exports declared by Russia's regions. The equivalent values for Sakhalin were $336.5 million and 0.5 per cent respectively. In 1997 Irkutsk's CIS exports were worth $47 million and Sakhalin's $2.5 million. On the import side, in 1997 the total value of non-CIS imports in Irkutsk was $393.9 million, 0.7 per cent of Russia's regional imports and for Sakhalin $302.8 million and 0.5 per cent respectively. Imports from elsewhere in the CIS totalled $244.3 million in Irkutsk and $9.8 million on Sakhalin. The large imbalance between exports and imports in the case of Irkutsk suggests that there are specialist export activities located within the oblast. The following sub-section looks at these foreign trade activities in more detail.

8.4.1 Irkutsk's Foreign Trade Activity

As transitional recession has struck and domestic demand for Irkutsk's industrial production has declined, so foreign economic relations have played a growing role in the region's economy. At the end of the 1980s the share of exports in industrial production stood at 6–8 per cent; by

1995 it had risen to 43 per cent (Chernikov 1998, p. 383). In August 1998 it was reported that 50 per cent of Irkutsk's products are exported (IEWS *Russian Regional Reporter* 20 August 1998). In 1995, according to local statistics, the value of exports was $2883.6 million and imports $934.5 million (Irkutsk Oblkomstat 1996b, p. 96). In 1995, 96.3 per cent of exports went to non-CIS states, but the CIS still accounted for 60 per cent of imports.

The dominant exports are aluminium, pulp and forest products. These three commodities accounted for 82 per cent of Irkutsk's exports in the first 11 months of 1998; but aluminium was by far the most important export earner, accounting for 63.4 per cent of total exports (Irkutsk Oblkomstat 1998, p. 42). Chernikov (1998, p. 383) reports that in 1995 aluminium accounted for 43.1 per cent of total exports; pulp and paper 16 per cent; chemicals 13.2 per cent; oil products 11.8 per cent; and forestry and timber products 7.0 per cent.

Imports are dominated by machinery and equipment and food products; however, as explained below, the true value of imports is probably depressed owing to the fact that internal tolling operations supply the aluminium industry with shipments of alumina via elsewhere in Russia and the CIS. The bulk of exports go to the Asia–Pacific region (65.1 per cent in 1995, of which Japan accounted 26.9 per cent). This represents a change from the Soviet period when exports were oriented towards fellow CMEA states. In fact, the Bratsk pulp and paper plant was a joint CMEA development project. This change in geographic orientation and an increasing reliance upon aluminium is a direct consequence of the expansion of tolling operations.

Classic tolling operations involve a company which processes raw materials that are provided by another company. In the current context, the other foreign company organizes the purchase of alumina which is then smelted in Siberia; the foreign company then arranges the sale of the aluminium. In Russia so-called 'internal tolling' has also become important. Here the foreign company provides the Russian company with credit which is then used to purchase alumina in Russia or elsewhere in the CIS. The credit is repaid when the aluminium is sold. Tolling operations have served to utilize excess capacity generated by the collapse in domestic demand; they have also allowed Russia's smelters to continue operating despite the fact that they have no real money to pay for raw materials. These operations have been made possible, in part, by the fact that the newly privatized companies have inherited the industrial capacity at a low cost and have no capital payments to service. At the same time, local prime costs are low by international standards. When tolling operations began, the foreign partner gained a profit of $300–400 per ton of exported aluminium.

However, there are also a number of problems associated with these tolling operations. First, they are vulnerable to increases in domestic costs, particularly for transportation. This is especially true of the operations in East Siberia, which are thousands of kilometres from ports on the Black Sea and in the Far East. In response to the financial crisis in August 1998, the federal Railways Ministry now sets shipping fees to foreign companies in US dollars. This is less of a problem for the aluminium industry as it has access to hard currency; however, it has been a major blow to the chemical industry in Irkutsk which has had to curtail exports to other CIS states.

Second, the sudden influx of cheap Russian aluminium on world markets, combined with depressed demand due to economic recession in the West, led to falling prices, accusations of dumping and EU sanctions. Third, the privatization of Russia's ferrous and non-ferrous metallurgical plants provided an opportunity for foreign investors to gain control of the production process within Russia, and this upset Russian business interests, who played the nationalist card. Eventually, the Russian government took action, some of it infringing shareholders' rights, to stop foreign companies gaining control of the aluminium smelting industry.

In the mid-1990s TransWorld Metals Ltd, a subsidiary of Trans-World Group (London), was able to gain controlling stakes in a number of Russian smelters, including the plant at Bratsk. The company had long been involved in smelting operations in the Soviet Union, but privatization offered an opportunity to control Russian production. Often shares were brought by a third party on behalf of TransWorld Metals Ltd. Some plant directors refused to recognize TransWorld's ownership rights. After much wrangling, TransWorld has reportedly lost control over the Novolipetsk and Sayansk plants, but retains control of the Bratsk aluminium plant.

A final problem with tolling is that it represents a substantial tax loss for the Russian government. Internal tolling operations free aluminium producers from paying tariffs on imported material and the final exported product as well as VAT on processed ore. Tax collectors estimate that tolling operations cost the state $300 million a year in lost revenue (IEWS *Russian Regional Reporter*, 5 November 1998). It is no surprise, then, that the short-lived Kiriyenko government tried to ban internal tolling; nor, perhaps, that the decision was later reversed and tolling allowed to continue through 1999. None the less, the future is still uncertain. The devaluation of the rouble has helped to keep domestic production costs low, but the capital stock is ageing and requires substantial new investment. If domestic production costs, particularly transport and electricity, reach world levels, then tolling in East Siberia will cease to be profitable simply because the smelters are too far from sources of supply and final markets. Perhaps by then domestic demand will have picked up.

Any decline in the profitability of the aluminium plants in Irkutsk would have an immediate impact on the local economy. The smelters at Bratsk and Irkutsk consume about half of locally produced electricity, they are the largest clients of the East Siberian Railroads and are major contributors to the oblast budget (IEWS *Russian Regional Reporter*, 23 April 1998). One solution for the region's economy is to develop new resources, but this requires the kind of capital investment that only foreign companies can provide. Thus, the region faces a dilemma: it needs to attract outside investors to diversify its economy and provide new revenue streams, but it wishes to retain close control over the activities of key region-forming enterprises and see them continue, regardless of their long-term profitability.

8.4.2 Foreign Investment Activity in Irkutsk

According to local statistics, during the period January–September 1998 there were 126 joint ventures operational in Irkutsk oblast (Irkutsk Oblkomstat 1998, p. 45). Information from Goskomstat Rossii (1999b, p. 252) indicates that there were 19 enterprises with foreign participation operating in Irkutsk oblast in 1998. These 19 enterprises represent a mere 0.5 per cent of the Russian total, but they accounted for 1.9 per cent of the total output of enterprises with foreign participation. Local statistics record that accumulated foreign investment at the beginning of 1998 was $134.2 million and 437.4 million roubles (the rouble figure being reinvested local profits). Between January and September 1998 a further $106.8 million and 90.1 million roubles were invested in the Oblast (Irkutsk Oblkomstat 1998, p. 40). According to Goskomstat Rossii (1999a, p. 382), during 1998 foreign investment in

Irkutsk totalled $135.2 million, including $51.9 million in the form of direct investment. This represents 79.3 per cent of total foreign investment in East Siberia, but only 1.2 per cent of total foreign investment in Russia.

These data on foreign economic activity reveal two things. First, that there are major problems with the statistics, particularly when comparing local data with data from Goskomstat Rossii. The net result is that we do not have a clear idea of the scale and impact of foreign investment in Russia's regions. Second, as unreliable as the data are, they do suggest that, given its industrial profile and level of foreign trade activity, Irkutsk oblast is underperforming when it comes to attracting foreign investment. The reasons for this become clear when one looks at the current status of the major foreign investment projects in the region.

There are two large-scale resource development projects in Irkutsk oblast whose future is dependent upon foreign investment: the Sukhoi Log gold mining project and the Kovytka natural gas project. Both have troubled histories and uncertain futures.

The Sukhoi Log gold field is located in the Bodaybo district in the north-west of Irkutsk oblast. The region comes under the jurisdiction of the Lenozoloto gold mining concern. In 1992 the Australian company Star Mining gained a foothold in Lenzoloto, acquiring 4.8 per cent of its shares by committing itself to provide bank guarantees for a credit of $500 million and paying another $250 million to increase its share ownership to 31 per cent (*Delovoy mir*, 4 December 1997, p. 1). Other shareholders included Atomredmetzoloto, the Irkutsk oblast administration, the workers' collective of Lenzoloto and the federal Ministry of State Property. Together, Star Mining and Lenzoloto were to develop the Sukhoi Log gold mines which have estimated reserves of 1025 tons of gold. However, an average of only 2.56 grammes per ton of ore means that the project has high extraction costs. Before the project had even started there was an ownership dispute between the federal government and the Irkustk oblast administration.

These problems aside, financial difficulties and the fact that the gold price was almost halved during 1996–7 forced Star Mining to refrain from making further financial injections. As a result, the management of Lenzoloto has had to give up its 49 per cent share in the Sukhoi Log gold mines. It was agreed that there should be a new tender for selling the rights to the Sukhoi Log gold deposits but the federal authority and the oblast administration could not agree on the conditions for the tender. The oblast will own 5 per cent of the company set up to do the actual mining. The successful bidder must pay Lenzoloto $50 million for the work already done; 3 per cent of what it mines for the right to work the deposit; and 7.8 per cent of sales for further exploitation of the raw material base (IEWS *Russian Regional Reporter* 9 April 1998). Moscow proposed a closed tender with only Russian bidders, while the oblast administration wanted an open tender to encourage foreign participation. Foreign observers considered the price high, given the low gold content of the deposit. The August 1998 financial crisis probably resolved the dispute between the centre and the region by removing many of the Russian bidders from contention. The tender process was further delayed, nevertheless, in the spring of 1999 a number of foreign companies registered interest in the project. In 1998 four foreign companies received licences to conduct geological explorations of the deposit and are reportedly convinced that the mine is very valuable. Agreement has also to be reached on the amount of compensation to be paid to Lenzoloto and Star Mining for the work already carried out. The Canadian company Placer Dome International has gone as far as registering a subsidiary Placer Dome Baykal to be in a position to participate in the tender (IEWS *Russian Regional Investor* 4 March 1999). The experience of Star Mining and other foreign resource companies in Russia (including those on Sakhalin) suggests that winning the tender is only the beginning and that there are many hurdles to be overcome before any project becomes a reality.

The second large-scale resource development project involves the exploitation of natural gas deposits in the Kovytka region 350 km north-east of the city of Irkutsk. In the early 1990s British Petroleum (BP) and Norway's Statoil carried out preliminary investigations into the possible development of the Kovytkinskoye gas fields discovered in 1987 with about 600–800 billion cu m of reserves and the Verkhnechonskoye oil fields, discovered in 1978 with an estimated 600–650 million metric tons of reserves (*Oil and Gas Journal* 1993, 9 (1), p. 30). After careful consideration, BP and Statoil concluded that 'there was no feasible way to export the province's oil or gas, thereby obtaining an adequate return in hard currency on the combine's investment'. Furthermore, the commercial conditions at that time were not right to justify further investment. First, the oil and gas reserves were modest. Second, the amount of capital required, in the region of $7 billion, was high and it was uncertain where the finance might come from. Third, the priority for the project seemed to be the development of the region's gas fields, but this required substantial infrastructure investment and secure markets.

Nevertheless, a joint-stock company called RUSIA-Petroleum was set up to develop what has become known as the Irkutsk Gas Programme. The initial aim of the company was to develop the oil deposits to supply crude oil to the Angarsk oil refinery, also owned by Sidanko. However, the Irkutsk Gas Programme is fast becoming a key component of improved economic relations between Russia and China (Andrews-Speed 1998). A project is now envisaged to develop the Kovytka gas fields and deliver gas by a 3700 km pipeline via Ulan-Bator in Mongolia to China's Pacific coast port of Lianyunggang and then possibly to South Korea and Japan. The possibility of a secured market for Irkutsk gas renewed BP's interest in the project. In late 1997 Sidanko and BP agreed to create a strategic alliance for exploration of the Kovytka gas fields. The project was part of a larger alliance that saw BP acquire a 10 per cent share in Sidanko at a cost of $650 million. On returning to Irkutsk, the vice-president of BP Exploration, Ian Rushby, said: 'One of the most decisive factors in BP's decision to revisit the deposit after a five-year break was the determination of the Chinese government to import natural gas' (IEWS *Russian Regional Reporter*, 29 January 1998).

Gaining access to the Kovytka project was a major reason for BP's 1997 strategic alliance with Sidanko. Unfortunately, Russia's financial crisis has dealt a severe blow to that alliance. Vladimir Potanin's Interros Group, which includes ONEXIMbank and owns 40 per cent of Sidanko, was very badly hit by the financial crisis. In addition, Sidanko has its own financial problems, which include the Angarsk refinery. On 18 May 1999 Sidanko was declared bankrupt and the Moscow court ordered that Sidanko be placed under external management. This decision was strongly resisted by BP (now BP-Amoco), but it remains to be seen what will happen to Sidanko's assets. It is possible that restructuring will see the spin-off of the Angarsk refinery and Kondpetroleum. Meanwhile, in February 1999, as part of a Russian–Chinese summit, agreement was reached to conduct a feasibility study of the Kovytka project. RUSIA-Petroleum and the China National United Oil Corporation signed an agreement to prepare a feasibility study that will take up to three years and cost $100–120 million. Clearly, there is a long way to go before this project becomes a reality and much will depend upon the outcome of the Sidanko situation. Meanwhile, Gazprom has hinted that it might be interested in supplying West Siberian gas to China.

8.4.3 Sakhalin's Foreign Trade Activity

During the 1990s there has been a substantial increase in the value of Sakhalin's foreign trade turnover, from $309.7 million in 1992 to $977.1 million in 1998.This growth can be explained by a reorientation of local production away from traditional markets elsewhere in Russia to markets in north-east Asia and an increased reliance on the import of food and consumer goods. Both these developments reflect the increasing isolation of Sakhalin from the European regions of Russia, mainly due to increases in transportation costs. In geographical terms, hitherto subsidized Sakhalin is no longer part of Russia's core economy.

Four branches of economic activity provide the bulk of Sakhalin's export: oil and oil products (35.4 per cent in 1997); fish and sea products (20.5 per cent); services (such as transportation, drilling wells and related work) (13 per cent); and timber and wood (7.8 per cent) (Sakhalin Oblkomstat 1998, pp. 8–9). Practically all of Sakhalin's exports go to non-CIS states. In 1998 Sakhalin exported 1.8 million tons of oil and oil products: 59.1 per cent of oil exports went to Ireland; 28 per cent to Singapore; and 8.8 per cent to China; while 52.6 per cent of oil product exports went to Singapore; 24.9 per cent to Hong Kong; and 22.5 per cent to Cyprus (Sakhalin Oblkomstat 1998, p. 95). In 1997, 90.5 per cent of oil exports went to Ireland. This can be explained by the fact that part of the financial assistance given to SMNG after the 1995 Neftegorsk earthquake included a licence to export West Siberian oil to Western Europe. Japan is the most important market for fish exports, receiving 43.1 per cent of total exports in 1998, followed by Germany (36.3 per cent), the USA (9.5 per cent) and South Korea (8.3 per cent) (Sakhalin Oblkomstat 1999, p. 93).

As noted earlier, the official figures for fish exports massively under-report the level of trade. In a recent announcement, the governor of Sakhalin has suggested the creation of an Economic Security Council on Sakhalin that would include all of the region's security agencies. One of the first targets for the Council would be the fishing industry for failing to report the actual size of their catches and avoiding paying taxes (IEWS *Russian Regional Report* 25 March 1999). This is done by selling part of the catch offshore and banking the proceeds abroad. (See Chapter 9, where the same practice is discussed for Kaliningrad and Primor'ye.) The fishing industry is closely related to organized crime and it will be a true test of the governor's resolve to improve tax collection.

Export earnings from oil- and gas-related service activities are tied to the offshore oil and gas projects and these are discussed below. The final export sector is forestry. During 1998, Sakhalin companies exported 407,000 cu m of timber, 3800 cu m of lumber, 9400 thousand cu m of low-grade wood and 100 tons of pulp. The most important markets for timber were Japan (67.4 per cent) and South Korea (31.7 per cent). Likewise Japan accounted for 72.9 per cent of lumber exports and South Korea the remaining 27.1 per cent (*Sakhalin Oil and Gas News* 13 June 1999, p. 2).

While the Sakhalin economy has increased its export orientation, the narrow specialization of the region's economy, combined with a heavy reliance upon Japan and South Korea, made it susceptible to the economic downturn caused by the Asian economic crisis in 1997 (see Figure 8.2). In fact, one could argue that the Asian crisis has been more

Figure 8.2   Sakhalin foreign trade, 1992–8

damaging to the island's economy than the Russian financial crisis that followed. Furthermore, Sakhalin has been hurt by the decline in oil prices, which have reduced the export earnings of SMNG and cast doubt on the economics of the offshore oil and gas projects.

Sakhalin's imports are dominated by machinery and equipment (1998 – 69.8 per cent) and food products (1998 – 9.9 per cent) (Sakhalin Oblkomstat 1999, p. 92). The growing importance of machinery and equipment imports is directly related to the progress of the offshore oil and gas products. In dollar terms the value of food imports actually fell between 1997 ($70 million) and 1998 ($48.4 million); this is probably due to the dramatic fall in the value of the rouble following the August 1998 financial crisis. The combination of depressed export markets, low commodity prices and currency devaluation means that Sakhalin cannot rely on its current foreign trade activities to rejuvenate the economy and maintain living standards.

8.4.4   Foreign Investment Activity on Sakhalin

As with Irkutsk, the level of foreign investment activity differs depending on whose statistics you believe. According the Goskomstat Rossii (1999b, p. 253), at the end of 1998 there were 51 enterprises with foreign capital operational on Sakhalin (1.2 per cent of the Russian total). However, these 51 enterprises accounted for 11.4 per cent of total investment in basic capital. This makes sense as many of the enterprises involved in oil and gas exploration are registered as joint ventures, particularly the sub-contractors. Goskomstat Rossii (1999b, p. 382) also reports that during 1998 Sakhalin received $136 million in foreign investment, 97 per cent of which was in the form of foreign direct investment (FDI). However, Sakhalin Oblkomstat (1999, p. 96) reports that during the first nine months of 1998 the region received $355.9 million in foreign investment, 96.3 per cent in the form of FDI. In 1996 the region received $131.4 million and in 1997 $163.6 million. Thus, there is a clear upward trajectory in the scale of foreign investment on Sakhalin. Most of the investment is in the energy sector: 84 per cent in 1997 and 72.1 per cent in the first nine months of 1998; but the food industry, construction and geological services are also important. Joint ventures and companies with foreign capital are active in the oil industry, in forestry and in fishing. Cable and Wireless (UK) also provide telecommunications services on the island. The United States is the most important source of investment, accounting for 78.1 per cent of total investment in the first nine months of 1998, followed by Cyprus (10.2 per cent), Great Britain (8.9 per cent) and Japan (1.5 per cent). It is necessary to examine the offshore oil and gas projects to understand this pattern of activity.

The history of Sakhalin's offshore oil and gas projects is complex, and a detailed analysis is beyond the scope of this chapter (for further details, see Paik 1995, pp. 206–21; Sagers 1995; and Bradshaw 1998). For our purposes it is sufficient to describe the nature of the current projects, their present stage of development and the short- and medium-term impacts that they will have on the Sakhalin economy. The various projects and their participants are shown in Table 8.4, while Map 8.3 shows the relative location of the various blocks. If nothing else, Table 8.4 illustrates the complexity of the Sakhalin projects, a situation that has been further complicated by the merger of EXXON and Mobil and the proposed merger between BP-Amoco and ARCO. Offshore exploration dates back to the mid-1970s when, in the aftermath of the 1974 energy crisis, Japan sought to diversify its energy supply. In 1975 a compensation agreement was reached between the USSR and the Sakhalin Oil Development Cooperation Company Ltd (Sodeco), a consortium of 18 Japanese companies created to represent Japanese interests. Under the terms of the agreement, the Japanese partners provided credit to fund exploration. These credits were to be paid off once economically viable fields were discovered. Exploration between 1976 and 1983 resulted in the discovery of the large Odoptu and Chayvo offshore oil, gas and condensate fields with total reserves of 67 million tons of oil and 172 billion cu m of gas. Unfortunately, these early successes soon fell foul of the changing geopolitical situation, low energy prices and the collapse of the USSR. Consequently, the project was put on hold without the Soviet Union repaying the loan, which stood at $276.6 million. None the less, between 1983 and 1990 SMNG continued exploration activity without direct foreign assistance.

In 1989–90 the then USSR Ministry of Oil and Gas Industry, in conjunction with McDermott (US), examined the possibility of setting up a joint venture to develop some of the fields discovered by SMNG. In late 1990, a proposal came from Palmco (US–Korean joint venture) to develop some of the Sakhalin field on a compensation basis. The proposal included plans to transport the oil and gas to Sakhalin and then to export a portion of the gas. The collapse of the Soviet Union also

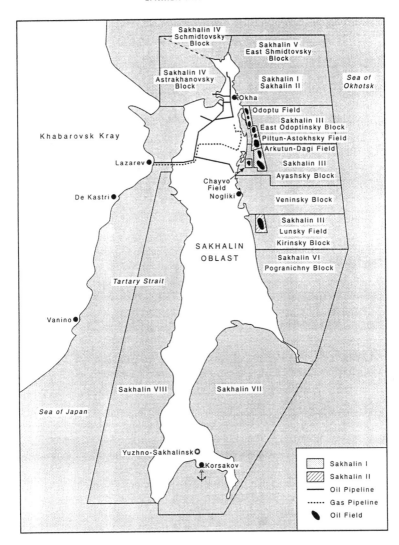

Map 8.3   Sakhalin: oil and gas projects

Table 8.4　Sakhalin offshore oil and gas projects and participants[a]

Project	Partners	
Sakhalin-1 PSA: Still in exploration phase	Sodeco (Japan) EXXON (US) Rosneft' (Russia) SMNG (Russia)	(30%) (30%) (17%) (23%)
Sakhalin-2 (Sakhalin Energy Investment Company) PSA: stage one: early oil July 1999	Marathon (US) Mitsui (Japan) Shell (UK/Netherlands) Mitsubishi (Japan)	(37.5%) (25%) (25%) (12.5%)
Sakhalin-3 (Kirinskii Block) (Pegastar) PSA: final agreement yet to be reached	Mobil (US) Texaco (US) Rosneft' (Russia) SMNG (Russia) (Sakhalin Oil Company) (Russia)	(33.3%) (33.3%)
Sakhalin–3 PSA: Awaiting approval of Federation 　Council and State Duma	EXXON (US) Rosneft' (Russia) SMNG (Russia)	(66.7%)
Sakhalin-4 Awaiting PSA and tender	ARCO (US) Rosneft' (Russia) SMNG (Russia)	
Sakhalin-5 Awaiting PSA and tender	BP-Amoco (UK) Rosneft' (Russia) SMNG (Russia)	
Sakhalin-6 Awaiting PSA and tender	Mobil (US) Texaco (US) Rosneft' (Russia) SMNG (Russia)	

Notes:
[a] As at June 1999.
At the time of writing EXXON and Mobil were in the process of merging and BP-Amoco were merging with ARCO.

Source: Based on information in Pacific Russia Information Group (1999).

promoted new foreign interest in Sakhalin as technological advances made offshore production less risky. In May 1991, a tender competition was held to develop the offshore fields. The governor of Sakhalin, then Valentin Fyodorov, sought to influence the tender process to gain maximum benefit for Sakhalin. He hoped that the foreign oil companies could be forced to build major infrastructure projects on the island. Six consortiums bid for the tender. The outcome of the tender process was delayed because of Fyodorov's interventions. In January 1992 the announcement was made that the McDermott–Marathon–Mitsui (MMM) bid was the winner. This was against the wishes of governor Fyodorov who favoured the EXXON–Sodeco bid. The Sakhalin administration tried to have the decision overturned, but failed. However, the tender was downgraded to the right to complete a feasibility study. In September 1992 Shell joined the consortium (creating MMMS) and in December 1992 Mitsubishi joined (creating MMMMS). At the end of 1992 the MMMMS consortium submitted its feasibility study. In March 1993 the study received the approval of the Russian government and the consortium created the Sakhalin Investment Energy Investment Company (hereafter Sakhalin Energy) to manage the development, production, financing and marketing of the project. In June 1993 the Sakhalin Energy Production Sharing Agreement (PSA) was signed and in December of that year the State Duma passed a Law on Production Sharing. However, it was recognized that the PSA law was an inadequate basis for large-scale capital investment as it was in contradiction to many existing Russian laws. Nevertheless, Sakhalin Energy pressed ahead with further exploration work and expects first oil to be produced in July 1999. This marks the first oil production in Russia under a PSA.

The project is known as Sakahlin-2 because the original Sodeco project is known as Sakhalin-1. The Sakhalin-2 development strategy envisages the early production of oil using an offshore production platform (the Molikpaq) and storage tanker (the Okha). The harsh operating conditions offshore restrict production to the summer months. Investment in stage one, known as the Vityaz complex, is in the region of $700 million. Financing for this first stage has come in part from the European Bank for Reconstruction and Development (EBRD), Japan's Export–Import Bank and the US Overseas Private Investment Corporation (OPIC) who together have signed loan agreements for $348 million during 1997 and 1998. The second stage of the project will involve the construction of oil and gas pipelines onshore and to the south of Sakhalin for processing prior to export. The cost of the pipelines is $1–1.5 billion and the cost of a liquefied natural gas (LNG) plant is in the region of $3 billion. The total budget of the Sakhalin-2 project is $10 billion (Pacific Russian Information Group 1999, p. 11). A decision to move to the second phase has yet to be made and will depend on market conditions and whether or not the infrastructure costs can be shared with other Sakhalin projects.

Not surprisingly, the development of Sakhalin-2 sparked renewed interest in the original Sodeco project. Now known as Sakhalin-1, this project involves a restructured version of the original Sodeco consortium, EXXON and Rosneft' and SMNG. Additional acreage has been given to the project to cover the outstanding Soviet debt. EXXON Neftegas Ltd operates the Sakhalin-1 project, which, unlike Sakhalin-2, has substantial Russian participation. All the partners are expected to contribute to the exploration and development costs of the project. A feasibility study was approved in 1994 and Sakhalin-1 was granted a PSA in June 1996. In September 1996 Sakhalin-1 drilled the first test well in Russia under a PSA. By their own admission, Sakhalin-1 has fallen behind Sakhalin-2. This is because they are having a difficult exploration phase that is still far from over. The consortium hoped for an oil project but has discovered far more gas. This has required a reconsideration of their development strategy. Added to this, financial crises in Asia and Russia have had an impact on some of the consortium members. Sodeco has confirmed its commitment to the project, but Rosneft' and SMNG are having problems financing their shares. To resolve this problem, in the spring of 1999 Rosneft' and SMNG put 49 per cent of their share of Sakhalin-2 up for sale. The outcome was expected in late summer 1999.

In the meantime, Sakhalin-1 is continuing its exploration programme and working on its development strategy. The Sakhalin-1 project seems to favour a pipeline-based strategy and is at present examining the feasibility of a pipeline route north-west to Khabarovsk Kray and then into China and a southern route to Japan. This plan seems to have the support of the federal government as it would solve the energy crisis on the mainland of the Russian Far East, but it might jeopardize Sakhalin Energy's LNG-based strategy.

The Sakhalin-3 fields are divided between two projects, the Pegastar Krinskii block and the EXXON Vostochno-Odoptinski and Ayashski blocks. While EXXON has signed an agreement with Rosneft' and SMNG to develop its two blocks, for the moment its focus is on Sakhalin-1. Progress on Sakhalin-3 Krinskii block has been held up by the project's failure to get a PSA. This was initially a Mobil–Texaco venture; the US partners came to realize that having a Russian partner was essential to getting on the PSA list. During 1998 Rosneft' and SMG were brought into the project and the US partners agreed to carry their Russian partners through the exploration phase. The Russian financial crisis served to focus the minds of Russia's legislators on the need to attract foreign investment. In the autumn of 1998 the long-awaited amendments to the PSA legislation and the so-called enabling laws were approved. In early 1999 Sakhalin-3 Krinskii block made it on to the Law of the Lists and was granted a PSA, but has yet to sign the necessary agreements with the Russian government. Having lost at least two drilling seasons due to delays over the PSA, the consortium must now be hoping that it can resolve the outstanding matters to enable it to begin drilling in 2000. On 14 April 1999 the PSA Conciliation Committee recommended that the EXXON blocks of Sakhalin-3 be included on the Law of the Lists. At the time of writing, this awaited the approval of the Federation Council and the State Duma.

The other three Sakhalin projects are some way from being a reality, but given rapid resolution of the legal and administrative matters they could soon be up for tender, perhaps with their PSAs already approved. The other consortia, all involving Rosneft' and SMNG, represent only a commitment to bid for the various blocks when they are tendered. There is no guarantee that they will all be successful. However, the Russian government has assigned Rosneft' the role of representing Russian interests in the PSAs and these agreements are likely to contain clauses that prohibit Rosneft' from bidding with other foreign companies. That said, the rule of law often fails to protect investor interests in Russia.

So what does all this activity add up to and what impact has it had on Sakhalin's economy? The answer to the first question is a lot more talk than action. The foreign oil companies have constantly had to deal with administrative and legal problems created by Moscow and by the oblast administration. For example, the original PSAs for Sakhalin-1 and -2 exempt imports of machinery and equipment from customs duties and VAT, yet the tax officials continue to collect VAT. It has been agreed that this will be repaid from the Russian royalty payments, but it should not have been charged in the first place. Clearly progress to date has been a learning process for all involved. Latecomers will undoubtedly benefit from the work done by the early projects. If the problems of investing in Russia were not enough, the Asian economic crisis and the related downturn in energy prices have also hampered the projects. Finally, the mergers of EXXON and Mobil and, to a lesser extent, BP–Amoco and ARCO will affect the pace and eventual scale of development. As a result of all these factors, the current level of activity on Sakhalin is actually quite modest and the future remains uncertain. Sakhalin-1 is still in the exploration phase and yet to declare a commercial development. Sakhalin-2 is about to produce first oil, a major achievement in its own right, but is some way off being able to commit to stage two. Sakhalin-3 Krinskii block has yet to finalize its PSA and will start exploration in the summer of 2000 if all goes well in Moscow. For most observers the question is no longer *whether* but *when* the Sakhalin fields will be developed. It may be that the economic and political risk in Russia, together with world market conditions, will delay any substantial capital commitments until well into the next decade. In the meantime, the various consortiums will want to carry out their exploration plans and conduct feasibility studies in order to know when the time is right.

The hoped-for oil and gas bonanza has yet to hit Sakhalin and this is a great source of frustration for the local politicians and residents. While Sakhalin-1 and -2 combined have spent well over $1 billion on their projects, much of the money has gone to pay for exploration services. This has been good news for the local geologists but has had a limited impact upon the local economy. It is only when large-scale infrastructure is required that the multiplier will start to tell. The PSA governing Sakhalin-2 requires 70 per cent Russian content over the duration of the project, but most of the big-ticket items in stage one have to be purchased outside Russia. This is unavoidable as the Russian Far East lacks the industrial base to supply the services needed. The shipyards at Komsomolsk-na-Amure did supply the large metal spacer on which the Moliqpaq now sits, but the steel had to be imported from Japan. The Russian content clause has required many international oil and gas service companies to come to Sakhalin in search of potential joint-venture partners. Suitable partners are few and far between and the search has now been extended to the Russian mainland. The oblast administration takes great interest in who gets what contract and has promoted the notion of 'Sakhalin first' when it comes to the award of tenders.

The PSAs also require various bonus payments to be made at certain stages and once a project has commenced for funds to be paid into the Sakhalin Development Fund. Both Sakhalin-1 and -2 have agreed to pay $100 million over the five years following commencement. Sakhalin-2 is already paying into the fund and will make a number of additional payments following production of first oil. The very nature of the PSA means that much of the early revenue will be used by the investors to pay off their initial investment. The Russian side has agreed that revenues will be split 60 per cent Sakhalin and 40 per cent Moscow. Profits will also go to Rosneft' and SMNG, but they will have to finance their share of the development costs. The bottom line is that it will be some time, possibly a decade or so, before there are substantial revenues flowing into the Sakhalin administration's budget. In the meantime, the demands on the Sakhalin Development Fund are sufficient to spend it many times over. The governor has used the funds to try to resolve the island's energy crisis and to promote prestige projects such as the airport and the Nogliki gas power station. This has brought criticism from those who would rather see the funds spent on addressing social issues, a strategy that the governor rejects as populist. The governor has to stand for re-election in the autumn of 2000 and the use of the Sakhalin Development Fund is bound to be a key issue.

8.5 CONCLUSIONS

Whilst Irkutsk and Sakhalin clearly vary in terms of their scale and economic importance, they have both inherited economic structures that are proving very difficult to sustain during the post-Soviet period. The initial benefits bestowed on such resource regions are fast disappearing, as the real economic viability of resource exploitation is becoming apparent. In the case of Irkutsk, dependence upon external supplies and high transportation costs have the potential to undermine the profitability of key region-forming industries. In the case of Sakhalin, the loss of central subsidies and reliance upon indigenous economic activity has resulted in economic collapse. In both instances local policy-makers are caught between a desire to prop up the traditional industries and the need to attract foreign investors to develop new resources. As across Russia, both regions are held hostage to the actions of the federal government in Moscow that sets the legal framework for investment and controls the licensing of resource development projects. However, they are also vulnerable to the volatility of international resource markets and the boardroom strategies of multinational resource corporations. This distinguishes them from other, more inward-looking regions whose fortunes are tied to the domestic market. Both regions seem to have little alternative but to continue to develop their natural resource potential in the hope that they can retain a fair share of the resource revenues. In both instances the oblast administration has sought to protect its interests by gaining equity ownership in future resource development. This is clear evidence that they mistrust the motivations of the federal government in Moscow as much as the multinational resource companies. They also hope that future resource exploitation can take place without the widespread environmental degradation associated with Soviet-style development. In both regions the environmental impact of a resource-based development strategy and the equitable division of resource rents are key issues with the electorate.

Summing up the post-Soviet experience of the two regions, it can be concluded that Irkutsk suffers from being at 'the right place at the wrong time', while Sakhalin has the potential to be at 'the right place at the right time'. Irkutsk is now suffering from having an economy that was constructed during the Soviet period without regard to production costs and market access. Thus, it finds itself a landlocked export-oriented region at the heart of the Eurasian landmass. Its only real hope is to secure new export markets in China, but it faces stiff competition. Sakhalin suffered from relative economic neglect during the Soviet period. It strategic role was far more important than its economic significance; much of the Soviet-era industrial infrastructure is now run down and inefficient: so much so that the island's economy is fast losing viability. However, it does have the major advantages of possessing oil and gas and of being located just offshore from Japan. Multinational oil companies are lining up to invest offshore of Sakhalin. Unfortunately, the incompetence of the federal government and changing global economic conditions have managed to slow the projects down to the extent that the energy bonanza may at best breathe new life into an economy that is on its last legs. The other danger is that Moscow, in various guises, will try and extract the majority of resource rents and orchestrate the further decline of Sakhalin's population. These two case studies show that while 'resource regions' as a category fared relatively well in the early years of the transitional recession, their economic recovery is now tied to the global economy as much as to the actions of the federal government. In such a situation the regional political elite find themselves trying to manage a centre–region relationship with Moscow, as well as a global–local relationship with major multinationals. For our two case-study regions, relations with London, Houston, Tokyo, Beijing and Melbourne matter just as much as those with Moscow.

9. Kaliningrad and Primorskiy Kray

Philip Hanson, Peter Kirkow, Douglas Sutherland and Tamara Troyakova

INTRODUCTION

The provinces of Kaliningrad and Primor'ye (or Primorskiy kray) are maritime gateway regions, situated at opposite ends of Russia. Many of their residents exploit their location. In both cases, an ocean-going fishing fleet sells large amounts of fish abroad, and those who control the fleets keep their money where their fish is – offshore. Another major activity has been second-hand car dealing: mainly German cars in Kaliningrad and Japanese cars in Primor'ye. The smuggling of amber out of Kaliningrad is another lucrative activity, but one for which a neat Primorskiy parallel is lacking. These activities are at the core of large informal sectors that seem to be underestimated in the official statistics. They also involve organized crime, with conspicuously lethal consequences in Primor'ye. Being head of the fisheries concern Primorybprom entails a high risk of assassination (see, for example, *OMRI Daily Digest*, 5 January 1996).

The politicians of the two regions are preoccupied, however, not with the opportunities that go with being a gateway to the outside world but with the disadvantages of remoteness from Moscow. That, at least, is what their public pronouncements say. They may well be directly or indirectly involved personally in some of the black and grey market activities available; but the public stance, at least, of these regional leaders is inward- not outward-looking.

Kaliningrad is nearer Moscow in mere kilometres than is much of Russia, but it is an exclave, cut off territorially from the rest of Russia and bordering Poland, Lithuania and the Baltic Sea (see Map 1.1 in the

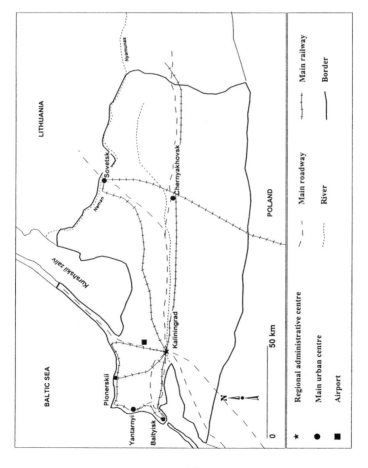

Map 9.1 Kaliningrad oblast

introductory chapter and Map 9.1 here). The political leadership has kept up a barrage of complaints about the disadvantages of being 'cut off' from the Russian homeland, and the Special Economic Zone status of Kaliningrad, an unstable and at best rather limited arrangement, is seen locally as a compensation for these supposed disadvantages (interviews with oblast officials, July 1997).

Primorskiy kray is simply a very long way indeed from Moscow (see Map 9.2). By the same token, it is a very long way from the centre of gravity of the Russian economy, which is west of the Urals. The collapse of communism threatened to end the very large subsidies to energy and transport that propped up development in Russia's Far North and Far East. It has been estimated that in the mid-1970s one-third of net material product utilized in the regions east of Lake Baykal was derived from transfers from the rest of Russia (Bradshaw 1999, citing Leslie Dienes). The exceptionally high cost of traditional Soviet-era economic activities in the Russian Far East has been exposed by the beginnings of transformation to the market. One response has been massive out-migration (see Chapter 4 and Kontorovich 1998).

Both regions had a major military role in Soviet times. They were therefore either partly or wholly closed to foreign visitors. The historical background is quite different, however, in the two cases. Kaliningrad, formerly East Prussia, with its capital known as Koenigsberg, was acquired from Germany by the USSR in the course of the Second World War. The German population was removed and Soviet citizens – mainly Russians – substituted. There are said to be only 6000 ethnic Germans in the region's present population (*Nezavisimaya gazeta* 3 February 1999, p. 9). Little of the German economic heritage remains. Some rural and suburban German housing still stands (the centre of the city of Kaliningrad was mostly flattened) and some factory buildings. But most of the capital assets stem from postwar Soviet investment. At the same time, Kaliningrad was not especially handicapped by high transport and energy costs during its Soviet development. Primor'ye, on the other hand, was a Russian imperial outpost, the rationale of whose development has long been geo-strategic, not economic (Kontorovich 1997).

Both regions might be thought to face similar challenges after the fall of communism. In both, people have had to cope with a degree of remoteness from Moscow which carries costs that previously were not borne by the inhabitants of the region. At the same time, both regions

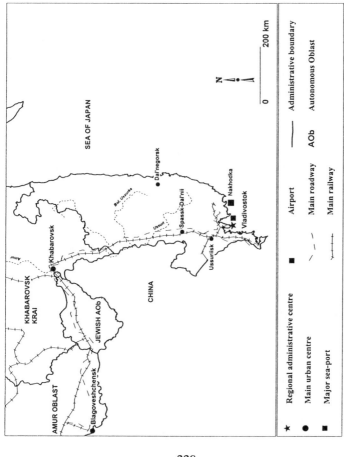

Map 9.2 Primorskiy kray

have opportunities that arise from their location between the Russian heartland and a major concentration of economic activity: Western and Central Europe in the case of Kaliningrad, and the Asia–Pacific area in the case of Primorskiy kray. If these were regions imbedded in a well-functioning market economy, the opportunities would probably have outweighed any disadvantage arising from their distance from their own nation's economic centre of gravity. But they have not been in this (comparatively) happy situation. Adapting to a new, less Moscow-centred society has been a common problem.

9.1   INHERITED ECONOMIC STRUCTURE

In both territory and population, Primorskiy kray is an order of magnitude larger than Kaliningrad: 2.20 million people against 943,000 at the beginning of 1999.[1] Thus Primor'ye is somewhat larger in population than the average Russian province, and Kaliningrad is about half the Russian average. And while the population of Primor'ye has been shrinking, that of Kaliningrad has been rising through net in-migration. Thus, both regions exhibit the excess of deaths over births that is characteristic of Russia as a whole, the natural decline in population is reinforced by net out-migration in the case of Primor'ye and offset by net in-migration in the case of Kaliningrad. In inherited economic structure, however, they are somewhat similar.

Both are slightly more urbanized than the Russian average, but both have, by Russian standards, relatively small main cities: the population of Vladivostok was 627,000 at the start of 1996, that of Kaliningrad city 422,000. One possible indicator of their inheritance of skills is that the development of their tertiary education systems has been rated as average for Kaliningrad and above average for Primorskiy kray (*Predprinimatel'skiy...* 1997, p. 103).

In both of them, the share of employment in transport and communications is well above the Russian average. This reflects their gateway locations. Even in the Soviet period, both probably had quite active black markets, stemming from the coming and going of ships. The saxophonist Aleksei Kozlov, who toured the Soviet Union

---

1.   As in the other case-study chapters, the reproduction of tables of numbers is kept to a minimum. Data on case-study regions are concentrated in the Appendix, where sources for them are given.

extensively in the 1980s with his band, Arsenal, inspected flea markets wherever he went; he rated Odessa's as the best supplied, with Kaliningrad second (Kozlov 1998, p. 332).

So far as the industrial sector is concerned, neither region had the typical Russian concentration on steel, non-ferrous metals or engineering. By Russian standards, these branches were rather little developed. Instead, fish-processing looms large in both of them, showing up in the data as an exceptionally large industrial-gross-output share for food-processing: 48.3 per cent in Primorskiy kray and 32.9 per cent in Kaliningrad in 1995. The only other distinctive feature about their industrial structures is the relatively large share of timber, woodworking, paper and pulp in the case of Kaliningrad; in fact, this consists mainly of activities downstream from logging, with much of the timber traditionally brought in from other Russian regions.

One consequence of their industrial structures is that neither of them houses giant enterprises. A listing of the 200 largest Russian enterprises in 1997 shows that these are concentrated in other regions (*Ekspert* 1998 no. 38 (12 October), p. 17). Such enterprises may typically be, as most Western economists assume, 'dinosaurs' and 'value-subtractors'. But they are concentrated in what have been traditionally regarded as economically strong regions, and those regions often have, in fact, adapted less badly than most Russian regions to the market (see the Introduction, Chapter 7 and the Conclusions).

One feature of the economies of the two regions is worth noting because of its subsequent importance in their development in the 1990s. Primorskiy kray, in common with the rest of the Russian Far East, is not linked to the 'single' electricity grid. The kray depends on coal-fired power stations, with much of the coal coming from a high-cost mine in the north of the region. Primor'ye has also had to 'import' coal from other regions (Bradshaw and Kirkow 1998). In the middle and late 1990s this has been a source of major disruptions to the regional economy, on which more below. Paradoxically, Kaliningrad, though territorially separated from the rest of Russia, is part of the (Soviet) single grid. Current plans to develop an electricity grid around the Baltic Sea, linking Scandinavian and former Soviet countries (Reuters from Moscow, 3 November 1998), would make electricity supply to Kaliningrad even more reliable, and perhaps lower in cost, than at present. Kaliningrad does have some oil extraction on its territory, but it has no need to depend on local resources of primary fuel and is not locked into high-cost energy as Primor'ye currently is.

In general, however, it is the similarities in the initial conditions of the two regions that are striking. Both Primor'ye and Kaliningrad had significant military roles in Russia – but housing military bases rather than large military production clusters; they contained major ports, ocean-going fishing fleets, fish-processing industries and not a great deal of heavy industry; both have experienced a shock from the sudden distancing of their economies from the hub of the old Soviet economy; neither contains a major conurbation in which agglomeration effects might be supposed to work strongly; but both have opportunities to develop as gateways opening on to large concentrations of economic activity in the wider world that Russia was expected by many to join.

The major initial differences between them were that Primor'ye occupied a rather precarious position in the inherited energy system while Kaliningrad did not; and that, on the other hand, Primor'ye has both a much larger internal market and the prospect of serving as a major hub of a Russian macro-region – the Russian Far East.

In these circumstances, it might be guessed that differences in outcomes should reflect differences in the policies of regional leaders.

9.2 ADAPTATION IN THE 1990s

The two regions both display a pattern of adaptation that is unusual for Russia. Primorskiy kray enjoys a reputation for possessing a particularly anti-reform and particularly corrupt administration. Its governor, Yevgenii Nazdratenko, has been a thorn in the side of several federal governments, disputing privatization policies, frequently being described in Moscow as corrupt, and latterly creating a lot of trouble over regional energy problems (Vacroux 1994; Kirkow 1997a; Bradshaw and Kirkow 1998). In a quieter, less conspicuous way, Leonid Gorbenko, the Kaliningrad governor since 1996, has been no friend of reform. Yet both regions exhibit in Table 9.1 some strong signs, by Russian standards, of market adaptation.

Per capita real incomes, as officially measured, appear very close to the national average if Moscow is excluded from the latter. In Kaliningrad, at least, anecdotal evidence suggests that the reality is well above

Table 9.1 Some indicators of outcomes and regional regimes,
Primorskiy kray and Kaliningrad oblast, late 1990s

Indicator	Primorskiy	Kaliningrad	RF[a]	RF – M[b]
Per capita real income, January 1999[c]	1.17	0.96	1.39	1.15
Change in industrial output, 1990–98 (%)[d]	–55	–61	–54	
Unemployment, December 1998 (%)[e]	3.8	3.5	3.2	
Employment in foreign firms, 1998 (%)[f]	0.7	1.2	1.2	1.1
Employment in small firms, 1998 (%)[g]	10.5	13.7	9.6	8.5
Per capita forex inflow, 1995 ($)[h]	438.0	392.0	435.0	300.0
Budget deficit/budget expenditure, 1997 (%)[i]	4.3	10.6		
Lavrov transfer balance, 1997 (RF = 100)[i]	6.1	33.5		
Production subsidies/budget expenditure, 1995 (%)[i]	19.8	11.3	(13.7)	
Strength of food-price controls (1 = lowest)[j]	15	1	(19.5)	

Notes and sources:
[a] RF denotes average for Russian Federation. RF figures in brackets are unweighted averages of data for all regions.
[b] RF – M denotes Russian Federation less Moscow city.
[c] Per capita real income is monetary income per head of population divided by the regional cost of the subsistence minimum. Derived from Goskomstat Rossii (1999a and 1999b).
[d] Shows the change in gross industrial output from 1990 to 1998 (approx). Derived from Goskomstat Rossii (1998d, table 14.6; 1998b, p. 318) (for Kaliningrad); and *Zolotoi rog* (Vladivostok) 9 February 1999. The 1998 year-on-year change is approximated by taking January 1999 over January 1998, for Kaliningrad only.
[e] The unemployment figure is especially approximate. It is the officially recorded 'unemployed and seeking work' figure for December 1998 as a percentage of average 1997 employment plus December 1998 unemployment. Derived from Goskomstat Rossii (1996, 1997d and 1999c, pp. 337–8).
[f] Employment in foreign firms (as defined in the text above) in 1998 is given as a per cent of the average 1997 total employment. Derived from Goskomstat Rossii (1998d, table 7.3, and 1999c, pp. 252–3).

g   Small-firm employment in 1998 is shown as % of all employment in 1997. Derived
    from Goskomstat Rossii (1998d, table 7.3, and 1999c, pp. 248–9).
h   Per cap forex inflow is *valyutnye postupleniya* (see Chapter 7) per head of
    population. Derived from Goskomstat (1996).
i   Lavrov transfer balance is remittance of tax collected to the centre minus explicit
    transfers back to region, per head of population (see Chapter 5), where 100 is the
    average for all regional budgets. This and the budget deficit and production
    subsidies ratios are derived from Lavrov (1998b).
j   Strength of food-price controls is an expert assessment. This is from *Predprinima-
    tel'skiy...* (1997).

the national average (Hanson 1998). The same was probably true of
Primor'ye until its energy problems took hold. Traditional industrial
activity apparently declined especially steeply in Kaliningrad. This
possibly reflects the sudden appearance of exclave costs for traditional
economic activities, over and above the reform shock for Russian
industry in general. The figures, however, are for large and medium
enterprises only – that is, for the traditional state enterprise reporting
base – and we shall show later that the news on the industrial front may
not be all bad. Reported unemployment rates, a bit higher in both
regions than the Russian average, also suggest a worse-than-average
situation. Again, however, there may be offsetting factors.

Before the 1998 financial crisis, Kaliningrad had markedly little
price control (and comparatively low prices, partly because of tariff
exemptions on imports consumed locally, under the Special Economic
Zone regime); Primorskiy kray had less than average. The employment
role of small firms was somewhat greater in both regions than the
Russian average. Subsidies to producers loomed larger than average in
the Primorskiy regional budget (see below on some probable reasons
for this) but were below average in Kaliningrad. And Kaliningrad
seems to have had a relatively strong development of foreign business
on its territory, while – somewhat surprisingly, in view of its gateway
location – Primor'ye has not. (One has, regrettably, to use the word
'seems' here because the data on employment in 'firms with foreign
investment', as Russian statistics label both wholly foreign-owned
firms and joint ventures, avowedly exclude firms with staffs of fewer
than 15 persons, and are in any case poor. Such firms may be on the
register but not operating; some foreign direct investments are not
recorded on the register.)

The picture that emerges is one of change stemming from the

gateway location, creating circumstances that allow – or perhaps enforce – a degree of liberalism with respect to pricing and the development of new business, despite a reputation for traditionalism that attaches to both the regional regimes.

9.3 POLICIES AND ADAPTATION

Primorskiy kray has become notorious for corruption, authoritarian rule and conflicts with the federal government. From 1991 to May 1993, the leadership under the first governor, Vladimir Kuznetsov, was considered to be broadly reformist. Both small-scale and large-scale privatization moved comparatively rapidly in the region in this period (Vacroux 1994). Kuznetsov, however, presided over a largely unreconstructed regional administration – the usual situation in Russia in that period. At the same time, he appears to have been regarded with suspicion by the managers of most of the region's large enterprises (Kirkow 1995). In the spring of 1993, when presidential control of the appointment of governors was somewhat relaxed, the kray council (legislature) managed to convince the authorities in Moscow that an election was appropriate, and that Yevgenii Nazdratenko, the general director of a local mining company, was a locally acceptable candidate. Nazdratenko was duly elected, and has been a thorn in Moscow's flesh ever since.

Nazdratenko was the local enterprise directors' man. In particular, he was a member of the PAKT association of 31 large enterprises, employing 9 per cent of the regional labour force, with activities extending from meat-processing to shipyards. PAKT sought to control the style of development of the regional economy, favouring 'cooperation' and 'integration', that is, monopoly, and striving to keep out investors from outside the region (Vacroux 1994; Kirkow 1995). Immediately after becoming governor, Nazdratenko appointed three other PAKT directors to deputy-governor posts (by 1997 there were 12 deputy governors: IEWS, *Russian Regional Report*, 29 May 1997). In August 1993 he tried to arrange for the regional administration to acquire controlling stakes in 172 enterprises, 64 of them previously of regional subordination and the rest federal. This led private investors to sell their shares, traders on the embryonic local stock exchange to halt business in protest, and the federal authorities eventually to block the move (Vacroux 1994). Anatolii Chubais, then heading the State Property Committee (GKI) emerged at this point as one of Naz-dratenko's strongest opponents in Moscow. Later, Nazdratenko found himself fighting Chubais again – this time, Chubais in his later incar-nation as the head of the national electricity company, YeES, not as privatization boss. Nazdratenko is quoted as deploying standard Russian provincial traditionalist language about Chubais, describing him as 'a hireling of American imperialism and Zionism' (P'yannikh 1998).

In the period 1993–8 Nazdratenko made a fairly consistent set of demands on the federal authorities: that the region should retain more of the tax collected on its territory and some of the customs revenue; that he be able to license fish and timber exports; that the centre should pay more to support the establishment of federal entities in the region; and that there should be large federal subsidies to support the high-cost regional energy system. At one point he tried, through the regional assembly, to use a unilateral declaration of republic status as a lever to get at least some of his demands granted (Kirkow 1997b; Troyakova 1998).

So far as economic policy is concerned, Nazdratenko has not been very different in his aims from many regional leaders. This point was forcefully made at an early stage by Irina Savvateyeva (1995). The title of her *Izvestiya* article sums it up: 'Yevgenii Nazdratenko as a mirror of Russian reforms'. Primor'ye really does have special economic problems, inherited from its Soviet and even Tsarist past, which the federal authorities should have done more to resolve. Developed as a military outpost, with an economy heavily subsidized to support its military role, the region has exceptionally high energy costs; for the same reason, it also has a large presence of federal military and other bodies on its territory, which it is hardly the regional administration's task to support.

It is not surprising, therefore, that Nazdratenko continued through 1998 to visit Moscow frequently and to 'bring back money and fuel for the kray' (*Zolotoi rog*, 29 December 1998, p. 2).

What has excited most criticism of the Nazdratenko regime, however, has been its authoritarian methods. The long-running ven-detta between Nazdratenko and the mayor of Vladivostok, Viktor Cherepkov, has many parallels in other Russian regions: big-city interests are more attuned to economic reform and political liberalism than those of smaller communities in Russian provinces, and the regional administration often draws much of its support from the latter. This antagonism is usually compounded by budgetary conflicts. The main city of a region is typically the tax milch-cow for the region as a whole, the development levels of most Russian regions being characteristically split between a more or less developed big city and a backward hinterland of villages and smaller towns. This is a standard source of friction between governors and the mayors of their main cities. (Such differences within Krasnodar kray are described in Chapter 7.) But the lengths to which Nazdratenko went to oust Cherepkov from his post (for a time) were remarkable. Similarly, his suppression of critical local media is generally regarded in Russia as harsher than the Russian provincial norm (for details, see Kirkow 1997b and Troyakova 1998).

Having prevented, for the time being at least, Cherepkov from returning to the post of mayor of Vladivostok, Nazdratenko next came into conflict with the chairman of the kray legislative assembly, Vladimir Dudnik. Dudnik had criticized the governor for trying to assert direct administrative control over all sub-regional administrative appointments. As a result, he has been subjected to a hostile press and letter-writing campaign (IEWS, *Russian Regional Reporter* 18 February 1999, and 1 April 1999). It was feared that Nazdratenko would rig the gubernatorial elections due in late 1999.

The fact remains that some indicators of economic liberalization in the region still looked quite favourable three years after Nazdratenko came to power, as Table 9.1 shows. Similarly, the extent of large-scale privatization was reckoned to be 'high' (the second of five categories) in a comparative appraisal of Russian regions in 1996 (*Predprinimatel'skiy...* 1997, p. 146) and that of small-scale privatization 'average' (ibid.). The state of play over privatization probably reflects two things: the presence of a reforming governor in 1992 and early 1993; and the small amount of production under the Military-Industrial Commission (VPK) in the region to begin with. That these changes were not rolled back may be due to the regional *nomenklatura* having got its hands on the most lucrative assets at an early stage. Vacroux (1994) noted that the region's managers, after initial opposition to privatization, quickly moved to form alliances with the regional GKI and Property Fund officials.

Another element in the situation may be that a border region with big money-making opportunities does not lend itself to very effective state control – or not, at any rate, to effective control by a weak and corrupt administration. In the 1998 crisis, the Nazdratenko regime predictably issued all sorts of instructions about price controls; but by the end of September it looked as though they were for the most part not being implemented (http://www.iep.doc.gov/bisnis/cables/981001ru.htm of 1 October 1998).

Corrupt authoritarian rule in Primorskiy kray is, it seems, compatible with a comparatively liberal *de facto* regime so far as the current operation of markets and perhaps small business is concerned. What it does not do is favour efficiency and freedom of market entry. The regional energy crisis, for example, is only in part the result of an economic inheritance of separation from the 'unified' grid and of high-cost generating capacity. According to an account (P'yannikh 1998) of the Chubais-led YeES tour of inspection of the Russian Far East in September 1998, the kray's electricity supply system was said by Vladimir Rumyantsev, head of the YeES power-station division, to be losing 50 per cent of its potential revenue. This was the result of cronyism in the provision of cheap electricity, including the acceptance of barter goods at nominally inflated prices (which has been standard Russian practice in the late 1990s), and also of exceptionally high 'leakage' of electricity. High-voltage power transmission can be expected to lose up to 7 per cent in the transmission process for technical reasons. According to Rumyantsev, the typical Russian level is 10–12 per cent, reflecting illegal tapping of the system, and this is the level observed in Sakhalin and Khabarovsk; but in Primorskiy kray the rate is 22 per cent.

The port services have been described as controlled by criminal gangs (Lloyd 1994). The region's fish-processing has been said to operate 75 per cent for the shadow economy (P'yannikh 1998).[2] This highly criminal environment will raise market entry costs to both foreign and Russian firms. The fact that the region has a relatively small presence, even by Russian standards, of joint ventures (see Table

2. This assessment is said to come from 'Japanese statistics'. This probably refers to a discrepancy between Russian officially recorded deliveries to Japan and Japanese officially recorded imports of Russian fish. That would seem likely, however, to stem from offshore selling, whether of raw fish from trawlers or of processed fish from factory vessels, rather than from on-shore processing facilities.

9.1) may simply be a sign of such high entry barriers. This is all the more striking in view of the fact that the region's location makes it more attractive than most of Russia to foreign investment. By the same token, the investment benefits forgone because of such barriers will be high. In addition, the deepening energy crisis of 1997–9, with frequent and extended power failures, has provided a new and powerful disincentive to invest in the region.

Adjustment to the August 1998 financial crisis shows a mixed picture. Gross regional product was officially reported to be 8.8 per cent lower in 1998 than in the previous year (*Zolotoi rog* 19 January 1999); this probably reflects a decline that started, as in most of Russia, after the first quarter of 1998, before the 17 August default and devaluation. Industrial output reportedly declined even more drastically, by 17 per cent (ibid.).

As in other regions, locally based banks have survived better than the local branches of Moscow banks. The latter typically had more foreign-currency liabilities and a higher exposure to the GKO (Treasury-bill) market (see *Zolotoi rog* 17 November 1998, p. 29). By April 1999 the leading locally based bank, the Far East Bank (FESbank), was negotiating to renew its links with the National Bank of Alaska and to establish cooperation with American Express (IEWS, *Russian Regional Investor,* 19 April 1999). Dalrybbank, however, remained in crisis (ibid.).

Food and other imports fell, of course, after the devaluation, but the short-term supply response of local producers was weak (*Zolotoi rog* 29 December 1998, pp. 3 and 8). The high costs of local production and its dependence on imported inputs remained a problem. For example, poultry meat from the region's only large-scale poultry farm was being sold at R25 per kilo in October 1998, below its unit cost (on Russian accounting) of R36 per kilo – blamed on the high cost of electricity and of imported feed and vitamin additives (*Zolotoi rog* 27 October 1998, p. 8). A local sausage producer was reported to use 90 per cent imported materials (*Zolotoi rog* 17 November, 1998, p. 1). Local food producers continue to look for state subsidies that do not materialize (*Zolotoi rog* 27 November 1998, p. 8); so does the major – and state-owned – wholesale agribusiness distribution (*Zolotoi rog* 27 October 1998, p. 11). A local law passed in January 1999 stipulated that the state (regional government) should have a majority stake in any wholesale market operating in the region. Clearly, the intention was one characteristic of a traditionalist local elite: when in doubt, increase state control. What it meant and how it would be implemented, remained unclear – the usual state of affairs with traditionalist economic measures in Russia.

In Kaliningrad, developments have been, mercifully, less dramatic.[3] As we have already indicated, however, they have not been entirely different in character. The conventional wisdom in the region, as we learnt from officials and some academic analysts there, is that the abrupt acquisition of exclave status imposed costs on the regional economy, over and above Russia-wide adjustment costs. The establishment of, first, a free, and later a special, economic zone in the region is conventionally seen as intended to compensate for what might be called exclave costs (considered as a continuing addition to regional operating costs, and not as a change requiring once-for-all adjustment). And the general view is that the special economic zone (SEZ) arrangements work poorly and do not do much to help the region.

What might these exclave and exclave-adjustment costs be? They are certainly not the enormous costs of daft location faced by producers in Primor'ye. The common assumption in the region – though it is seldom voiced in these terms – is that the transaction costs of dealing with firms and households in the rest of Russia were permanently increased by the break-up of the Soviet Union. Both individuals and freight cargoes may now encounter documentation delays in crossing the Lithuanian border: in preliminary paperwork to be completed and in monitoring checks at the border. Transactions with firms and households in the Baltic states themselves involve currency conversion costs that were not present before. Freight going through one or more Baltic states may also have to pay duties. And there is uncertainty about several of these things.

The imposition of these costs on transactions with suppliers or customers in other parts of Russia would presumably add to a transformation cost, described by Blanchard and Kremer (1997). A final-stage producer relying on a number of input suppliers assigned to him under central planning may find his supply chains disintegrating even when switching to the alternative outlets now available to his suppliers yields a lower total output than would be provided by a continuation of traditional links. Blanchard and Kremer show how this can happen

---

3. The sub-section on Kaliningrad is a summary of Hanson and Sutherland (1999).

when information along the supply chain is imperfect and it is not possible to write effective contracts to reduce the resulting uncertainties. Supply chains working in both directions – in and out of Kaliningrad – might be expected to be affected in such ways more severely than equivalent linkages within 'mainland' Russia.

Some scepticism is in order about this characterization of Kaliningrad's problems. In the first place, we are not convinced that the Blanchard and Kremer model is a very useful one for understanding Russia's output collapse in general. If much of traditional manufacturing activity on Russian territory was value-subtracting, and established networks have tended to preserve it, the breaking of Soviet-era links might do more good than harm. There certainly is an information problem in the search for new configurations of Russian economic activity, but there is also much evidence that the preservation of traditional linkages by means of tolerated payment arrears, barter and money-surrogate transactions has carried very high costs. Looked at in this way, the sudden appearance of an international boundary around Kaliningrad oblast might be a blessing in disguise.

Moreover, the evidence about continuing exclave costs is not very persuasive. In fact, sealed containers dispatched to Moscow by rail or road via Lithuania do not incur duties; nor, apparently, are they delayed on the Lithuanian side.[4] Russian railway freight charges have been specially reduced for cargoes between Kaliningrad and the 'mainland'. The freight costs to Moscow for a cargo that comes into the Lithuanian port of Klaipeda (not far from the Kaliningrad border) have been lower, none the less, than the charges from the port of Kaliningrad (Fisher Associates 1997; *Initial Report...* n.d.; interview with an adviser to the Kaliningrad administration, January 1998). But international competition is not an exclave cost.

Our scepticism about exclave costs is supported, so far as the industrial sector is concerned, by shift-share analysis of employment by branch of industry, 1990–95. This shows that the changes in Kaliningrad can be accounted for largely by the branch composition of its industrial sector: in other words, the decline in industrial employment, at any rate over that period, was roughly what one would have expected if each branch faced much the same proportional changes in

---

4. We were told that there are delays on the Russian (Kaliningrad) side. If so, that is just normal Russian bureaucratic sniping at one's own feet.

employment levels in the region as it did nationally. Moreover, an analysis of the extent of structural change in the industrial sector, using the Lilien measure, suggests that it has been significantly greater in Kaliningrad than in Russia as a whole (Hanson and Sutherland 1999). That might be interpreted as a favourable indication of adjustment. The question remains open.

One cost arising from the region's new situation as an exclave is, however, undeniable. This is the political uncertainty specific to the region, over and above Russian political uncertainty in general. This is evident from both Russian and European debates about the status of Kaliningrad, especially in the light of NATO and EU expansion. In Poland there have been calls for the region to be handed over to Poland in reparation for past Soviet treatment of the Polish nation. In Germany especially, but also in other north-eastern EU member-states, there has been serious discussion of a special status for the region, whether it be a special EU associate status or a regime of shared administration by neighbouring states. In Russia the civil rights activist Sergei Kovalev has said that Kaliningrad belongs by rights to Germany. All these propositions elicit a predictable response from Russian politicians: that Kaliningrad is a vital Russian military outpost and should receive more subsidies.

Opinion within the region is divided. In a July 1998 survey of 1158 residents, the percentages supporting various changes in status were: an independent republic outside Russia 7; republic status within the Russian Federation 10; special status with enhanced powers entrenched in the Russian constitution 35. Only 10 per cent considered the present status desirable (Danilov 1999, from whom other material in this and the preceding paragraph is summarized).

At all events, residents of Kaliningrad benefit from being next to two economies that are in better shape than that of Russia: those of Lithuania and Poland. A great deal of the region's food supply, as well as other products, comes from these neighbouring countries. The competitive character of production in the two neighbouring countries, plus the duty-free arrangements of the Special Economic Zone, made Kaliningrad one of the cheapest of Russian regions – up to the August 1998 rouble devaluation.

The SEZ arrangements consist chiefly of allowing in duty-free imports to the region. If imports are processed in Kaliningrad, they may be sold on to the rest of Russia if some value is added locally: 30 per cent for many products and less for supposedly high-tech processing (which might, for example, be car or computer assembly).

Nobody is enthralled by the SEZ rules. They have been subject to much alteration over time and have come to be regarded as a source of uncertainty in themselves. Indeed, the free economic zone status was cancelled in 1995 by President Yeltsin, and a special economic zone was instated in January 1996. The quantities that may be imported duty-free are subject to quotas. The duty-free arrangements leave producers with 14 federal, 4 regional and 23 local taxes to pay (Widgery 1997).

In 1997 and early 1998, before the Russian devaluation and default later in the latter year, we observed three favourable developments in Kaliningrad which seem to be the results of its location and relative openness. The evidence is far from conclusive about the region's progress as a whole, but it is suggestive. The information cited here comes from interviews with enterprise managers in January 1998; perusal of the local press in 1997–8; and internal Tacis project reports. Little or none of this information could be derived from official statistics.

First, the grey economy of border trade, especially the highly organized motor vehicle trade, in which Kaliningrad acts as an entrepôt between Western Europe and the Russian mainland, is clearly a source of substantial income for many people. The earnings in this field were cited by industrial managers, in interviews, as making it difficult for them to attract and retain good staff. Press advertisements of a 24-hour service of *rastamorzhanie* (sorting out of customs arrangements) for vehicles purchased in the region and to be shipped to mainland Russia indicate a large and highly developed car-trade sector; so does the choice of the name *Novye kolesa* (New Wheels) for a local business newspaper that is not especially devoted to the motor trade. In addition, the possibility of importing motor vehicles duty-free to Kaliningrad has encouraged Russian road haulage firms to use Kaliningrad as an administrative base, registering imported vehicles there. These may be used elsewhere in Russia, but their Kaliningrad registration saves on the payment of tariffs.

Second, reports on a number of state and ex-state enterprises, and our own visits to two of them, conveyed very strongly the impression that in industry getting by, and even in some cases getting ahead, in the new environment was linked with having a Western partner. That did not necessarily mean foreign direct investment. It might take the form of a strategic alliance or merely of imports of equipment and know-how from the West. Thus Gazavtomatika, a Gazprom subsidiary which makes electrical equipment for the gas industry, has not drastically altered its product profile or its market, but it has acquired Western components and know-how through an alliance with the French company Schneider SA. Baltkran, which produces and exports port equipment, is 20 per cent owned by Noel Preussag of Germany, through whose marketing channels they have increased their exports substantially. Both these companies had been increasing their sales for some time by early 1998 after earlier declines. In contrast, a visit to the Yantarnyi amber mine showed an isolated, still state-owned enterprise in what looked to be terminal decline.

Foreign direct investment is only one form of such cooperation with foreign business partners, but it is probably of special importance as a channel for the acquisition of foreign technology and managerial know-how. It provides the foreign partner with a direct and long-term interest in making these transfers work. The data on such investment are problematic (see above). They seem, at least, to be slightly better for Kaliningrad than for Primorskiy kray (Table 9.1). However, there are some large question marks over regional policies on foreign investment. These will be discussed below.

Third, there is at least one branch in which new private firms predominate and are thriving. At the time of our interviews (January 1998), the regional Association of Furniture Manufacturers grouped 22 firms, ranging in employment size from 2 to 100 staff, and their sales to mainland Russia were booming. Nimaks, employing 50 staff in two shifts, was at the time of our interview selling in 30 Russian regions. Its director considered that their only real competition on the Russian market was foreign firms. The development of this *de novo* industry has been based on Western inputs: at first, components and then just Western equipment. One large, pre-existing state furniture factory in the region was in an advanced state of decay, while Nimaks and a cluster of new firms in the same industry were growing fast. The reason given for this contrast was that the Soviet-era state furniture factory had equipment that was grossly energy-inefficient, and could not compete on cost. The director of Nimaks was almost alone among our Kaliningrad informants in considering that the SEZ was useful: it had enabled him and his counterparts to start up with an advantage over equivalent

*Table 9.2   Employment in some large Kaliningrad enterprises, 1990
and 1996–7*

Enterprise	Employment c. 1990	Employment in 1996–7
Kvarts	10,000	1,000
Stroidormash	3,000	450
Gazavtomatika	2,000	800
Mikrodvugatel'	1,800	400
Svetotekhnika	3,500	800
Sudoremmashavtomatika	1,000	400
Kalininbummash	1,000	300
Total	22,300	4,150

Sources: Widgery (1997); interviews (January 1998).

firms in other regions because they could acquire foreign components and equipment duty-free. He also had, he said, no problems with transport to mainland Russian markets.

Developments of this kind are under-represented in the official statistics. They may, however, help to explain the prosperity that was evident on the streets of Kaliningrad city and in Svetlogorsk. It would appear from our (not necessarily representative) evidence on the industrial sector that the shift of labour out of manufacturing may have been even greater in reality than the statistics depict. Table 9.2 shows employment data for seven 'leading' large enterprises of the region (large, that is, by the rather modest standards of this particular region).

Far from seeing such reductions as lamentable, we suspect that they reveal as much as anything the presence of alternative, more attractive employment in the commercial hub, Kaliningrad city. Job quits were routinely described as voluntary, and any declaration of mass redundancies was denied. That is in line with what is known generally about Russian industrial enterprise adjustment. Moreover, one enterprise at a physically isolated location, the amber mine at Yantarnyi, claimed a workforce decline from about 2000 only to about 1700 (interview at Yantarnyi, January 1998).

One tentative conclusion about adjustment in Kaliningrad region is that there has probably been a great deal more successful adaptation than the official statistics would reveal – at least up to the financial crisis of 1998. This does not seem to be due to especially reformist or outward-looking policies on the part of the regional administration. The current administration's general orientation is probably best exemplified by the governor's reported greeting on being introduced to a Western business executive engaged in complicated and much-delayed negotiations over a major telecommunications deal in the region: 'So you've come to make money out of us, have you?' (interview with the executive concerned, January 1998). Interviews with other Western business people conveyed the same impression: of a suspicious and unhelpful administration.

In general, the stance of the present governor, Leonid Gorbenko, is traditionalist. In a 1998 interview he called for greater regional powers to set quantitative limits on duty-free imports into the region, giving the reduction of smuggling from Kaliningrad to the Russian 'mainland' as the justification. (As noted above, such quotas already exist, but they are set in Moscow. They were made more restrictive after the August 1998 crisis.) In the same interview, it is true, Gorbenko espoused some liberalization of the legislation on land ownership and sales, though he has not followed the lead of Saratov and Samara in introducing regional legislation to that effect.

Otherwise, he spoke in the standard, ex-Soviet style of most Russian regional leaders. He complained that his power to hire and fire officials was less than that of an *obkom* first secretary in Soviet times; this was (by implication) to do with the officials of local branches of federal government agencies. He also complained that the centre was not meeting its promises over transfers from the federal to the regional budget. In 1997, he said, the oblast had been promised 240 billion (old) roubles, and received 72 billion (*Nezavisimaya gazeta – Regiony* 1998 (6), p. 4). Of course, nobody can be criticized for complaining when a purported beneficiary does not keep promises; but the federal government has been failing to meet its payment obligations to suppliers, employees and regional budgets for several years, and to go on whingeing about this in 1998 as if it were some shocking and unexpected blow is disingenuous.

Traditionalism may not be the most important characteristic of the Gorbenko regime. Sadly, there are other resemblances to the Nazdratenko regime in Primor'ye: extensive accusations of corruption and of repression of opposition. These accusations have been set out at length in *Izvestiya* (Korol'kov 1998). They have not, to our knowledge, been challenged as libellous in the Russian courts. In what looks to be a substantial piece of investigative reporting, Igor' Korol'kov interviewed business and other notables in the region, many of whom requested anonymity, according to Korol'kov, for fear of reprisals by the Gorbenko regime.

The story Korol'kov unfolds can be summarized as follows. Gorbenko was elected governor in October 1996. His predecessor, Yuri Matochkin, was an intellectual and a reformer who had, among other things, worked to restore the special economic zone advantages, had got them in place in January 1996, and had negotiated for the first major investment project: car assembly by Kia Baltika, a Moscow company using the Korean Kia company's technology. (The exact nature of Kia's direct involvement, if any, in Kaliningrad is not clear, but they would have supplied cars in kit form.) An area at the Yantar' shipyard had been adapted for car assembly. Meanwhile, however, people were experiencing the economic turmoil common to all of Russia, and the gubernatorial election produced a majority for a non-reformer: Gorbenko had headed the fishing port of Kaliningrad and was regarded as a practical manager who got employees' wages paid on time. Perhaps he would be better at getting money out of Moscow.

Korol'kov describes Gorbenko's team as corrupt and Gorbenko himself as erratic and vindictive. He describes insider deals and suspected money laundering involving members of that team, the Baltika Bank and a Fund for Development of the Oblast headed by a Gorbenko associate. Officials who were not compliant were allegedly intimidated. The editor of an opposition paper, *Novye kolesa*, was beaten up and his offices bombed.

The Kia-Baltika project was halted by the regional customs imposing standard duties on car parts, in breach of the Special Economic Zone arrangements.[5] That was enough to make the project unprofitable. This was allegedly Gorbenko's doing; he did not want, according to Korol'kov's informants, to see a project identified with his predecessor succeed. Volkswagen, who had been interested in investing in Kaliningrad, were reportedly put off by the Kia-Baltika fiasco. The

5. It has to be said that the Kia company was approaching bankruptcy at the time, and that might have been a sufficient cause of the project's failure. However, our understanding is that Kia were not direct investors in the project but were supplying technology and kits via Avtotor-Holding, a Russian company.

quotas imposed on duty-free imports by the federal government were introduced, according to Korol'kov, at Gorbenko's urging.

In an interview after the August 1998 crisis, Gorbenko showed some signs of having learnt about the need to look outwards as well as back towards Mother Russia (*Nezavisimaya gazeta – Regiony*, 1999 (3), p. 1). He dwelt on the need for stability to encourage investors and on the benefits he expected from closer cooperation with Poland, Lithuania, Denmark and Germany. But his traditionalist inclinations were still apparent. He spoke of the regional administration's success in bringing prices under control after the crisis, and he expressed a hope that Prime Minister Primakov would appreciate the strategic importance of Kaliningrad and 'support' it appropriately.

The region had certainly suffered more than most from the devaluation of the rouble, as Gorbenko claimed. It is, after all, unusually dependent on foreign trade. However, in so far as the region has enjoyed some success in adapting to the new circumstances, this is probably in spite of the policies of the regional administration.

In 1998–9 BMW was negotiating with Avtotor-Holding (who had also been involved in the abortive Kia-Baltika project) and the regional administration to establish assembly of Land Rovers in Kaliningrad, with an initial investment of DM50 million. The August 1998 devaluation and default put this project on ice for seven months, but the go-ahead was announced in March and the deal formally signed in April 1999 (*Guardian* 18 March 1999, p. 21; IEWS *Russian Regional Investor* 15 March 1999). The same space at the Yantar' shipyard would be used as would have been used in the Kia-Baltika project. Presumably, BMW expected to get the special economic zone benefits which were denied, according to Korol'kov, to Kia-Baltika. If this project goes ahead, it will be the first large foreign direct investment project in Kaliningrad. A second-stage investment of DM75 million is planned.

9.4   CONCLUSIONS

Russian border regions, like border regions in most parts of the world, are hospitable to informal, shadow-economy activities. What has been striking about Russian gateway regions in the 1990s, other than

St Petersburg, is that their political leaders have not sought to facilitate more regular kinds of foreign trade and inward investment. Rather, they have been inward-looking, protectionist and even xenophobic.

In the case of Primorskiy kray, and also of Kaliningrad, this might be ascribed to their history as military outposts. People now in office there grew up in communities administratively closed to foreigners and were taught, quite truthfully, that their region defended the USSR against a hostile outside world. But that may not be the whole story. After all, governor Kondratenko in Krasnodar is now the all-Russian provincial xenophobia champion (see Chapter 7), and his region was not a military bastion. And it is striking that the only region in which a representative of Vladimir Zhirinovsky's hyper-nationalist party has gained gubernatorial office is Pskov, on the border with Estonia. Suspicion of the outside world and a constant looking to Moscow as the source of benefits are perhaps rather widespread characteristics of the Russian regional political elite; those who run gateway regions simply air their views more fervently because of their exposed position.

If Kaliningrad had, by early 1998, been more successful in economic adjustment than Primorskiy kray – and neither had done brilliantly – we suggest that this may be for two reasons. In the first place, the scale of the long-term adjustment needed in the latter is exceptionally daunting and the inherited economic structure exceptionally distorted. Second, the Nazdratenko leadership in Primor'ye has sought aggressively to entrench the monopoly power of the local business establishment, creating especially large barriers to market entry and fostering corruption of epic dimensions. In Kaliningrad, in contrast, foreign trade and investment may not have been actively encouraged, but the region's economy has been rather more open, though the intertwining of the local political and red-managerial elites is similar.

The governors' teams in both regions have been the subject of accusations of corruption, embezzlement and intimidation of political opponents. These accusations have been made in some detail and have not to our knowledge elicited libel suits.

Both regions have been severely affected by the 1998 crisis, which has been particularly damaging for foreign trade and investment. Meanwhile, Kaliningrad had already begun to be affected by a new source of uncertainty: the prospect of European Union enlargement. In preparation for its EU membership application, Poland had begun to tighten up on border controls, impeding border trade with Kaliningrad

(*Kaliningradskaya pravda*, 13 January 1998, p. 1, and 14 January 1998, p. 1).

The sad truth is that, for all the gains available from trade, foreign investment, technology transfer and the free movement of people, opening to the outside world does entail opening up to new sources of uncertainty and turbulence. Border regions are more exposed than the hinterland to such turbulence. Suspicion of the outside world is mostly, but not entirely, misplaced. Extensive and high-level corruption probably compound the problems. Location on a Russian border provides opportunities for grey-market activities that may usefully boost the incomes of the population. Unfortunately, gateway regions are also a natural habitat for gate-keepers. The above-average opportunities for high-level market-rigging, embezzlement and money-laundering in the Russian environment can easily shape the kind of regional political regime that flourishes in these places.

10. Conclusions

Philip Hanson and Michael Bradshaw

In the Introduction we listed the questions that we were trying to answer. In summary, and with a little rearrangement, they were as follows. Is there a single Russian economic space, or are there regional barriers to the movement of goods and factors of production, and even major differences across regions in the rules of the economic game? Are the diverging economic fortunes of different regions such as to threaten Russia with political fragmentation?

In so far as resources are being reallocated across regions, is this happening in ways that resemble those to be found in established market economies? Can inter-regional migration and capital flows be accounted for by firms and households responding to more or less 'standard' incentives in more or less 'standard' ways?

Why have some regions adapted better than others to the new circumstances? Are the regional patterns of change largely attributable to differences in initial conditions and subsequent autonomous adaptation by firms and households? Or, on the contrary, has the regional pattern of change been substantially influenced by differences in the policies of regional administrations? Do regional leaders make a difference?

What role, if any, has the federal government played in these diverging regional outcomes?

What role has the opening to foreign trade and investment played in these regional patterns of change?

Finally, there was a cluster of questions about how the political economy of regional change fed back to national economic policies and, more broadly - and other than by mere aggregation - to Russia's overall economic mess. In 1995-8 monetary tightening reduced inflation while the public finances continued to show a large deficit and monetary discipline in aggregate failed to translate into hard-budget constraints on large enterprises and banks. To what extent can the failures in tax collection, in the trimming of public spending, in the restructuring of large enterprises, along with the pervasive corruption and lack of confidence in the state and in Russia's future be ascribed to the activities of regional actors – regional political and business elites?

The details of our provisional answers to these questions can be found in Chapters 3–9 above. Pulling these details together, we suggest the following broad conclusions.

First, much of the observed adjustment across Russia's main administrative regions is the result of households and entrepreneurs (the founders of new firms) behaving in the way that standard economic theory assumes. In particular, migration flows amongst regions (Chapter 4) and regional differences in the rate of formation of new firms (Chapter 3) can be accounted for in standard ways. There was also some evidence, albeit rather weak, against the proposition that there were large differences in regime (monetized or unmonetized) across regions (Chapter 3). The case-studies (Chapters 6–9), as well as some of the quantitative analysis of Chapter 3, support the view that a region's initial economic conditions were a dominant factor in accounting for the differences in outcomes through 1998. They also suggest that regional administrative barriers to the movement of goods were weak and, probably, declining. Nevertheless, regional average real income levels had not begun to converge by 1998; they were, on the contrary, still diverging. Those inequalities amongst regional averages, however, were dwarfed by inequalities of real income within regions (Chapter 3).

Chapter 5 showed the federal government exerting very little influence on this divergence of regional levels of income and of public provision. True, poorer regions have tended to receive larger per capita net budgetary transfers than less-poor regions. But the scale of net transfers has been small and their effect in reducing inequalities of public provision has been very weak. As for the special federal development programmes announced for a number of regions, these have in recent years not been financed (Chapters 5, 7, 8). All of this contributes to the lack of credibility of federal institutions in the eyes of regional elites.

The role of regional leaders themselves in influencing the fortunes of their territories also appears to be small and, when not small, malign.

That is a judgement derived chiefly from our case-studies, and not the result of hypothesis-testing. At the same time, it is compatible with our quantitative analysis.

All four of our two-region comparisons testify to the importance of a region's initial economic conditions. Some governors make speeches decrying Chubaisian privatization, foreign investors and Moscow reformers; others do not. All are inclined to micro-manage, to protect 'their' enterprises and to seek direct control over any large assets on their turf. In three of the four 'gateway' regions in our case-studies (Kaliningrad, Primorskiy kray and Krasnodar) regional leaders have looked inwards rather than outwards: back to Moscow for help in the face of their exposure to the outside world, rather than to the outside world to promote trade and investment. At least two of those three regions also have regimes that are corrupt and oppressive. In the fourth of our gateway regions, St Petersburg, the environment has been more market-friendly, more open to foreign business; but there we find that regional administration policy under Sobchak probably hindered, albeit unintentionally, adaptation to take advantage of the city's location.

We have found, then, that differences across Russian regions in economic adjustment show clearly the effects of 'standard' market adaptation by new firms and households; that national policies designed to affect regional outcomes have little influence, and that the policies of regional leaders themselves, though often unhelpful, have less to do with regional outcomes than do each region's initial conditions. In other words, our particular angle on Russian post-communist economic change shows this to be a country in which market forces play a considerable role and government policies are apt to be ineffectual.

That is not the same as saying that Russian economic change exhibits the expected characteristics of a well-functioning market economy. Between government policies and market behaviour of new firms and households there is something else, and it is profoundly discouraging. The administrative, legal and social rules governing the economic game in 1990s' Russia have been inimical to successful adjustment and output recovery. The pathology in question has been widely discussed, especially since the 1998 financial crisis: in particular, unclear property rights, weak state governance, defective corporate governance, pervasive embezzlement and corruption, a lack of trust in institutions and a lack of confidence in the country's economic future.

This is not the place to discuss this pathology in general. What is relevant here is the role of regional actors in the Russian economic mess. Regional business and political elites have been an important part of the problem. The growth of new firms is impeded by official corruption; failing large enterprises have been propped up by tax offsets, tax arrears, the use of barter and money surrogates; tax collection has been weak (including the collection of personal income tax, all of which can be retained by regions); public spending has been wasteful, subject to embezzlement and poorly accounted for. Much of this pathology stems from tacit arrangements between regional politicians and the bosses of large enterprises to preserve the inherited population of firms (Chapters 6–9).

It is true that a Russian governor who pursued strict free-market policies would be going against the present Russian grain: of distributional coalitions inherited from the old order; of a general disregard for the law; and of pervasive patron–client relations. Similarly, the director of a large, privatized firm who sought to restructure and to invest for the future, in the absence of effective banks and securities markets, would have to be a visionary with deep pockets and lots of strong-arm protection. In other words, regional actors have had to operate in an environment inimical to constructive development – and especially to creative destruction. To depict members of the regional elites merely as passive victims of corruption and policy errors at national levels of government, however, would be misleading.

Any sustained improvement in the Russian economy will require changes in the incentives and constraints faced by businesses and administrations in the provinces. How might such changes come about?

One component of constructive change, barely touched upon in this study, must be the functioning of the courts: not (mainly) new legislation, but effective implementation of the existing commercial legislation and laws to do with abuse of power, through independent and competent courts in the provinces as well as the capital. That would be one topic deserving of further study: just how courts in the provinces operate at present, and how their working might be strengthened.

In Chapter 5 we discussed another way forward: reforms of the budgetary system. Here there are two important elements that have been left as black boxes in the present study and that merit further information-digging and analysis. They are the relations between regional and local (sub-regional) budgets and the nature, size and dynamics of regional and local off-budget funds. We need to know more about what drives local spending and how regional authorities' incentives are affected by their ability to operate off-budget funds. A recent pioneering study sheds some light on these questions for one region (Arai and Belov 1999). As we would have guessed, this study shows the regional administration under great pressure both to pass funds down to local level and to maximize its transfers from Moscow – relaxing its tax effort and keeping funds off-budget to assist with the latter aim.

That study reinforces a conclusion that we would draw from our review of fiscal-federal arrangements (Chapter 5): the Russian government and, when appropriate, Western aid agencies should insist on transparency in sub-national finances. Western aid has too often been made conditional on measures related exclusively to the federal budget, to the neglect of what happens in the devolution of spending responsibilities and public borrowing at sub-national levels.

However, even if public-finance reform and reform of the courts are possible ways forward, it remains the case that there is no single key that will unlock Russia's economic potential. Our research has emphasized the pervasive and mutually connected character of Russia's economic problems. Some regions have done less badly than others, but the handicaps of weak government machinery and weak social capital are present everywhere.

Appendix. Key Statistical Indicators for Case-study Regions

Table A.1 *Demographic characteristics of case-study regions*

	Population (000) 1998	% in capital 1998	Urban % 1998	Average in-migration 1993–6	Share of in-migration from Russia	Average out-migration 1993–6	Share of out-migration to Russia	Dependency ratio 1997
Russia	147,105		73.1	1.55	61.5	1.18	79.0	42.2
St Petersburg	4,749	88.3	100	2.07	64.9	1.95	71.3	40.3
Kostroma	797	36.5	65	1.56	65.1	1.05	83.2	44.5
Samara	3,309	35.2	81	1.75	58.8	0.88	82.7	40.8
Krasnodar	5,075	13.0	54	2.34	59.3	0.91	75.4	44.5
Irkutsk	2,774	21.3	80	1.28	71.7	1.28	83.8	40.8
Sakhalin	620	28.5	86	1.37	74.6	3.74	84.1	35.6
Primorskiy kray	2,216	27.8	78	1.46	71.7	1.72	80.4	37.7
Kaliningrad	943	45.1	78	2.71	44.3	1.43	67.4	39.8

Note: The dependency ratio is the percentage of the population of non-working age.
Sources: Calculations based on Goskomstat (1997 and 1999).

Table A.2 Electoral results for case-study regions (%)

	1996 presidential election, second round		1995 Duma election, party list				Gubernatorial election	
	Yeltsin	Zyuganov	Left	Democratic	Patriotic		Turnout	Vote
Russia	73.9	21.1	34.8	32.0	18.1		44.2	47.5
St Petersburg	61.3	32.3	30.5	35.5	16.7		34.4	53.4
Kostroma	49.9	53.8	38.5	26.8	18.4		53.1	64.1
Samara	51.9	42.7	32.3	31.7	20.1		50.7	63.4
Krasnodar	43.9	51.5	38.2	24.3	26.7		48.6	82.0
Irkutsk	52.6	39.8	28.3	32.0	21.3		46.0	78.2
Sakhalin	53.4	38.8	32.6	25.6	22.4		33.7	39.5
Primorskiy kray	52.3	39.4	31.3	22.8	27.4		62.2	68.6
Kaliningrad	57.7	35.3	26.7	32.7	23.1		43.6	49.6

Source: Territorial'noe... (1997).

257

Table A.3 *Budgetary characteristics of case-study regions*

	Tax receipts per capita 1997	Federal funds % of budget 1996	Tax share retained 1996	Balance of transfers 1996	Share of FFPR 1999
Russia	1.00	11.7			
St Petersburg	1.35	3.1	54	1140	0
Kostroma	0.87	35.0	66	–16	0.9128
Samara	1.47	0.8	55	1308	0
Krasnodar	0.63	19.1	61	300	1.8459
Irkutsk	1.12	2.5	60	831	0.9210
Sakhalin	1.50	28.5	68	110	1.9166
Primorskiy kray	0.94	18.9	67	286	3.9785
Kaliningrad	0.69	8.1	62	397	0.6109

Sources: Calculations based on Goskomstat (1999), Lavrov (1997a) and Sobranie Zakonodatel'stva (1999).

Table A.4 Gross regional product (per capita) and industrial output

| | Gross regional product (per capita) | | | | Industrial output (change %) | Industrial labour productivity |
	1994	1995	1996	1997	1990–97	1997
Russia	1.00	1.00	1.00	1.00	−51	1.00
St Petersburg	1.05	1.16	1.15	1.17	−66	0.59
Kostroma	0.85	0.88	0.76	0.81	−67	0.68
Samara	1.55	1.63	1.58	1.62	−38	2.14
Krasnodar	0.68	0.74	0.77	0.71	−55	0.31
Irkutsk	1.31	1.47	1.41	1.49	−53	1.29
Sakhalin	1.39	1.23	1.26	1.56	−52	1.34
Primorskiy kray	0.98	1.02	0.94	1.01	−52	0.70
Kaliningrad	0.76	0.68	0.67	0.67	−69	0.42

Notes: All normalization is based on the Russian regional average. The reported gross regional product excludes measures of non-market collective services provided by the state to the population as a whole; certain non-market services financed by the federal budget; services of financial intermediaries; and services for foreign trade operations (see Granberg *et al.* 1998).

Source: Calculations based on Goskomstat (1999).

259

Table A.5   Industrial branch structure in terms of output in 1997

	Electricity	Fuel	Metals	Chemicals and petrochemical	Engineering	Timber and paper	Light	Food processing	Other
Russia	17.1	17.4	13.4	7.2	18.8	3.7	1.8	14.5	6.1
St Petersburg	16.3	0.3	3.5	3.9	34.6	2.9	2.7	28.8	7.0
Kostroma	49.6	0.2	0.3	1.4	12.3	11.5	4.2	10.8	9.7
Samara	13.1	9.0	1.7	9.3	54.1	0.4	0.4	8.5	3.5
Krasnodar	20.1	7.0	0.2	1.8	10.3	4.6	1.8	43.6	10.6
Irkutsk	17.5	12.3	22.5	5.1	12.2	15.4	0.5	10.3	4.2
Sakhalin	21.7	34.7	0.3	0.0	4.5	6.5	0.3	30.0	2.0
Primorskiy kray	29.4	9.4	1.6	1.7	8.4	4.1	0.5	39.8	5.1
Kaliningrad	18.0	7.8	0.4	0.6	16.0	7.1	1.3	43.8	5.0

Source: Goskomstat (1999).

Table A.6 Small enterprises at the start of 1998

	No. of enterprises	No. of small enterprises	Residents per enterprise	Small enterprise employment ('000)	% of total employment	Employment growth 1993–8
Russia	2,727,146	861,063	170.8	6514.8	10.1	28.4
St Petersburg	148,261	102,717	46.2	532.2	22.7	146.6
Kostroma	13,179	2,609	305.5	22.5	6.7	–22.9
Samara	56,608	19,612	168.7	130.9	9.0	–5.7
Krasnodar	96,961	26,917	188.5	226.6	11.8	21.8
Irkutsk	38,827	12,586	220.4	120.7	10.4	67.6
Sakhalin	13,675	3,305	187.6	42.3	15.2	29.4
Primorskiy kray	37,826	10,350	214.1	100.3	10.6	51.5
Kaliningrad	22,896	6,616	142.5	45.5	11.1	131.0

Note: Small enterprises data exclude small enterprises with more that 25 per cent state ownership, small private farms, and individual activity. Employment growth is only indicative. Because of frequent methodological changes the growth rate cannot be precise. The measure used here is small enterprise employment in at the start of 1998 and the employment in private sector small enterprises at the end of 1993.

Source: Calculations based on Goskomstat (1994, 1999).

Table A.7 *Banking activity*

	Banks		Branches in 1999		Deposits		Bank Credits	
	1998	1999	Regional	Outside bank	Per capita	Share in hard currency	1996	1997
Russia	1697	1474			1.00	52.2	1.00	1.00
St Petersburg	43	40	36	62	1.63	56.9	0.47	0.30
Kostroma	9	6	0	25	0.01	0.0	0.26	0.15
Samara	24	24	36	63 [a]	0.39	46.2	1.27	1.66
Krasnodar	42	30	49	81	0.14	29.7	0.61	0.47
Irkutsk	16	14	36	50	0.24	23.8	0.78	0.61
Sakhalin	7	6	8	21	0.11	60.3	0.87	0.68
Primorskiy kray	16	11	26	38	0.39	65.0	0.91	0.91
Kaliningrad	15	14	7	27	0.28	75.7	1.24	1.10

Notes: [a] Includes a branch of a foreign bank

The number of banks registered is at the start of the year. Regional per capita bank deposits and bank credits are normalized by the regional average. Apart from the registration of branches from banks outside the region the activities of the largest Moscow-based banks are excluded from the regional banking statistics. The regional data give a measure of local banking sector development.

Source: Calculations based on Tsentral'nyi Bank Rossiiskoy Federatsii (1999).

262

Table A.8 Foreign economic activity in 1997

	Cumulative total foreign investment	Exports	Joint Ventures				
			No.	Employment	Output	Exports
Russia	1.00	1.00	14,734	1.00	1.00	1.00
St Petersburg	1.18	0.66	1,467	0.30	0.30	3.87
Kostroma	0.00	0.13	56	0.12	0.39	0.02
Samara	0.64	1.11	99	0.05	0.29	0.17
Krasnodar	0.25	1.35	257	0.05	0.37	0.04
Irkutsk	0.43	1.50	87	0.90	0.34	0.11
Sakhalin	2.92	0.99	89	0.16	0.93	0.85
Primorskiy kray	0.60	0.51	323	0.12	0.57	0.76
Kaliningrad	0.66	0.63	317	0.28	0.94	1.86

Notes: All figures are per capita, except for the total number of joint ventures, and are normalized by the regional average. Output is the recorded output for sales on the domestic market. Cumulative foreign investment is the amount of actual investment made in a region, regardless of whether the representative office is registered in another region.

Source: Calculations based on Goskomstat (1999).

Table A.9 Income and unemployment, 1997

	Real income	Real wage	Poverty	Unemployment	Official unemployment
Russia	1.00	1.00	20.8	11.3	2.8
St Petersburg	0.97	0.98	23.1	9.0	1.1
Kostroma	0.79	0.90	20.8	9.2	3.2
Samara	1.16	1.28	18.3	9.3	3.2
Krasnodar	0.90	0.95	25.0	15.6	1.6
Irkutsk	0.92	1.17	27.0	13.9	2.1
Sakhalin	0.64	0.97	33.7	15.3	3.2
Primorskiy kray	0.78	1.03	27.2	13.5	2.9
Kaliningrad	0.78	0.90	24.2	11.5	2.5

Notes: Real income and real wage are the average monthly per capita monetary income and wage income deflated by the regional income necessary to sustain a minimal standard of living, and are normalized by the regional average. Poverty is the percentage of the population with an income below the income necessary to sustain a minimal standard of income. Unemployment is the ILO measure of unemployment, whereas official unemployment is the share of the labour force which is officially registered at the Federal Employment Service.

Source: Calculations based on Goskomstat (1999).

Table A.10 Employment in different sectors of the economy, 1990 and 1997

	Industry		Agriculture		Construction		Transport and communications		Trade and catering		Education		Other	
	1990	1997	1990	1997	1990	1997	1990	1997	1990	1997	1990	1997	1990	1997
Russia	30.3	23.0	13.2	13.7	12.0	8.7	7.7	7.9	7.8	13.5	13.3	13.3	15.7	19.9
St Petersburg	33.1	22.7	0.5	0.5	11.1	9.3	8.8	11.2	8.1	16.0	21.3	17.6	17.1	22.7
Kostroma	30.2	23.7	13.6	11.8	12.8	4.1	7.7	9.5	8.3	13.2	11.8	14.2	15.6	23.5
Samara	36.4	30.8	8.9	7.7	12.3	9.7	8.0	8.8	7.0	11.7	11.9	11.6	15.5	19.7
Krasnodar	23.1	16.6	20.6	20.7	10.5	9.4	8.4	8.3	8.8	13.9	10.6	11.6	18.0	19.5
Irkutsk	29.9	26.7	8.3	8.1	15.1	9.5	9.7	8.0	8.1	14.1	12.1	13.2	16.8	20.4
Sakhalin	26.8	22.8	5.1	5.8	14.2	11.3	11.2	7.2	10.6	15.8	10.3	12.1	21.8	25.0
Primorskiy kray	29.9	19.6	7.7	7.3	12.7	12.0	12.3	6.7	9.0	19.9	11.5	12.5	16.9	22.0
Kaliningrad	30.3	19.9	12.0	10.5	9.6	7.9	8.8	6.8	9.0	18.7	13.3	11.7	17.0	24.5

Source: Goskomstat (1999).

References

Abalkina, I. (1994), 'Analiz regional'nykh razlichiy formirovaniya zhilishch-nogo rynka', *Voprosy ekonomiki* 4, 111–19.

Abraham, Filip (1996), 'Regional Adjustment and Wage Flexibility in the European Union', *Regional Science and Urban Economics* 26, 51–75.

Adamesku, A. A. *et al.* (1996), 'O sovershenstvovanii administrativno-territorial'nogo ustroystva Rossiyskoy Federatsii', in *Problemy kompleks-nogo regional'nogo razvitiya Rossii*, vol. 2, Moscow: SOPS, 31–56.

Afanas'yev, M. [N.] (1994), 'Izmeneniya v mekhanizme funktsionirovaniya pravyashchikh regional'nykh elit', *Polis* 6, 6–18.

—— (1997), *Klientelizm i rossiyskaya gosudarstvennost'*, Moscow: Mos-kovskiy Obshchestvennyy Nauchnyy Fond.

—— (1998), 'V Rossii sformirovany predstavitel'nye sobraniya pravyashchikh regional'nykh grupp', in *Kuda idyot Rossiya? Transformatsiya sotsial'noy sfery i sotsial'naya politika*, Moscow: Delo, 140–44.

Agafonov, N. T. and Yu. N. Gladkiy (1994), 'Postperestroyechnaya obsh-chestvennaya geografiya: iskushenie rynkom i preyemstvennost'', *Izvestiya RGO* 126 (4), 23–32.

Alimova, T., V. Buev, P. Vakurov, V. Golikova and L. Korbut (1995), 'Strategii povedeniya semeynykh fermerskikh khozyaystv', *Voprosy ekonomiki* 1, 47–56.

Analysis of Tendencies of Russia's Regions Development in 1992–1995 (1996), Moscow: Ekspert Institute.

Andrews, J. and K. Stoner-Weiss (1995), 'Regionalism and Reform in Provin-cial Russia', *Post-Soviet Affairs* 11 (4), 384–406.

Andrews-Speed, P. (1998), 'Natural Gas in East Siberia and the Russian Far East: A View from the Chinese Corner', *Cambridge Review of Inter-national Affairs* 12 (1), 77–95.

Animitsa, E. G. (1993), *Ekonomicheskaya reforma v Rossii: obshchenatsio-nal'nye i regional'nye aspekty*, Yekaterinburg: Urals State University Press.

Arai, N. and A. Belov (1999), 'Osobennosti byudzhetnoy sistemy Sakhalin-skoy oblasti v 1996–1998gg', paper presented at Hokkaido University Slavic Research Centre Symposium on 'Russian Regions: Economic Growth and Environment', Sapporo, July.

Arsen'yev, V. (1998), 'Vesti pro 200 krupneyshikh kompaniy Rossii', *Den'gi* 4 February, 38–43.

Baburin, V. L. and V. E. Shuvalov (1996), 'Transformatsiya ponyatiynokontseptual'nogo apparata sotsial'no-ekonomicheskoy geografii v uslovi-yakh realizatsii ekonomicheskoy reformy', *Izvestiya RGO* 124 (1), 31-9.

Bahry, D. (1987), *Outside Moscow: Power, Politics, and Budgetary Policy in the Soviet Republics*, New York: Columbia University Press.

Balzer, H. (1997), 'A Shadow Middle Class for a Shadow Economy', paper presented at the XXIX Annual Conference of the American Association for the Advancement of Slavic Studies (AAASS), Seattle, November.

―― (1998), 'Russia's Middle Classes', *Post-Soviet Affairs* 14 (2), 165-87.

Balzer, M. M. (1995), 'Homelands, Leadership, and Self Rule: Observations on Interethnic Relations in the Sakha Republic', *Polar Geography* 19 (4), 284-305.

―― and U. A. Vinokurova (1996), 'Nationalism, Interethnic Relations and Federalism: The Case of Sakha Republic (Yakutia)', *Europe–Asia Studies* 48 (1), 101-20.

Bandman, M. K. (1998), 'Sibir'' v sisteme ekonomicheskikh rayonov SSSR-Rossii', *Region: Ekonomika i Sotsiologiya* 2, 3-27.

Barro, R. J. and X. Sala-I-Martin (1991), 'Convergence Across States and Regions', *Brookings Papers in Economic Activity*, 1, 107-82.

Barteneva, A. (1999), 'Poteryannye milliardy', *Ekspert*, 5 April, 15-20.

Bayoumi, T. A. and A. K. Rose (1993), 'Domestic Savings and Intra-National Capital Flows', *European Economic Review* 37, 1197-202.

Belandi, H. and C. A. Ingene (1994), 'A General Equilibrium Analysis of Rural–Urban Migration under Uncertainty', *Journal of Regional Science* 34 (1), 91-103.

Belokurova, E. V., V. Ya. Gel'man and M. V. Nozhenko (1997), *Regional Profile: Saint Petersburg and Leningrad Oblast*, Russian Regional Research Group Working Paper 12, Birmingham: University of Birmingham.

Belyakov, D. E. (1997), 'Ekonomicheskiy potentsyal razvitiya regionov', *Regionologiya*, 4, 195-207.

Berkowitz, D. (1994a), 'Local Support for Market Reform: Implications of a Consumption Bias', in T. H. Friedgut and J. W. Hahn (eds), *Local Power and Post-Soviet Politics*, Armonk, NY: M.E. Sharpe, 192-207.

―― (1994b), *Russia: Market Integration Against the Odds*, Washington, DC: National Council for Soviet and East European Research.

―― (1996), 'On the Persistence of Rationing Following Liberalization: A Theory for Economies in Transition', mimeo.

―― (1997), 'Regional Income and Secession: Center–Periphery Relations in Emerging Market Economies', *Regional Science and Urban Economics*, 27, 17-45.

―― and D. DeJong (1997), *Accounting for Growth in Post-Soviet Russia*, Department of Economics Working Paper 318, Pittsburgh, PA: University of Pittsburgh.

―― and S. Husted (1995), 'Market Integration Against the Odds: Evidence from Russia's Big Bang', mimeo.

Bertaud, A. and R. Bertrand (1997), 'Socialist Cities without Land Markets', *Journal of Urban Economics*, 41, 137-51.

Bil'chak, V. S. and V. F. Zakharov (1998), *Regional'naya ekonomika*, Kaliningrad: Yantarnyy Skaz.
Bird, R. M. (1992), *Tax Policy and Economic Development*, Baltimore, MD: Johns Hopkins University Press.
Blanchard, O. and M. Kremer (1997), 'Disorganization', *Quarterly Journal of Economics*, 112 (4), 1091–127.
Blanchflower, D. G. and A. J. Oswald (1994), *The Wage Curve*, Cambridge, MA: MIT Press.
Blow, L., J. Hall and S. Smith (1996), 'Financing Regional Government in the UK: Some Issues', *Fiscal Studies* 17 (4), 99–120.
Botkin, O. I. (ed.) (1997), *Ekonomika Udmurtii*, Izhevsk: Udmurt University Press.
Brade, I. *et al.* (1999), 'Izmeneniya v sisteme gorodov Rossii v 1990-kh gg.', *Izvestiya AN – Seriya Geografiya* (forthcoming).
Bradshaw, M. J. (1992), 'Siberia Poses a Challenge to Russian Federalism', *RFE/RL Research Report* 1 (41) (16 October), 6–14.
—— (1995), *Regional Patterns of Foreign Investment in Russia*, London: Post-Soviet Business Forum, Royal Institute of International Affairs.
—— (1996), *Russia's Regions: A Business Analysis*, London: The Economist Intelligence Unit.
—— (1997a), 'The Geography of Foreign Investment in Russia: 1993–1995', *Tijdschrift voor Economische en Sociale Geografie* 88 (1), 77–84.
—— (1997b), 'Sakhalin: The Right Place at the Right Time', *Russian and Euro-Asian Bulletin* 6 (9), 1–7.
—— (1998), 'Going Global: The Political Economy of Oil and Gas Development Offshore of Sakhalin', *Cambridge Review of International Affairs* 12 (1), 147–76.
—— (1999), *The Russian Far East: Prospects for the Millennium*, Discussion Paper 80, London: Royal Institute of International Affairs.
—— and P. Hanson (1994), 'Regions, Local Power and Reform in Russia', in R. Campbell (ed.), *Issues in the Transformation of Centrally Planned Economies: Essays in Honour of Gregory Grossman*, Boulder, CO: Westview Press, 133–63.
—— and J. A. Palacin (1996), *An Atlas of Economic Performance of Russia's Regions*, Russian Regional Research Group Working Paper 2, Birmingham: University of Birmingham.
—— and D. J. B. Shaw (eds) (1996), *Regional Problems During Economic Transition in Russia: Case Studies*, Russian Regional Research Group Working Paper 1, Birmingham: University of Birmingham.
—— and P. Kirkow (1998), 'The Energy Crisis in the Russian Far East: Origins and Possible Solutions', *Europe–Asia Studies* 50 (6), 1043–63.
——, A. Stenning and D. J. Sutherland (1998), 'Economic Restructuring and Regional Change in Russia', in J. Pickles and A. Smith (eds), *Theorising Transition: The Political Economy of Post-Communist Transformations*, London: Routledge, 147–71.
Brown, K. (1993), 'Nizhnii Novgorod: A Regional Solution to National Problems?', *RFE/RL Research Report* 2 (5), 17–23.

Broxup, M. B. (1996), 'Tatarstan and the Tatars', in G. Smith (ed.), *The Nationalities Question on the Post-Soviet States*, London: Longman, 75–93.

Buckley, R. M. and E. N. Gurenko (1997), 'Housing and Income Distribution in Russia: Zhivago's Legacy', *The World Bank Research Observer* 12 (1), 19–32.

Bylov, G. and D. Sutherland (1998), 'Statistical Overview', *Communist Economies and Economic Transformation* 10 (3), 305–18.

Callejon, M. and M. T. Costa (1997), 'Agglomeration Economies and the Location of Industry', paper presented at the European Network for Industrial Policy International Conference on Industrial Policy for Europe, London, June.

Campbell, A. (1994), 'Local Government Policy Making and Management in Russia: The Case of St Petersburg (Leningrad)', *Policy Studies Journal* 21 (1), 133–42.

—— (1995), 'Power and Structure in Nizhnii Novgorod, St. Petersburg and Moscow', in A. Coulson (ed.), *Local Government in Eastern Europe*, Aldershot, UK: Edward Elgar, 238–63.

Chernikov, A. (1998), 'Resource-Rich Regions: Irkutsk Oblast' on the Road to the Market', *Communist Economies and Economic Transformation* 24 (3), 375–89.

Clarke, S. (1997), 'Structural Adjustment without Mass Unemployment?' in S. Clarke (ed.), *Structural Adjustment without Mass Unemployment? Lessons from Russia*, Cheltenham, UK: Edward Elgar, 9–87.

Clem, R. S. and P. R. Craumer (1995), 'A Rayon-Level Analysis of the Russian Election and Constitutional Plebiscite of December 1995', *Post-Soviet Geography* 36 (8), 459–75.

—— (1996), 'Roadmap to Victory: Boris Yel'stin and the Russian Presidential Elections of 1996', *Post-Soviet Geography and Economics* 37 (6), 335–54.

Cline, M. (1994), 'Nizhnii Novgorod: A Regional View of the Russian Elections', *RFE/RL Research Report* 3 (4), 48–54.

Colombatto, E. and J. R. Macey (1995), 'Path-Dependence, Public Choice, and Transition in Russia: A Bargaining Approach', *Cornell Journal of Law and Public Policy* 4 (8) (Spring), 379–414.

Commander, S. and C. Mummsen (1999), *Understanding Barter in Russia*, EBRD Working Paper 37, London: European Bank for Reconstruction and Development.

——, Q. Fan and M. E. Schaffer (eds) (1996), *Enterprise Restructuring and Economic Policy in Russia*, Washington, DC: World Bank.

Cooper, J. M. R. (1994), 'Migration and Market Wage Risk', *Journal of Regional Science* 34 (4), 563–82.

Danilov, D. (1999), 'Kaliningradskaya dilemma', *Nezavisimaya Gazeta – Regiony*, 4, 14.

Daveri, F. and R. Faini (1998), 'Where Do Migrants Go?', mimeo.

Debardeleben, J. (1997), 'The Development of Federalism in Russia', in P. Stavrakis, J. Debardeleben and L. Black (eds), *Beyond the Monolith: The Emergence of Regionalism in Post-Soviet Russia*, Baltimore, MD:

Woodrow Wilson Center and Johns Hopkins University Press, 35–56.

—— and A. A. Galkin (1997), 'Electoral Behavior and Attitudes in Russia: Do Regions Make a Difference or Do Regions Just Differ?', in P. Stavrakis, J. Debardeleben and L. Black (eds), *Beyond the Monolith: The Emergence of Regionalism in Post-Soviet Russia*, Baltimore, MD: Woodrow Wilson Center and Johns Hopkins University Press, 57–81.

De Masi, P. and V. Koen (1996), 'Relative Price Convergence in Russia', *IMF Staff Papers* 43 (1), 97–122.

De Melo, M. and G. Ofer (1999), 'Reforms Along the Volga: Initial Conditions, Policies and Outcomes in Ten Regional Capitals', mimeo.

——, —— and O. Sandler (1995), 'Pioneers for Profit: St Petersburg Entrepreneurs in Services', *World Bank Economic Review* 9 (3), 425–50.

Dmitrieva, O. G. (1992), *Regional'naya ekonomicheskaya diagnostika*, St Petersburg: St Petersburg University of Economics and Finance.

Dronov, V. P. (1998), *Infrastruktura i territoriya*, Moscow: Moscow State Pedagogical University.

Duka, A. V. (1995), 'Transformatsiya mestnykh elit (institutsionalizatsiya obshchestvennykh dvizheniy: ot protesta k uchastiyu)', *Mir Rossii*, 2, 34–45.

Earle, J. S. and S. Estrin (1997), 'After Voucher Privatisation: The Structure of Corporate Ownership in Russian Manufacturing Industry', London Business School, mimeo.

EBRD (European Bank for Reconstruction and Development) (1998), *Transition Report 1998*, London: EBRD.

Eckert, D. and A. Treyvish (1995), 'La géographie industrielle, discipline en crise dans la recherche russe', *L'Espace géographique* 24 (2), 169–80.

Ekonomicheskie reformy v Rossii: itogi pervykh let· (1991–1996) (1997), Moscow: Nauka.

Ekspert (1997), 'Investitsionnyy reyting rossiyskikh regionov, 1996–1997 gody', *Ekspert* 47 (8 December), 18–40.

—— (1998), 'Investitsionnyy reyting rossiyskikh regionov v 1998 godu', *Ekspert*, available from http://wint.decsy.ru/expert/expert/regions/reg98/data/reg98nc.htm.

Ellman, M. (1997), 'Transformation as a Demographic Crisis', in S. Zecchini (ed.), *Lessons from the Economic Transition: Central and Eastern Europe in the 1990s*, London: Kluwer Academic Publisheres, 351–71.

European Commission (1994), *Competitiveness and Cohesion: Trends in the Regions*, Luxembourg: European Union.

Feldstein, M. and C. Horioka (1980), 'Domestic Savings and International Capital Flows', *The Economic Journal* 90, 314–29.

Field, M. G. (1997), 'Health in Russia: The Regional and National Dimensions', in P. Stavrakis, J. Debardeleben and L. Black (eds), *Beyond the Monolith: The Emergence of Regionalism in Post-Soviet Russia*, Baltimore, MD: Woodrow Wilson Center and Johns Hopkins University Press, 165–80.

Filatotchev, I. V. and R. P. Bradshaw (1995), 'The Geographical Impact of the Russian Privatisation Program', *Post-Soviet Geography* 36 (6), 371–84.

Fisher Associates (1997), *Support to the Kaliningrad Oblast' Within the Context of the Special Economic Zone*, EDRUS 9404, Tacis report, mimeo.

Fondahl, G. A. (1996), 'Contested Terrain: Changing Boundaries and Identities in Southeastern Siberia', *Post-Soviet Geography and Economics* 37 (1), 3–15.

—— (1997), 'Siberia: Assimilation and its Discontents', in I. Bremmer and R. Taras (eds), *New States, New Politics: Building the Post-Soviet Nations*, Cambridge: Cambridge University Press, 190–234.

Frank, A. and R. Wixman (1997), 'The Middle Volga: Exploring the Limits of Sovereignty', in I. Bremmer and R. Taras (eds), *New States, New Politics: Building the Post-Soviet Nations*, Cambridge: Cambridge University Press, 140–189.

Freinkman, L. and M. Haney (1997), *What Affects the Russian Regional Government's Propensity to Subsidize?*, Policy Research Working Paper 1818, Washington, DC: The World Bank.

—— and P. Yossifov (1999), *Decentralization in Regional Fiscal Systems in Russia: Trends and Links to Economic Performance*, Policy Research Working Paper 2100, Washington, DC: World Bank .

Gaddy, C. G. (1996), *The Price of the Past: Russia's Struggle with the Legacy of a Militarized Economy*, Washington, DC: Brookings Institution Press.

—— and B. W. Ickes (1998), 'Beyond a Bailout: Time to Face Reality about Russia's "Virtual Economy"', Washington, DC: Brookings Institution, mimeo.

Gel'man, V. (1997), 'Konsolidatsiya regional'noy elity i mestnaya demokratiya v Rossii: Sankt-Peterburg v sravnitel'noy perspektive', mimeo.

—— and M. McAuley (1994), 'The Politics of City Government: Leningrad/ St. Petersburg, 1990-1992', in T. H. Friedgut and J. W. Hahn (eds), *Local Power and Post-Soviet Politics*, Armonk, NY: M. E. Sharpe, 15–42.

—— and O. Senatova (1995), 'Sub-National Politics in Russia in the Post Communist Transition Period: A View from Moscow', *Regional and Federal Studies* (Summer), 211–23.

—— and V. Ryzhenkov (1998), 'Politicheskaya regionalistika: ot obshchest-vennogo interesa l otrasli znaniya?' in I. Oswald, R. Possekel, P. Sykow and J. Wielgohs (eds), *Sotsial'nye issledovaniya v Rossii*, Moscow: Polis.

Geograficheskie osnovy tipologii regionov dlya formirovaniya regional'noy politiki Rossii (1995), Moscow: Institut Geografii RAN.

Gibson, J. and P. Hanson (eds) (1996), *Transformation from Below: Local Power and the Political Economy of Post-Communist Transformations*, Cheltenham, UK: Edward Elgar.

Gimpelson, V., D. Slider and S. Churgov (1994), 'Political Tendencies in Russia's Regions: Evidence from the 1993 Parliamentary Elections', *Slavic Review* 53 (2), 711–32.

Gladkiy, Yu. N. (1992), 'Obshchestvennaya geografiya: starye mifologemy i novye orientiry', *Izvestiya RGO* 124 (2), 139–45.

Glaz'yev, S. (1998), 'Krakh "stabilizatsionnoy programmy" i imperativ pere-khoda k mobilizatsionnoy modeli', *Rossiyskiy ekonomicheskiy zhurnal* (9–10), 8–19.

Golobokova, G. M. (1997), *Strategicheskoye upravlenyie regionom v tranzitivnoy ekonomike*, Irkutsk: Izdatel'stvo IGEA.

Goskomstat Rossii (1992), *Pokazateli ekonomicheskogo razvitiya respublik, krayov i oblastey Rossiyskoy Federatsii*, Moscow: Goskomstat Rossii.

—— (1994), *Rossiyskiy statisticheskiy ezhegodnik 1994*, Moscow: Goskomstat Rossii.

—— (1995), *Sravnitel'nye pokazateli ekonomicheskogo polozheniya regionov Rossiyskoy Federatsii*, Moscow: Goskomstat Rossii.

—— (1996), *Rossiyskiy statisticheskiy ezhegodnik 1996*, Moscow: Goskomstat Rossii.

—— (1997a), *Demograficheskiy ezhegodnik Rossii*, Moscow: Goskomstat Rossii.

—— (1997b), *Regiony Rossii: statisticheskiy sbornik*, vol. 1, Moscow: Goskomstat Rossii.

—— (1997c), *Regiony Rossii: statisticheskiy sbornik*, vol. 2, Moscow: Goskomstat Rossii.

—— (1997d), *Sotsial'no-ekonomicheskoye polozhenie Rossiyskoy Federatsii*, Moscow: Goskomstat Rossii.

—— (1998a), *Regiony Rossii: statisticheskiy sbornik*, vol. 1, Moscow: Goskomstat Rossii.

—— (1998b), *Regiony Rossii: statisticheskiy sbornik*, vol. 2, Moscow: Goskomstat Rossii.

—— (1998c), *Rossiya v tsifrakh 1998*, Moscow: Goskomstat Rossii.

—— (1998d), *Rossiyskiy statisticheskiy ezhegodnik 1998*, Moscow: Goskomstat Rossii.

—— (1999a), *Obzor regionov Rossiyskoy Federatsii*, Moscow: Goskomstat Rossii.

—— (1999b), *Sotsial'no-ekonomicheskoye polozhenie Rossii, yanvar' 1999 goda*, Moscow: Goskomstat Rossii.

—— (1999c), *Sotsial'no-ekonomicheskoye polozhenie Rossii, yanvar'-fevral' 1999 goda*, Moscow: Goskomstat Rossii.

Gosudarstvennyy doklad o sostoyanii i ispol'zovanii zemel' Rossiyskoy Federatsii za 1995 god (1996), Moscow: Komitet po zemel'nym resursam i zemleustroystvu.

Govoryonkova, T. *et al.* (1997), 'Chto sulit i chem grozit administrativno-territorial'naya reforma v Rossii', *Federalizm* 3, 109–28.

Gramlich, E. M. (1977), 'Intergovernmental Grants: A Review of the Empirical Literature', in W. E. Oates (ed.), *The Political Economy of Fiscal Federalism*, Lexington, MA: Lexington Books, 219–39.

Granberg, A. G. (1994), 'Regional'naya ekonomika i regional'naya ekonomicheskaya nauka v SSSR i Rossii', *Region: ekonomika i sotsiologiya* 1, 3–26.

—— (1995), *Regional'naya politika v programme ekonomicheskikh reform*, Moscow: Sovet po razmeshcheniyu proizvoditel'nykh sil i ekonomicheskomu sotrudnichestvu.

——, A. I. Masakova and Yu. Zaitseva (1998), 'Valcvoi regional'nyi produkt kak indikator differentsiatsii ekonomicheskogo razvitiya regionov',

Voprosy statistiki (9), 3–11.

Grandstaff, P. J. (1980), *Interregional Migration in the U.S.S.R.: Economic Aspects, 1959–1970*, Durham, NC: Duke University Press.

Grant, E. K. and J. Vanderkamp (1976), *The Economic Causes and Effects of Migration: Canada, 1965–71*, Ottawa: Economic Council of Canada.

Gritsay, O. V. (1996), 'Postindustrial'nye sdvigi v Moskve: kontseptsiya global'nogo goroda i strukturnaya perestroyka ekonomiki', *Izvestiya AN – Seriya Geografiya*, 5, 90–7.

——, G. V. Ioffe and A. I. Treyvish (1991), *Tsentr i periferiya v regional'nom razvitii*, Moscow: Nauka.

Hahn, J. W. (1991), 'Local Politics and Political Power in Russia: The Case of Yaroslavl', *Soviet Economy* 7 (1), 322–41.

—— (1993), 'Attitudes Toward Reform Among Provincial Russian Politicians', *Post-Soviet Affairs* 9 (1), 66–85.

—— (1994a), 'How Demoractic are Local Russian Deputies?', in C. Saivetz and A. Jones (eds), *In Search of Pluralism: Soviet and Post-Soviet Politics*, Boulder, CO: Westview Press, 74–9.

—— (1994b), 'Reforming Post-Soviet Russia: The Attitudes of Local Politicians', in T. H. Friedgut and J. W. Hahn (eds), *Local Power and Post-Soviet Politics*, Armonk, NY: M. E. Sharpe, 208–38.

—— (1997a), 'Democratization and Political Participation in Russia's Regions', in K. Dawisha and B. Parrott (eds), *Democractic Changes and Authoritarian Regimes in Russia, Ukraine, Belarus and Moldova*, Cambridge: Cambridge University Press, 130–74.

—— (1997b), 'Regional Elections and Political Stability in Russia', *Post-Soviet Geography and Economics* 38 (5), 251–63.

Hanson, Philip (1981), *Trade and Technology in Soviet–Western Relations*, London: Macmillan.

—— (1993), 'Local Power and Market Reform in Russia', *Communist Economies and Economic Transformation* 5 (1), 45–60.

—— (1994a), 'The Center versus the Periphery in Russian Economic Policy', *RFE/RL Research Report* 3 (17), 23–8.

—— (1994b), *Regions, Local Power and Economic Change in Russia*, London: Post-Soviet Business Forum, Royal Institute of International Affairs.

—— (1996), 'Economic Change in the Russian Provinces', in J. Gibson and P. Hanson (eds), *Transformation from Below: Local Power and the Political Economy of Post-Communist Transitions*, Cheltenham, UK: Edward Elgar, 179–216.

—— (1997a), 'How Many Russias? Russia's Regions and their Adjustment to Economic Change', *International Spectator* 31 (1), 39–53.

—— (1997b), 'Samara: A Preliminary Profile of a Russian Region and its Adaptation to the Market', *Europe–Asia Studies* 49 (3), 407–29.

—— (1997c), 'What Sort of Capitalism is Developing in Russia?' *Communist Economies and Economic Transformation* 9 (1), 27–43.

—— (1998), 'What Can be Learnt from Case Studies of Russian Regions?' paper presented at American Association for the Advancement of Slavic

Studies conference, Boca Raton, September.

—— (1999), 'Regional Income Differences', forthcoming in B. Granville and P. Oppenheimer (eds), *The Russian Economy in the 1990s*, Oxford: Oxford University Press.

—— and P. Kirkow (1997), 'Tomsk: Federal–Regional Relations', paper presented at the OECD–Tomsk Regional Administration conference on industrial restructuring in the Tomsk oblast'.

—— (1998), 'Tomsk: Federal–Regional Relations', in OECD, *Industrial Restructuring in Tomsk Oblast'*, Paris: OECD.

—— and D. J. Sutherland (1998), 'Kaliningrad: Industrial Sectoral Overview', Report for Tacis: Promotee II, mimeo.

—— (1999), *Economic Restructuring in Kaliningrad*, Russian Regional Research Group Working Paper 16, Birmingham: University of Birmingham.

Harris, J. R. and M. P. Todaro (1970), 'Migration, Unemployment and Development: A Two Sector Analysis', *American Economic Review* 60, 126–42.

Heleniak, T. (1994), 'The Projected Population of Russia in 2005', *Post-Soviet Geography* 35 (10), 608–14.

—— (1995), 'Economic Transition and Demographic Change in Russia, 1989–1995', *Post-Soviet Geography* 36 (7), 446–58.

—— (1997), 'Internal Migration in Russia during the Economic Transition', *Post-Soviet Geography and Economics* 38 (2), 81–104.

Helf, G. (1994), 'All the Russians: Centre, Core and Periphery in Soviet and Post-Soviet Russia', unpublished PhD dissertation, University of California at Berkeley.

—— and J. W. Hahn (1992), 'Old Dogs and New Tricks: Party Elites in the Russian Regional Elections of 1990', *Slavic Review*, 51 (3), 511–30.

Hughes, J. (1994), 'Regionalism in Russia: The Rise and Fall of the Siberian Agreement', *Europe–Asia Studies* 46 (7), 1133–61.

IEPPP (Institut Ekonomicheskikh Problem Perekhodnogo Perioda) (1998), *Osnovnye voprosy kontseptsii razvitiya otnosheniy mezhdu Federal'nym byudzhetom i byudzhetami sub"ektov RF (analiticheskie materialy k dokladu na zasedanii Kommissii Pravitel'stva RF po ekonomicheskoy reforme)*, Moscow: IEPPP.

Ilaldinov, I. (1997), 'Ekonomicheskie reformy v Tatarstane: "tretiy put'"'?', *Panorama-Forum* 16, 102–8.

'Initial report on the situation in the transport sector and its potentialities' (n.d.), Tacis report, mimeo (probably 1997).

Ioffe, G. and T. Nefyodova (1997), *Continuity and Change in Rural Russia: A Geographical Perspective*, Boulder, CO: Westview Press.

Irkutsk Oblkomstat (1996a), *Sotsial'no-ekonomicheskoye polozhenie Irkutskoy oblasti*, 12, Irkutsk: Irkutsk Oblkomstat.

—— (1996b), *Irkutskaya oblast' za gody reformy 1990–1996g.g.*, Irkutsk: Irkutsk Oblkomstat.

—— (1998), *Sotsial'no-ekonomicheskoye polozhenie Irkutskoy oblasti*, 12, Irkutsk: Irkutsk Oblkomstat.

Johnson, D. Gale (1993), 'Trade Effects of Dismantling the Socialized Agriculture in the Former Soviet Union', *Comparative Economic Studies* 35 (4), 21–31.

Kaganskiy, V. L. (1995), 'Ideologemy rossiyskogo neosovetskogo prostranstva', in *Kuda idyot Rossiya? Al'ternativy obshchestvennogo razvitiya*, Moscow: Aspekt-Press, 466–71.

—— (1996), 'Neosovetskoye prostranstvo: osnovnye struktury, transformatsiya', in *Kuda idyot Rossiya? Sotsial'naya transformatsiya postsovetskogo prostranstva*, Moscow: Aspekt-Press, 59–69.

—— (1997), 'Neopredelyonnost' sovremennogo rossiyskogo prostranstva', in *Kuda idyot Rossiya? Obshcheye i osobennoye v sovremennom razvitii*, Moscow: Aspekt-Press, 63–8.

—— and B. B. Rodoman (1995), 'Nauka o kul'ture: itogi i perspektivy', Issue 3, Supplement to *Panorama kul'turnoy zhizni stran SNG i Baltiki*, Moscow: Izdatel'stvo Rossiyskoy Gosudarstvennoy Biblioteki.

Karasyov, A. V. (1997), *Anatomiya politicheskoy vlasti (regional'nyy aspekt)*, Tver': RIK TsGR.

Karelina, I. A., L. E. Limonov and B. S. Zhikharevich (1998), 'Strategic Planning in St. Petersburg', *Communist Economies and Economic Transformation* 10 (1), 5–19.

Karpov, V. V. (1996), *Regional'naya rynochnaya ekonomika: problemy i analiz*, Omsk (publisher not avaiilable).

Katanian, K. (1998), 'The Propiska and the Constitutional Court', *East European Constitutional Review* 7 (2), 52–7.

Katanyan, K. (1998), 'Luzhkov predlagayet peredel Rossii', *Izvestiya*, 18 September.

Kayanova, O. and A. Mal'gin (1994), 'Chto proiskhodit na zhilishchnom rynke S. Peterburga', *Voprosy ekonomiki* 10, 120–30.

Kazantsev, S. V. (1996), 'Promyshlennoye razvitie regionov Rossiyskoy Federatsii', in *Rossiyskie regiony v novykh ekonomicheskikh usloviyakh*, Moscow: Mezhdunarodnaya Akademiya Regional'nogo Razvitiya i Sotrudnichestva RAN, 20–26.

Khakimov, S. (1996), 'Prospects of Federalism in Russia: A View from Tatarstan', *Security Dialogue* 27 (1), 69–80.

Khrushchyov, S. (1994), 'The Political Economy of Russia's Regional Fragmentation', in D. Blum (ed.), *Russia's Future: Consolidation or Disintegration?*, Boulder, CO: Westview Press, 91–107.

Khursevich, S. (1998), 'O nekotorykh usloviyakh rezul'tativnosti reformy mezhbyudzhetnykh otnosheniy', *Voprosy ekonomiki* 10, 127–39.

Kirkow, P. (1994), 'Regional Politics and Market Reform in Russia: The Case of the Altay', *Europe–Asia Studies* 46 (7), 1163–87.

—— (1995), 'Regional Warlordism in Russia: The Case of Primorskiy Kray', *Europe–Asia Studies* 47 (6), 923–47.

—— (1996a), 'Distributional Coalitions, Budgetary Problems and Fiscal Federalism in Russia', *Communist Economies and Economic Transformation* 8 (3), 277–98.

—— (1996b), 'The Siberian and Far Eastern Challenge to Centre-Periphery

Relations in Russia: A Comaprison between Altaiskiy and Primorskiy Krays', in J. Gibson and P. Hanson (eds), *Transformation from Below: Local Power and the Political Economy of Post-Communist Transitions*, Cheltenham, UK: Edward Elgar, 217–60.

—— (1996c), *Economic Change in Novosibirsk Province: From Depressed Rust Belt to Siberia's Financial and Distributional Centre?* Russian Regional Research Group Working Paper 6, Birmingham: University of Birmingham.

—— (1997a), 'Transition in Russia's Principal Coastal Gateways', *Post-Soviet Geography and Economics* 38 (5), 296–314.

—— (1997b), 'Local Self-government in Russia: Awakening from Slumber?', *Europe–Asia Studies* 49 (1), 43–58.

—— (1998), *Russia's Provinces: Authoritarian Transformation versus Local Autonomy?*, London: Macmillan.

—— and P. Hanson (1994), 'The Potential for Autonomous Regional Development in Russia: The Case of Primorskiy Kray', *Post-Soviet Geography* 35 (2), 63–88.

—— and —— (1998), 'Tomsk: Centre–Regional Relations', in OECD, *Industrial Restructuring in Tomsk Oblast'*, Paris: OECD.

——, —— and A. Treivish (1998), 'Networks, Linkages and Legacies: Evidence from an Elite Survey in Seven Russian Regions, 1996–97', *Communist Economies and Economic Transformation* 10 (3), 405–14.

Kleyner, G. (1996), 'Sovremennaya ekonomika Rossii kak "ekonomika fizicheskikh lits"', *Voprosy ekonomiki* 4, 81–90.

Klotsvog, F. and I. Kushnikova (1998), 'Resursnyy potentsial sub"ektov Federatsii i ego ispol'zovanie', *Ekonomist* 12, 33–9.

Klyuyev, N. N. (1996), *Ekologo-geograficheskoye polozhenie Rossii i eyo regionov*, Moscow: Institut Geografii RAN.

Kobuzan, V. M. (1996), 'Russkaya etnicheskaya territoriya v blizhnem zarubezh'ye i sub"ektakh Rossiyskoy Federatsii v XVIII–XX vv', *Mir Rossii* 2, 43–62.

Kolosov, V. A. *et al.* (1996), 'Rossiyskaya obshchestvennaya geografiya pervoy poloviny 90-kh godov', *Izvestiya AN – Seriya Geografiya* 3, 7–34.

Kontorovich, V. (1997), 'The Russian Far East as Imperial Legacy', paper presented at American Association for the Advancement of Slavic Studies conference, Seattle, November.

—— (1998), 'How Much Will Russian Far East Shrink?', paper presented at Australia and New Zealand Slavic Association conference, Melbourne, July.

'Kontseptsiya reformirovaniya mezhbyudzhetnykh otnosheniy v Rossiyskoy Federatsii na 1999 god i na period do 2001 goda' (1998), report approved in April by the Russian Government Commission on Economic Reform.

Korol'kov, I. (1998), 'Vsya gubernatorskaya rat'', *Izvestiya*, 29 July, 4.

Kostroma Oblkomstat (1994), *Narodnoye khozyaystvo Kostromskoy oblasti (k 50-letiyu obrazovaniya oblasti)*, Kostroma: Kostroma Oblkomstat.

Kotlyakov, V. M. and V. S. Preobrazhenskiy (eds) (1996), *Geography in Russia (1992–1995)*, Moscow: Institut Geografii RAN.

Kouznetsova, O., P. Hanson and D. Sutherland (1999), *Reforming Centre–Region Budgetary Relations*, Russian Regional Research Group Working Paper 17, Birmingham: University of Birmingham.

Kovalyov, Ye. M. (1995), *Gumanitarnaya geografiya Rossii. Posobie dlya studentov VUZov*, Moscow: LA Varyag.

Kozlov, A. (1998), *Kozyol na sakse*, Moscow: Vagrius.

Kuklinski, A. (ed.) (1990), *Globality versus Locality*, Warsaw: University of Warsaw.

Lapidus, G. W. (1999), 'Asymmetrical Federalism and State Breakdown in Russia', *Post Soviet Affairs* 15 (1), 74–82.

—— and E. W. Walker (1995), 'Nationalism, Regionalism, and Federalism: Center–Periphery Relations in Post-Communist Russia', in G. W. Lapidus (ed.), *Russia's Troubled Transition*, Cambridge: Cambridge University Press, 395–480.

Latynina, Yu. (1998), 'Regions Look to Hamurabi for Crisis Plan', *Moscow Times*, 27 October.

Lavrov, A. (1997a), *Mify i rify rossiyskogo byudzhetnogo federalizma*, Moscow: Magistr.

—— (1997b), 'Konflikty mezhdu tsentrom i regionami v rossiyskoy modeli byudzhetnogo federalizma', in *Evolyutsiya vzaimootnosheniy tsentra i regionov Rossii: ot konfliktov k poisku soglasiya*, Moscow (publisher not avaiilable), 101–31.

—— (1998a), 'Nedenezhnoye ispolnenie regional'nykh byudzhetov v Rossiyskoy Federatsii', mimeo.

—— (1998b), 'Nekotorye problemy mezhbyudzhetnykh otnosheniy v Rossii', paper presented at Economic and Social Research Council seminar on Russian Regional Transformations, May, mimeo.

—— and O. Kuznetsova (1996), 'Ekonomicheskaya politika regionov: liberal'naya i konservativnaya modeli', *Politiya* 1 (3), 57–64.

—— and V. Shuvalov (1997), *Predprinimatel'skiy klimat regionov Rossii*, Moscow: Nachala-Press.

Layard, R., O. Blanchard, R. Dornbusch and P. Krugman (1992), *East–West Migration: The Alternatives*, London: MIT Press.

Laykam, K. (1998), 'Optimizatsiya raspredeleniya nalogov mezhdu federal'nym i regional'nym urovnyami byudzhetnoy sistemy', *Voprosy ekonomiki* 10, 139–43.

Lebedev, G. (1996), 'St Petersburg in the Baltic Expanse of Europe: Prerequisites and Genesis of the Megapolis', in E. Varis and S. Porter (eds), *Karelia and St Petersburg: From Lakeland Interior to European Metropolis*, Joensuu: Joensuu University Press, 39–55.

Le Houerou, P. and M. Rutkowski (1996), 'Federal Transfers in Russia: Their Impact on Regional Revenues and Incomes', *Comparative Economic Studies* 38 (2/3), 21–47.

Leksin, V. and A. Shvetsov (1995), 'State Regulation and Selective Support for Regional Development', *Problems of Economic Transition* 37 (12) and 38 (1).

Levada, Yu. A. (1996), 'Sotsial'no-prostranstvennaya struktura rossiyskogo

obshchestva: tsentr i regiony', in *Kuda idyot Rossiya? Sotsial'naya trans-formatsiya postsovetskogo prostranstva*, Moscow: Aspekt-Press, 276–85.
Liefert, W. M., R. B. Kooperman and E. C. Cook (1993), 'Agricultural Reform in the Former USSR', *Comparative Economic Studies* 35 (2), 49–58.
Liuhto, Kari (1998), 'Statistical Illusions of Joint-Ventures in Russia: St Petersburg: New Klondyke or Unusual Flower-Growing Swamp?', *Slovo*, 8 (1), 102–17.
Lloyd, J. (1994), 'Challenge to Russia's Democracy on the Waterfront', *Financial Times*, 27 October, 3.
Löwenhardt, J. and S. White (1999), 'Beyond the Garden Ring: A Bibliography', mimeo.
Loy, J.-P. and P. Wehrheim (1997), *Spatial Food Market Integration in Russia*, The Russian Food Economy in Transition Discussion Paper no. 6, Christian-Albrechts-Universität.
Lynn, N. J. and A. V. Novikov (1997), 'Refederalizing Russia: Debates on the Idea of Federalism in Russia', *Publius: The Journal of Federalism* 27 (2), 187–203.
Lysenko, V. N. and V. N. Podoprigora (eds) (1998), *Ekonomicheskie reformy v regionakh Rossiyskoy Federatsii: opyt i perspektivy*, Moscow: Institut Sovremennoy Politiki.
Lyubovnyy, V. Ya. and B. T. Lagutenko (1994), 'Federal'naya ekonomicheskaya politika po ozdorovleniyu krizisnykh regionov', *Izvestiya AN – Seriya Geografiya* 5, 18–23.
Magomedov, A. (1998), 'Krasnodar Kray: A Growth Pole in the Transitional Economy of Russia?', *Communist Economies and Economic Transformation* 10 (3), 363–75.
Makfol, M. and N. Petrov (eds) (1998), *Politicheskiy Al'manakh Rossii 1997*, vol 1: Vybory i Politicheskoye Razvitie, Moscow: Moskovskiy Tsentr Karnegi.
'Makroekonomicheskie modeli perekhodnogo perioda: mirovoy opyt i rossiyskaya spetsifika' (1996), Proceedings of the interdisciplinary seminar of 1 March 1996, Moscow: Analiticheskiy Tsentr PANINTER.
Malle, S. (1986), 'Heterogeneity of the Soviet Labour Market as a Limit to More Efficient Utilisation of Manpower', in D. Lane (ed.), *Labour and Employment in the USSR*, Brighton, Sussex: Wheatsheaf, 122–42.
Marchenko, G. (1996), *Regional'nye problemy stanovleniya novoy rossiyskoy gosudarstvennosti*, Moscow: Moskovskiy Obshchestvennyy Nauchnyy Fond.
—— and O. Machul'skaya (1997), 'Vyravnivanie ili pereraspredelenie?' *Ekonomika i zhizn'* 50 (December), 30.
Matayev, D. (1998), 'Ekonomicheskaya politika pri vozvrate k mobilizatsionnoy modeli razvitiya', *Rossiyskiy ekonomicheskiy zhurnal* 4, 11–27.
Mau, V. and V. Stupin (1997), 'The Political Economy of Russian Regionalism', *Communist Economies and Economic Transformation* 9 (1), 5–25.
McAuley, A. (1997), 'The Determinants of Russian Federal Regional Fiscal Relations: Equity or Political Influence?', *Europe–Asia Studies* 49 (3), 431–44.

McAuley, M. (1992), 'Politics, Economics and Elite Realignment in Russia: A Regional Perspective', *Soviet Economy* 8 (1), 46–88.

—— (1997), *Russia's Politics of Uncertainty*, Cambridge: Cambridge University Press.

McIntyre, R. (1998), 'Regional Stabilisation Policy under Transition Period Conditions in Russia: Price Controls, Regional Trade Barriers and Other Local-level Measures', *Europe–Asia Studies* 50 (5) 859–71.

Melvin, N. J. (1998), 'The Consolidation of a New Regional Elite: The Case of Omsk, 1987–1995', *Europe–Asia Studies* 50 (4), 619–50.

Men'shikov, S. (1990), *Sovetskaya ekonomika: katastrofa ili katarsis?* Moscow: Inter-Verso.

MinEkon (Ministry of the Economy) (1998), *Kontseptsiya razvitiya mezhbyudzhetnykh otnosheniy mezhdu federal'nym i territorial'nymi byudzhetami*, Report to the Russian Government Commission on Economic Reform.

Mitchneck, B. (1994), 'The Changing Role of the Local Budget in Russian Cities: The Case of Yaroslavl'', in T. H. Friedgut and J. W. Hahn (eds), *Local Power and Post-Soviet Politics*, Armonk, NY: M.E. Sharpe, 73–95.

—— (1995), 'An Assessment of the Growing Local Economic Development Function of Local Authorities in Russia', *Economic Geography* 71 (2), 150–70.

—— (1997a), 'The Emergence of Local Government in Russia', in M. Bradshaw (ed.), *Geography and Transition in the Post-Soviet Republic*, Chichester, Sussex: Wiley, 89–108.

—— (1997b), *Regional Governance in Russia: The Role of Accumulation Alliances*, Department of Geography and Regional Development, Discussion Paper 97-4, Tucson, AZ: University of Arizona.

—— (1997c), *Regional Governance Regimes in Russia: The Case of Udmurtia and Yaroslavl'*, Department of Geography and Regional Development, Discussion Paper 97-5, Tucson, AZ: University of Arizona.

—— (1997d), 'Restructuring Russian Urban Budgets: 1991–1995', *Europe–Asia Studies* 49 (6), 989–1015.

MMVB and Expert Institute (1997), *Regiony Rossii: finansovye aspekty razvitiya*, Moscow: Agentstvo Infomart.

Mokhov, V. P. (1997), 'Transformatsiya regional'noy politicheskoy elity v perekhodnyy period', in *Na putyakh politicheskoy transformatsii (politicheskie partii i politicheskie etapy postsovetskogo perioda)*, 2nd part, Moscow (publisher not avaiilable), 90–96.

Moltz, J. C. (1996), 'Core and Periphery in the Evolving Russian Economy: Integration or Isolation of the Far East?', *Post-Soviet Geography and Economics* 37 (3), 175–94.

Morozov, A. (1996), 'Tax Administration in Russia', *East European Constitutional Review* Spring/Summer, 39–48.

Moses, J. C. (1994), 'Saratov and Volgograd, 1990–1992: A Tale of Two Russian Provinces', in T. H. Friedgut and J. W. Hahn (eds), *Local Power and Post-Soviet Politics*, Armonk, NY: M.E. Sharpe, 96–137.

Moukhariamov, M. M. (1997), 'The Tatarstan Model: A Situational Dynamic', in P. Stavrakis, J. Debardeleben and L. Black (eds), *Beyond the Monolith: The Emergence of Regionalism in Post-Soviet Russia*, Baltimore, MD: Woodrow Wilson Center and Johns Hopkins University Press, 213–32.

Murrell, P. (1991), 'Public Choice and the Transformation of Socialism', *Journal of Comparative Economics* 14, 203–10.

Musgrave, R. A. (1959), *The Theory of Public Finance: A Study in Public Economy*, New York: McGraw Hill.

Muzdybayev, K. (1995), *Dinamika urovnya zhizni v Peterburge 1992–1994*, St Petersburg: SMART.

Nagaev, S. A. and A. Worgotter (1995), *Regional Risk Rating in Russia*, Vienna: Bank of Austria.

Nefyodova, T. G. (1997), 'Sel'skoye khozyaystvo Rossii: sotsial'no-infrastrukturnye i drugie faktory riska', in *Problemy rasseleniya: istoriya i sovremennost'. Seriya Rossiya 90-kh: problemy regional'nogo razvitiya*, Moscow: Institut Geografii RAN, 54–62.

—— (1998), 'Rossiyskie prigorody: spetsifika rasseleniya i stanovlenie zhilishchno-zemel'nogo rynka', *Izvestiya AN – Seriya Geografiya* 3, 69–84.

—— and A. Treyvish (1994), 'Rayony Rossii i drugikh yevropeyskikh stran s perekhodnoy ekonomikoy v nachale 90-kh godov', in *Seriya Rossiya 90-kh: problemy regional'nogo razvitiya*, Moscow: Institut Geografii RAN.

—— (1996), 'Postsovetskoye prostranstvo Rossii', *Mir Rossii* 2, 3–42.

—— (1998), '"Sil'nye" i "slabye" goroda Rossii', in *Polyusa i tsentry rosta v regional'nom razvitii*, Moscow: Mezhdunarodnaya Akademiya Regional'nogo Razvitiya i Sotrudnichestva RAN, 136–43.

Newbery, D. M. (1997), 'Optimal Tax Rates and Tax Design during Systemic Reform', *Journal of Public Economics* 63 (2), 177–206.

NIFI (Nauchno-issledovatel'skiy finansovyy institut) (1998), *Predlozheniya po soderzhaniyu kontsepstii mezhbyudzhetnykh otnosheniy Rossiyskoy Federatsii na 1999 i posleduyushchie gody*, Report to the Russian Government Commission on Economic Reform.

Nizhegorodskiy prolog. Ekonomika i politika v Rossii (1992), Nizhniy Novgorod and Moscow: EPItsentr and Koordinatsionnyy Sovet Nizhegorodskoy Oblasti.

Nordhaus, W. D. (1990), 'Soviet Economic Reform: The Longest Road', *Brookings Paper on Economic Activity* (Papers and proceedings of the 49th Brookings Panel on Economic Activity), 287–317.

Northern Economics (1998), *Sakhalin Island Infrastructure Development Plan*, Anchorage, AK: Northern Economics Inc.

Novikov, A. (1997), 'Between Space and Race: Rediscovering Russian Cultural Geography', in M. J. Bradshaw (ed.), *Geography and Transition in the Post-Soviet Republic*, Chichester, Sussex: Wiley, 43–57.

—— (1998), *Risk Factors Associated with Russian Regions and Municipalities*, Moscow: Institute for Urban Economics.

O plane-grafike mer po realizatsii kontseptsii reformirovaniya mezhbyudzhet-

nykh otnosheniy v Rossiyskoy Federatsii v 1999–2000 godakh (1998), Russian Federal Government Resolution no. 1718 of 4 December, Moscow.

Oates, W. (1972), *Fiscal Federalism*, New York: Harcourt Brace Jovanovich.

—— (1977), 'An Economist's Perspective on Fiscal Federalism', in W. Oates (ed.), *The Political Economy of Fiscal Federalism*, Lexington, MA: Lexington Books, 3–20.

—— (1991), *Principles of Fiscal Federalism: A Survey of Recent Theoretical and Empirical Research*, Center for Institutional Reform and the Informal Sector Working Paper 21, College Park, MD: University of Maryland.

OECD (1997), *Economic Survey of Russia*, Paris: OECD.

Oleynik, A. (1998), 'Domashnie khozyaystva v perekhodnoy ekonomike: tipy i osobennosti povedeniya na rynke', *Voprosy ekonomiki* 12, 56–66.

O'Loughlin, J., M. Shin and P. Talbot (1996), 'Political Geographies and Cleavages in the Russian Parliamentary Elections', *Post-Soviet Geography and Economics* 37 (6), 355–85.

Olson, M. (1995), 'Russian Reforms: Established Interests and Practical Alternatives', in R. Skidelsky (ed.), *Russia's Stormy Path to Reform*, London: Social Market Foundation, 9–42.

Ormond, J. (1997), 'The North Caucasus: Confederation in Conflict', in I. Bremmer and R. Taras (eds), *New States, New Politics: Building the Post-Soviet Nations*, Cambridge: Cambridge University Press, 96–139.

Ottaviano, G. I. P. and Diego Puga (1997), *Agglomeration in the Global Economy: A Survey of the 'New Economic Geography'*, Centre for Economic Performance Discussion Paper no. 356, London: Centre for Economic Performance.

Pacific Russia Information Group (1999), *The Oil and Gas Industry of Sakhalin Island: Annual Review – Spring 1999*, Anchorage, AK: Pacific Russia Information Group.

Paik, K. W. (1995), *Gas and Oil in Northeast Asia: Policies, Prospects and Projects*, London: Royal Institute of International Affairs.

Pavlenko, S. (1997), 'Novyy federalizm: intriga i kontrintriga', *Pro et Contra* 2 (2), 20–46.

Perekhod k rynku. Kotseptsiya i programma, (1990), Moscow: Ministerstvo pechati i massovoy informatsii RSFSR (Working Group headed by S. S. Shatalin, created by joint decision of presidents M. S. Gorbachyov and B. N. Yeltsin).

Petrov, N. and A. Treyvish (1994), 'Riski regional'noy dezintegratsii', Moscow, mimeo.

—— et al. (1992), 'Rossiyskie regiony v period krizisa i reform', *Politicheskiy Monitoring Rossii*, 3, 4–62.

—— (1993), 'Regional'noe razvitie Rossii i zadachi regional'noy politiki', in *Rayonirovanie i regional'nye problemy*, Yekaterinburg: Nauchnyy Sovet RAN po Problemam Regional'noy Ekonomiki, 85–105.

Petrov, V. V. (1998), 'Tendentsii v izmenenii tematiki po ekonomicheskoy i sotsial'noy geografii (analiz publikatsiy v serii "RZh-Geografiya")', *Vestnik Moskovskogo Universiteta, Seriya 5 – Geografiya* 1, 68–74.

Pivovarov, Yu. L. (1996), 'Al'ternativnaya kontseptsiya makroregional'nogo razvitiya Rossii: szhatie intensivno ispol'zuyemogo prostranstva', *Mir Rossii* 2, 63–74.

Polishchuk, A. (1998), 'Rossiyskaya model' "peregovornogo federalizma" (politiko-ekonomicheskiy analiz)', *Voprosy ekonomiki* 6, 68–79.

Polishchuk, L. (1996), *Russian Federalism: Economic Reform and Political Behavior*, Pasadena, CA: California Institute of Technology.

—— (1997), 'Missed Markets: Implications for Economic Behavior and Institutional Change', in J. M. Nelson, C. Tilly and L. Walker (eds), *Transforming Post-Communist Political Economies*, Washington, DC: National Academy Press, 80–101.

Popov, V. (1998), 'Shokoterapiya protiv gradualizma: konets diskussii', *Ekspert* 35, 14–19.

Pozdnyakov, A. *et al.* (1998), *Metodologicheskoye i metodicheskoye obespechenie sovershenstvovaniya mezhbyudzhetnykh otnosheniy*, Moscow: Minnats RF and Insan.

Predprinimatel'skiy klimat regionov Rossii (1997), Moscow: Nachala-Press.

Primorskiy Goskomstat (1998), *Primorskiy Kray v 1997 g.*, Vladivostok: Primorskiy Goskomstat.

Privalovskaya, G. *et al.* (1995), *Territorial'naya struktura khozyaystva staroosvoyennykh rayonov*, Moscow: Nauka.

Problemnoye napravlenie v geografii (Sbornik statey) (1993), Chita–Irkutsk: Sibirskoye otdelenie RAN.

Proyekt srednesrochnoy programmy Pravitel'stva RF, Strukturnaya perestroyka i ekonomicheskiy rost v 1998–2000 godakh (1998), Moscow.

Pryde, P. (1991), *Environmental Management in the Soviet Union*, Cambridge: Cambridge University Press.

—— (1995), 'Russia: An Overview of the Federation', in P. Pryde (ed.), *Environmental Constraints in the Former Soviet Republic*, Boulder, CO: Westview Press, 1–24.

Puga, Diego (1996), *The Rise and Fall of Regional Inequalities*, Centre for Economic Performance Discussion Paper no. 314, London: Centre for Economic Perfomance.

P'yannikh, G. (1998), 'Energonositel'', *Kommersant" Vlast'*, 29 September, 34–8.

Pyle, W. (1997), 'Inter-regional Credit Markets in Russia', *Post-Soviet Geography and Economics* 38 (8), 478–98.

Radvanyi, J. (1992), 'And What if Russia Breaks Up?', *Post-Soviet Geography* 33 (2), 69–77.

Ratner, N. M. *et al.* (1993), 'Metody regulirovaniya razvitiya rayonov v rynochnykh usloviyakh', in *Rayonirovanie i regional'nye problemy*, Yekaterinburg: Nauchnyy Sovet RAN po Problemam Regional'noy Ekonomiki, 131–44.

'Regional Policy Addressing Economic, Social and Legal Asymmetries in Russia' (1999), in *Tacis Phase Two Report: Regional Economic and Social Policy*, vol. 2a, Moscow: Ministry of Regional Policy.

Regional'nye issledovaniya ekonomiki SSSR: novye podkhody. Sbornik nauch-

nykh trudov (1991), Moscow: Sovet po Izucheniyu Proizvoditel'nykh Sil pri Gosplane SSSR.

Regiony Rossii v perekhodnyy period (1993), Moscow: Expert Institute.

Regiony Rossii: finansovye aspekty razvitiya (1997), Moscow: Infomart.

'Reyting rossiyskikh regionov. 1996–1997 gody' (1997), *Ekspert* 47 (8 December), 18–40.

'Reyting...' (1999), 'Investitionnyi reyting regionov Rossii', *Ekspert* 39 (18 October), 26–45.

Rimashevskaya, N. M. and E. N. Yakovleva (eds) (1998), *Rossiya–1997. Sotsial'no-demograficheskaya situatsiya*, 7th Annual Report, Moscow: Institut Sotsial'no-Ekonomicheskikh Problem Narodonaseleniya RAN.

Risnes, B. (1998), 'Can Law Keep Russia Together?', paper presented at the NUPI–Fridtjof Nansen Institute Conference on Perspectives of Russia as a Federation, Oslo, January.

Rodoman, B. B. (1993), 'Rayonirovanie v nauke i praktike', in *Rayonirovanie i regional'nye problemy*, Yekaterinburg: Nauchnyy Sovet RAN po Problemam Regional'noy Ekonomiki, 178–82.

—— (1998), 'Prostranstvennaya polyarizatsiya i pereorientatsiya', in *Kuda idyot Rossiya? Transformatsiya sotsial'noy sfery i sotsial'naya politika*, Moscow: Delo, 140–44.

Romanov, P. and I. Tartakovskaya (1998), 'Samara oblast': A Governor and his Guberniya', *Communist Economies and Economic Transformation* 10 (3), 341–63.

Rozman, G. (1997), 'The Crisis of the Russian Far East, Who is to Blame?', *Problems of Post-Communism* 44 (5) (September/October), 3–12.

Sagers, M. J. (1995), 'Prospects for Oil and Gas in Russia's Sakhalin Oblast'', *Post-Soviet Geography* 36 (5), 274–90.

Sakhalin Oblkomstat (1996), *50 let Sakhalinskoy Oblasti*, Yuzhno-Sakhalinsk: Sakhalin Goskomstat.

—— (1998), *Vneshneyekonomicheskaya deyatel'nost' predpriyatiy i organziatsiy Sakhalinskoy oblasti za 1997 god*, Yuzhno-Sakhalinsk: Sakhalin Oblkomstat.

—— (1999), *Doklad o Sotsial'no-ekonomicheskom polozhenii Sakhalinskoy Oblasti za yanvar'–dekabr' 1998 goda*, Yuzhno-Sakhalinsk: Sakhalin Oblkomstat.

Samara Oblkomstat (1997), *Sotsial'no-ekonomicheskoye polozhenie Samarskoy oblasti, yanvar'–noyabr' 1997goda*, Samara: Samara Oblkomstat.

Samokhvalov, A. (1996), 'Ekonomicheskie osnovy federativnykh otnosheniy', special issue of *Promyshlenniy Vestnik Rossii*, 1.

Sapir, Jacques (1996), 'Is There Still a Unified Russian Economic System?', Paris: Centre des hautes études en sciences sociales, mimeo.

Savvateyeva, I. (1995), 'Yevgeniy Nazdratenko kak zerkalo rossiyskikh reform', *Izvestiya*, 1 December, p. 5.

Schiffer, J. R. (1988), *Soviet Economic Policy: The East–West Debate over Pacific Siberian Development*, London: Macmillan.

Schrumpf, H. (1998), 'Possibilities and Limits of Regional Policy in the Russian Federation', in European Policies Research Centre, *Options for*

Regional Policy in Russia, Interim Report to the Tacis ACE Programme, Glasgow: University of Strathclyde, 47–51.

Selivyorstov, V. E. *et al.* (1996), 'Metodologicheskie osnovy razrabotki federal'noy programmy pomoshchi depressivnym i otstalym regionam', *Region: Ekonomika i Sotsiologiya* 1, 3–43.

Serova, E. (1999), 'Russian Agrarian Sector: Development and Prospects', *Russian Economic Trends*, Monthly Update (January), 1–9.

Shabad, T. and V. Mote (1977), *Gateway to Siberian Resources (The BAM)*, New York: Wiley.

Shleifer, A. and M. Boycko (1994), 'Next Steps in Privatization: Six Major Challenges', in I. W. Lieberman and J. Nellis (eds), *Russia: Creating Private Enterprises and Efficient Markets*, Washington, DC: World Bank, 75–86.

Shtayner, M. (1996), 'Raznoobraznye formy adaptatsii regionov i ikh znachenie dlya regional'noy politiki', in *Gosudarstvennaya Sluzhba. Tsentr i Regiony. Zarubezhnyy Opyt*, Moscow (publisher not avaiilable), 79–88.

Slider, Darrell (1994a), 'Federalism, Discord, and Accommodation: Intergovernmental Relations in Post-Soviet Russia', in T. H. Friedgut and J. W. Hahn (eds), *Local Power and Post-Soviet Politics*, Armonk, NY: M.E. Sharpe, 239–69.

—— (1994b), 'Privatization in Russia's Regions', *Post-Soviet Affairs* 10 (4), 367–96.

—— (1996), 'Elections to Russia's Regional Assemblies', *Post-Soviet Affairs* 12 (3), 243–63.

—— (1997a), 'Russia's Market-Distorting Federalism', *Post-Soviet Geography and Economics* 38 (8), 445–60.

—— (1997b), 'Regional Aspects of Privatisation in Russia', in P. Stavrakis, J. Debardeleben, and L. Black (eds), *Beyond the Monolith: The Emergence of Regionalism in Post-Soviet Russia*, Baltimore, MD: Woodrow Wilson Center and Johns Hopkins University Press, 105–17.

Smith, G. E. (1995a), 'Federalism, Defederation and Refederation: From the Soviet Union to Russian Statehood', in G. Smith (ed.), *Federalism: the Multi-ethnic Challenge*, London: Longman, 157–79.

—— (1995b), 'The Ethnopolitics of Federation without Federation', in D. Lane (ed.), *Russia in Transition*, London: Longman.

—— (1999), *The Post-Soviet States: Mapping the Politics of Transition*. London: Edward Arnold.

Smith, J.-P. (1998), 'Strategy: Russia. How Much Reform and How Soon?', *Morgan Stanley Dean Witter Emerging Markets Investment Research*, 10 July.

Solnick, S. L. (1995), 'Federal Bargaining in Russia', *East European Constitutional Review* 4 (4), 52–8.

—— (1996), 'The Political Economy of Russian Federalism: A Framework for Analysis', *Problems of Post-Communism* 46 (6), 13–25.

—— (1998), 'The 1996–97 Gubernatorial Elections in Russia: Outcomes and Implications', *Post-Soviet Affairs* 14 (1), 48–81.

Sotsial'no-ekonomicheskie problemy regiona v perekhodnyy period (1996),

Tyumen': Tyumen' State University Press.

Stark, D. (1992), 'Path Dependence and Privatisation Strategies in East–Central Europe', *East European Politics and Societies* 4, 351–92.

Stavrakis, P. J., J. Debardeleben and L. Black (1997), *Beyond the Monolith: The Emergence of Regionalism in Post-Soviet Russia*, Baltimore, MD: Woodrow Wilson Center Press and Johns Hopkins University Press.

Stenning, A. C. (1997), 'Economic Restructuring and Local Change in the Russian Federation', in M. J. Bradshaw (ed.), *Geography and Transition in the Post-Soviet Republics*, Chichester, Sussex: Wiley, 145–62.

Stephan, J. (1971), *Sakhalin: A History*, Oxford: Clarendon Press.

Stewart, K. (1997), *Are Intergovernmental Transfers in Russia Equalizing?* Innocenti Occasional Papers, Economic and Social Policy Series no. 59, Florence: UNICEF International Child Development Centre.

Stiglitz, J. (1999), 'Whither Reform? Ten Years of the Transition', keynote address at the World Bank Annual Conference on Development Economics, Washington, DC.

Stoner-Weiss, K. (1997), *Local Heroes: The Political Economy of Russian Regional Governance*, Princeton, NJ: Princeton University Press.

—— (1999), 'Central Weaknesses and Provincial Autonomy: Observations on Devolution', *Post-Soviet Affairs* 15 (1), 87–106.

Stroyev, Ye. (1997), 'Region i predpriyatie: vzaimodeystvie v usloviyakh stanovleniya rynochnoy ekonomiki', *Federalizm* 2, 71–88.

Sutherland, D. (1996), *Small and Medium Sized Enterprises in the Russian Regions: Employment Constraints and Incentives*, Russian Regional Research Group Working Paper 7, Birmingham: University of Birmingham.

—— (1997), 'Regional Economic Structure and the Process of Economic Transformation in the Russian Federation', unpublished PhD Thesis, Centre for Russian and East European Studies, University of Birmingham.

—— and P. Hanson (1996), 'Structural Change in the Economies of Russia's Regions', *Europe–Asia Studies* 48 (3), 367–92.

Tabata, S. (1998), 'Transfers from Federal to Regional Budgets in Russia: A Statistical Analysis', *Post-Soviet Geography and Economics* 39 (8), 447–60.

Talbott, S. (1998), 'O strategicheskom terpenii v trudnye vremena', *Izvestiya*, 21 November.

Tarkhov, S. (1995), 'Tipy rayonov i dinamika vospriimchivosti k innovatsiyam', in *Geograficheskie osnovy tipologii regionov dlya formirovaniya regional'noy politiki Rossii*, Moscow: Institut Geografii RAN, 84–92.

—— and A. Treyvish (1992), 'Geographical Location and Diffusion of Basic Innovations (The Case of the European USSR)', *GeoJournal* 26 (3), 341–8.

Tartakovskaya, I. (1998), 'Ekonomika Samarskoy oblasti. Yanvar' – Iyul' 1998 g. Prilozhenie: Krizis', mimeo.

Tatarinov, A. (1998), 'Problemy otsenki rekreatsionno-turistskogo produkta na regional'nom urovne', Sochi State University, mimeo.

Tatarkin, A. I. (ed.) (1997), *Sotsial'no-ekonomicheskiy potentsial regiona:*

problemy otsenki, ispol'zovaniya i upravleniya, Yekaterinburg: Ural'skoe Otdelenie RAN.

—— and A. N. Silin (1997), *Regional'nye aspekty ekonomicheskogo rosta*, Yekaterinburg: Institut Ekonomiki Ural'skogo Otdeleniya RAN.

Teague, E. (1996), 'Russia and the Regions: The Uses of Ambiguity', in J. Gibson and P. Hanson (eds), *Transformation from Below: Local Power and the Political Economy of Post-Communist Transitions*, Cheltenham, UK: Edward Elgar, 13–38.

Territorial'noye Upravlenie prezidenta Rossiskoye Federatsii (1997), *Rossiyskie regiony posle vyborov–96*, Moscow: Yuridicheskaya Literatura.

Tikhomirov, V. (1997), 'Food Balance in the Russian Far East', *Polar Geography* 21 (3), 155–202.

Tikhomirova, I. (1997), *Investitsionnyy klimat v Rossii: regional'nye riski*, Moscow: Federal'nyy Fond Podderzhki Malogo Predprinimatel'stva.

Tikhonov, V. (1996), *Anti-economics i zhizn' posle 'smerti rynka'*, Moscow: Riza-M.

Tolz, Vera (1993a), 'The Role of the Republics and Regions', *RFE/RL Research Report* 2 (15) (9 April), 8–13.

—— (1993b), 'Regionalism in Russia: The Case of Siberia', *REF/RL Research Report* 2 (9), 1–10.

Transformatsiya rossiyskikh regional'nykh elit v sravnitel'noy perspektive. Materialy mezhdunarodnogo seminara (Tver' 20–22 February, 1998) (1999), Seriya Nauchnye Doklady, Issue 71, Moscow: Moskovskiy Obshchestvennyy Nauchnyy Fond.

Treisman, D. (1995), 'The Politics of Soft Credit in Post-Soviet Russia', *Europe–Asia Studies* 47, 949–76.

—— (1996a), 'Moscow's Struggle to Control Regions Through Taxation', *Transition* 20 September, 45–9.

—— (1996b), 'The Politics of Intergovernmental Transfers in Post-Soviet Russia', *British Journal of Political Science* 26, 299–335.

—— (1996c), 'Why Yeltsin Won', *Foreign Affairs* 75 (5), 64–77.

—— (1997), 'Russia's "Ethnic Revival": The Separatist Activism of Regional Leaders in a Post-Communist Order', *World Politics* 49 (2), 212–49.

—— (1998), 'Fiscal Redistribution in a Fragile Federation: Moscow and the Regions in 1994', *British Journal of Political Science* 28, 185–200.

Treyvish, A. I. (1994), 'Ekonomika: poisk modeley', *Vash Vybor* 2 (9), 6–8.

—— (1998a), 'Geografiya rossiyskogo krizisa i zanyatost' naseleniya', in *Problemy naseleniya i rynkov truda Rossii i Kavkazskogo regiona. Seriya Rossiya 90-kh: problemy regional'nogo razvitiya*, Stavropol', 13–19.

—— (1998b), 'Kostroma Oblast': an Average-Russian, Averagely-Depressed Region', *Communist Economies and Economic Transformation* 10 (3), 319–40.

—— (1998c), 'Rossiyskie goroda na perekhode k rynku: tendentsii, problemy, paradoksy', *Era Gorodov – Urban Age*, 1, Regional Supplement no. 1.

Troyakova, T. (1995), 'Regional Policy in the Russian Far East and the Rise of Localism in Primorye', *Journal of East Asian Affairs* 9 (2), 428–61.

—— (1998), 'A Prmorskiy Republic: Myth or Reality?', *Communist Economies and Economic Transformation*, 10 (3), 391–405.

Tsentral'nyi Bank Rossiyskoy Federatsii (1999), *Byulleten' bankovskoy statistiki*, 2 (69).

Ulanova, S. (1995), 'O vozdeystvii mestnykh organov upravleniya v otdel'nykh regionakh na protsessy formirovaniya tsen na tovary narodnogo potrebleniya i platnye uslugi naseleniyu v III kvartale 1995 goda', *Voprosy Statistiki* 12, 57–60.

Vacroux, A. (1994), 'Privatization in the Regions: Primorskiy Kray', in I. W. Lieberman and J. Nellis (eds), *Russia: Creating Private Enterprises and Efficient Markets*, Washington, DC: World Bank, 35–45.

Van Atta, D. (1994), 'Agrarian Reform in Post-Soviet Russia', *Post-Soviet Affairs* 10 (2), 159–90.

Van Selm, B. (1998), 'Economic Performance in Russia's Regions', *Europe–Asia Studies* 50 (4), 603–18.

Vardomskiy, L. B. (1997), *Otkrytie rossiyskoy ekonomiki: regional'noe izmerenie*, Moscow: Institut Mezhdunarodnykh Ekonomicheskikh Issledovaniy RAN.

Vendina, O. I. (1998), 'Protivorechiya rynka truda, ili poisk modeli adaptatsii k proiskhodyashchim izmeneniyam', in *Problemy naseleniya i rynkov truda Rossii i Kavkazskogo regiona. Seriya Rossiya 90-kh: problemy regional'nogo razvitiya*, Stavropol', 38–44.

Vishnevskiy, A. (1998), *Serp i rubl': konservativnaya modernizatsiya v SSSR*, Moscow: Ob"edinyonnoye Gumanitarnoye Izdatel'stvo.

Vitebskiy, P. (1996), 'The Northern Minorities', in G. Smith (ed.), *The Nationalities Question on the Post-Soviet States*, London: Longman, 94–112.

Voronov, Yu. (1997), 'Geograficheskiy profil' tseny', *EKO* 12, 161–9.

Vrublevskaya, O. V. and N. G. Ivanova (1994), 'Formirovanie byudzheta Sankt-Peterburga: problemy i protivorechiya', *Finansy* 7, 9–14.

Vtoraya mezhdunarodnaya konferentsiya po federalizmu (1997), *Materialy dlya obsuzhdeniya*, Moscow.

Vysokov, M. (1996), *A Brief History of Sakhalin and the Kurils*, Yuzhno-Sakhalinsk: Sakhalin Publishing House.

Walberg, P., M. McKee, V. Shkolnikov, L. Chenet and D. A. Leon (1998), 'Economic Change, Crime, and the Russian Mortality Crisis: A Regional Analysis', *British Medical Journal* 31 (7), 312–18.

Wallich, C. I. (1992), *Fiscal Decentralization: Intergovernmental Relations in Russia*, Studies of Economies in Transformation, Paper no. 6, Washington, DC: World Bank.

—— (ed.) (1995), *Russia and the Challenge of Fiscal Federalism*, Washington, DC: World Bank.

Webster, L. and J. Charap (1994), 'Private Sector Manufacturing in St Petersburg', in I. W. Lieberman and J. Nellis (eds), *Russia: Creating Private Enterprises and Efficient Markets*, Washington, DC: World Bank, 203–19.

Wegren, S. K. (1996), 'From Farm to Table: The Food System in Post-Communist Russia', *Communist Economies and Economic Trans-*

formation 8 (2), 149–83.

—— (1997), 'Land Reform and the Land Market in Russia: Operation, Constraints and Prospects', *Europe–Asia Studies* 49 (6), 959–87.

White, S., R. Rose and I. McAllister (1997), *How Russia Votes*, Chatham, NJ: Chatham House Publishers.

Widgery, A. (1997), 'Support to the Kaliningrad Oblast within the Context of the Special Economic Zone, EDRUS 9404, Initial Review of Engineering and Electronics', Tacis report, mimeo.

World Bank (1996a), *Fiscal Management in Russia*, Washington, DC: World Bank.

—— (1996b), *From Plan to Market: World Bank Development Report 1996*, Washington, DC: World Bank.

Young, J. F. (1994), 'Institutions, Elites and Local Politics in Russia: The Case of Omsk', in T. H. Friedgut and J. W. Hahn (eds), *Local Power and Post-Soviet Politics*, Armonk, NY: M.E. Sharpe, 138–61.

—— (1997), 'At the Bottom of the Heap: Local Self-Government and Regional Politics in the Russian Federation', in P. J. Stavrakis, J. Debardeleben and L. Black (eds), *Beyond the Monolith: The Emergence of Regionalism in Post-Soviet Russia*, Baltimore, MD: Woodrow Wilson Center and Johns Hopkins University Press, 81–102.

Zelent, I. (1997), Podderzhka sobstvennykh tovarproizvoditelei – klyuchevaya zadacha', *Ekonomist* 5, 32–7.

Zhdanov, V. A. (1995), 'Contemporary Siberian Regionalism', in S. Kotkin and D. Wolff (eds), *Rediscovering Russia in Asia: Siberia and the Russian Far East*, Armonk, NY: M.E.Sharpe, 120–32.

Zhideleva, V. V. (1997), *Ekonomika regiona: formirovanie sotsial'no-ustoychivoy strategii razvitiya*, Syktyvkar: Syktyvkar State University.

Zimine, D. A. (1998), *Economic Development in the City of Novgorod and in Novgorod Oblast: An Overview of Main Patterns and Public Policies*, Russian Regional Research Group Working Paper 14, Birmingham: University of Birmingham.

—— (1999), *Economic Development of St Petersburg: A Challenging Case of Economic Restructuring*, Russian Regional Research Group Working Paper 18, Birmingham: University of Birmingham.

—— and M. J. Bradshaw (1999), 'The Novgorod Region: "Success Story" or Adaptation to Economic Crisis?', *Post-Soviet Geography and Economics* 40 (5), 309–27.

Zlotnik, Mark (1996), 'Russia's Governors: All the President's Men?' *Problems of Post-Communism* 43 (6), 26–34.

Index